POWER STRUCTURE RESEARCH

SAGE FOCUS EDITIONS

POWER STRUCTURE RESEARCH

Edited by

G. WILLIAM DOMHOFF

 SAGE PUBLICATIONS   Beverly Hills   London

For information address:

SAGE Publications, Inc.
275 South Beverly Drive
Beverly Hills, California 90212

SAGE Publications Ltd
28 Banner Street
London EC1Y 8QE, England

Printed in the United States of America

Library of Congress Cataloging in Publication Data
Main entry under title:

Power Structure Research

   (Sage Focus Editions; v. 17)
   Bibliography: p.
1. Social classes—United States—Addresses, essays, lectures. 2. Power (Social sciences) —Addresses, essays, lectures. 3. United States—Politics and Government—1974— Addresses, essays, lectures. I. Domhoff, G. William II. Series.
HN90.S6P68   301.44'0973   79.25255
ISBN 0-8039-1431-8
ISBN 0-8039-1432-6 pbk.

FIRST PRINTING

CONTENTS

INTRODUCTION

G. William Domhoff

This volume of original essays and new research findings inaugurates the fourth decade of systematic work in the exciting and burgeoning field known as "power structure research." Each of the studies herein deals with one or more of the several basic questions concerning the distribution and exercise of power which have imbued power structure research with a keen sense of relevance since its beginnings in the otherwise Silent Fifties. At the same time, these essays often build upon the more recent debates that gave renewed theoretical vigor to power structure research in the 1970s.

A brief recapitulation of the arguments that focused power structure research in its first three decades will provide a context for introducing the specific essays in this volume, essays which present new findings and contribute greatly to the resolution of long standing problems. Power structure research, unlike most fields of inquiry, did not grow slowly or develop over time. It appeared all of a sudden and with much fanfare between the years 1953 and 1956 in widely read books by sociologists Floyd Hunter and C. Wright Mills. Hunter, new to academic sociology after many years working for community agencies in various cities, arrived upon the scene unexpectedly with *Community Power Structure* (1953), a book which gave the field its name and offered a new method of discovering power networks and their functioning through systematic interviews. The publication of Mills's *The Power Elite* (1956), on the other hand, was not entirely unexpected, for

Mills's earlier articles and books had made it clear that he intended to construct an overall portrait of American society which included the level he also called "the high and the mighty" and "the higher circles" (Gillam, 1975).

Hunter's finding that power in Atlanta was in the hands of a relatively few corporate leaders deeply disturbed many members of the social science community, and especially the political scientists, who had enjoyed a near-monopoly on the study of policy formation and the workings of government. Convinced that American government was run by nearly everyone for the sake of most, they denied that power could be so concentrated, and even more that power could be studied by a sociologist who had arrived at his basic findings by asking upper-middle-class professionals and the allegedly powerful themselves to tell him who, in their opinions, were the most powerful people in a city or community. They dubbed this sociometric interview method "the reputational method," and heaped scorn upon it even as sociologists were using and refining it in dozens of new community studies inspired by the Hunter example. A few of these political scientists even ventured into the cities near their universities to determine how specific decisions are "really" made, and emerged with the conviction that their "decisional method" of tracing the specific influences on a variety of decisions had yielded the more valid conclusion that power in America was multibased, issue-specific, and shifting—in a word, pluralistic. The best and most important of these decisional studies was reported in Robert A. Dahl's *Who Governs?* (1961), which won a foundation prize as the best political science book of the year and quickly became one of the most frequently quoted books within the social science community.

If Hunter's book caused consternation within the social sciences because of its reputational method and disconcerting conclusions, Mills's *The Power Elite* created waves in the larger academic community and even spilled onto the pages of popular magazines and political journals. Claiming that the great mass of Americans were dominated by a small triumvirate of corporate rich, political insiders, and military warlords who came together at the top of their institutional pyramids as an interlocking and overlapping power elite, Mills criticized both the "higher immorality" of this power elite and the emptiness of pluralist formulations about power in America.

But it would be wrong to overemphasize tone and style in assessing the impact of *The Power Elite,* for lurking beneath the angry metaphors was a new theory of power that challenged both liberals and Marxists, a theory which took seriously the vast corporate, military, and administrative hierarchies of twentieth-century America. Moreover, this theory was buttressed by information on the social and economic connections of those in positions of authority in each of his three domains. This "positional method" of studying power, as it came to be known, was only one aspect of the problem as far as Mills was concerned (1956: 280-281), but even that aspect was no more acceptable to the pluralists than was Hunter's reputational method. They emphasized even more than Mills that there is no direct relationship between political decision-making and the social origins and occupational careers of policy-makers. "Now it is a remarkable and indeed astounding fact," intoned political scientist Dahl, really speaking for all pluralists on this point, "that neither Professor Mills nor Professor Hunter has seriously attempted to examine an array of specific cases to test his major hypothesis" (Dahl, 1958: 31).

Although Mills's major attack was on the pluralist theory advocated by the Cold War liberals, his own theory annoyed Marxists almost as much as it did liberals, for Mills rejected their class-based perspective of a still-dominant ruling capitalist class that was locked in constant struggle with a growing and restive working class. He dismissed their view in a single footnote as "a rather simple theory," claiming that the phrase "ruling class" was a "badly loaded" one which assumed what needed to be studied and demonstrated, namely, that a particular economic class was able to turn its wealth and status into political power (Mills, 1956: 277). More generally, Mills did not think the idea of a "ruling class" allowed enough "autonomy to the political order and its agents, and it says nothing about the military as such" (1956: 277). Mills also doubted that the working class was in inevitable opposition to a power elite or ruling class, but it was not until a few years later that he expressed his doubts more dramatically by calling the Marxian faith in the eventual victory of the working class a "labor metaphysic."

More than Marxists generally realize, however, power structure research has been influenced by the questions they ask. Hunter had become familiar with Marxism as a member of the Progressive Party in Atlanta in the late 1940s, a time when he also learned about the power structure firsthand by bumping up against it, losing his position as head of a community agency for allowing 1948 Progressive presidential candidate Henry Wallace to speak in the community center. And Mills, as a socialist intellectual highly eager to see egalitarian social change, also was quite alive to the tenets of Marxism. But neither Hunter nor Mills was a full-blown Marxist, and therein lay the seeds of future conflict between Marxism and power structure research. Therein also lay the peculiar strength and appeal of power structure research. Marxism had helped to formulate its questions, but had not dictated its answers. Power structure researchers felt the need to do empirical work on what Marxists took for granted. They tried to study the workings of power, whereas Marxists tended to focus on the workings of the economy.

The conflicts between the founders and critics of power structure research in the second half of the 1950s carved out the general issues and lines of research that have persisted in one form or another down to the present. However, the intensity of these conflicts subsided somewhat in the late 1960s, partly because they were getting to be old hat, partly because power structure research was being shaped to some extent by the needs of civil rights and antiwar activists. Some of the pluralists even moderated their views as they observed the intransigence of the American power structure in the face of calls for greater social justice and an end to clandestine and militaristic intervention in Cuba, Brazil, the Dominican Republic, Vietnam, and other parts of the globe.

However, as the conflicts with pluralists declined in importance, the questions raised by a new generation of Marxists became a primary focus of debate and research. This Marxist critique first appeared in reviews of *The State in Capitalist Society* (1969) by Ralph Miliband, one of Mills's closest Marxist friends between 1957 and Mills's death in 1962 (Miliband, 1962). A British political scientist born on the European continent, Miliband brought together a great variety of information on the social and occupational backgrounds of government officials and on the workings of the social and political institutions of capitalist countries. He used this information to argue that a ruling class based in the ownership and control of income-producing private property dominates in these countries. Miliband, careful to keep his distance from power structure researchers, saw his book as a more Marxian answer to the pluralists than had been given hitherto, but some Marxists saw it as an inadequate presentation of what they felt to be the true Marxian view. They believed it was a flawed treatment that did not transcend the categories of pluralists and power structure researchers, and that might have been infected by some of Mills's "elitist" ideas (Balbus, 1971; Poulantzas, 1969).

For Isaac Balbus, Miliband's failure to appreciate fully the role of class struggle in shaping modern capitalist society made him pessimistic about social change and one-dimensional and overly manipulative in his understanding of power. In fact, according to Balbus (1971: 45), Miliband was not a real Marxist at all, but only a self-proclaimed one: "This is not the first work by a serious and highly respected thinker on the Left in which a self-proclaimed Marxist class analysis turns out at bottom to be yet another variant of ruling elite analysis." Balbus's theme became a favorite one for Marxists of the 1970s, who often quoted him when reading Miliband out of their fraternity even while they forgot that Balbus had rejected traditional workers as agents of change and proclaimed "students and intellectuals" as the key elements in the "subordinate" class. It was a surprising emphasis for a Marxist so hostile to "elitism," for Mills had discussed the role of students in less apocalyptic terms in the late 1950s.

The critique by French Marxist Nicos Poulantzas raised other questions. While he too questioned the residual elitism in the Miliband analysis, he stressed that work on the involvement of members of the ruling class in government was beside the point. His most famous statement on the matter read as follows:

> *Direct* participation of members of the capitalist class in the State apparatus and in the government, even where it exists, is not the important side of the matter. The relation between the bourgeois class and the State is an *objective relation*. This means that if the *function* of the State in a determinate social formation and the *interests* of the dominant class in this formation *coincide*, it is by reason of the system itself: the direct participation of members of the ruling class in the State apparatus is not the *cause* but the *effect*, and moreover a chance and contingent one, of this objective coincidence [1969:73; all italics in this quote are in the original—GWD].

The general reproaches visited upon Miliband and power structure research by Balbus and Poulantzas were echoed and elaborated over the next few years by the American Marxist economist James O'Connor (1973) and the German political philosopher Claus Offe (1974). O'Connor and Offe had come to know each other during a visit to West Germany by O'Connor, and out of their intellectual interactions there grew several discussion groups and a journal—*Kapitalistate*—devoted to the development of a Marxist theory of the state. It was *Kapitalistate* groups, and not Poulantzas, that were to have the greatest effect on power structure research in the 1970s. These groups, and in particular the San Francisco group, created the dichotomy of "instrumentalist" and "structuralist" as a way of categorizing various Marxist views of "the state" (Gold et al., 1975). The instrumentalist view was characterized as one which saw government as a mere committee of the ruling class, directly manipulated by leading members of that class. Instrumentalists were said to be under the influence of an overly crude or "economistic" Marxism that did not appreciate the "relative autonomy" of government. Miliband was singled out as the most sophisticated exponent of this view. Structuralists, on the other hand, were said to be interested in the systematic functional interrelationships among the institutions of a society, and especially the underlying functional relationships between the economy and the state. Poulantzas was said to be the exemplar of this category, although aspects of his work were found wanting by the American structuralists (Esping-Anderson et al., 1976). Poulantzas (1976) rejected the categorization in any case, explaining how he had been misinterpreted by his American admirers.

Power structure research was drawn into this Marxist debate because it was said to fall squarely within the instrumentalist category. Indeed, it was seen as a crude form of Marxian instrumentalism, a somewhat surprising charge against a field of research which had been started by a radical structural-functionalist, Floyd Hunter, and a radical Weberian, C. Wright Mills, and which owed more to Mills's rejection of the concept of ruling class because it does not allow enough "autonomy" to the "political order" than it did to the phrase in The Communist Manifesto where Marx and Engels write that "the modern state is but a committee for managing the common affairs of the whole bourgeoisie."

The result of this dichotimization, of course, was to leave the alleged instrumentalists somewhat dismayed (e.g., Miliband, 1970, 1973). As far as power structure research is concerned, however, not too much should be made of the protests expressed by the so-called instrumentalists, for in the end the various claims and counterclaims sharpened the questions asked by power structure researchers and led to further studies, including several of those reported in this volume.

Given this tumultuous history, perhaps it is not surprising that the essays in this volume continue to address basic questions raised by and about power structure research over the past three decades. The "pluralist" versus "power elite" versus "ruling class" argument lies just off stage when it is not the central focus, and the more recent "instrumentalist" versus "structuralist" debate is an explicit concern in many of the contributions. What is gratifying about these essays is that they respond to the theoretical debates with original empirical findings that are often the result of new research techniques. It is this fact which gives hope that power structure research will continue to play the unique and relatively independent role it has carved out during its first three decades.

Marvin Dunn's opening essay describes a relatively unknown mechanism of ruling-class coordination, the family office. Dunn learned about the existence of this office somewhat inadvertently, for he began only with the interesting idea that studying a wealthy family in detail might cast light on many of the questions that concern power structure researchers. He soon discovered that the large family in question coordinates much of its economic, philanthropic, and political activity through a common office. Thus, Dunn is able to use his new information to call into question the claim that there is no longer a ruling class in America because wealthy families are unable to solidify their positions of power.

Richard Zweigenhaft brings new perspectives to general questions of ruling-class flexibility and class consciousness by examining the assimilation of successful businesspeople of Jewish background into the social organizations of the upper class. Not only does he give us original substantive information on upper-class anti-Semitism, but he shows us that what Jewish businesspeople do and do not list in a who's who biography is very revealing about their economic position and class consciousness. Consciousness from who's who biographies? But I'll let you read it for yourself.

Susan Ostrander gets her information on class consciousness in one of the ways we might expect someone to get such information—by interviewing. But she adds an interesting twist by interviewing women of the upper class, which gives her a rather unique vantage point. Moreover, Ostrander stresses that she did not learn about class consciousness by asking about it directly. Instead, she learned about it from questions that she didn't think related to class consciousness at all. She was as surprised by many of her findings as you will be, which not only affirmed her in the belief that members of the upper class are class conscious, but led her to an original formulation of what we should mean by the concept itself. It is at the least a provocative approach that she suggests, and it nicely encompasses the kinds of findings presented in the essays by Dunn and Zweigenhaft.

Allen Whitt's essay on the involvement of corporate leaders in one aspect of California politics in effect builds on the understandings solidified in Ostrander's essay. Whitt studied in detail the activities of California business leaders in relation to several ballot initiatives concerning highways and mass transit. He found that these corporate capitalists were quite organized and purposeful in their behavior right down to the last gallon of gas and bank asset, which determined how much they gave in cash contributions to various political campaigns. But it is not gallons of gas or bank assets that ultimately interest Whitt, and he uses his findings to make insightful observations about the instrumentalist-structuralist dichotomy.

The next essay, by Richard Ratcliff, uses his dimensions of "social prominence" and "economic power" to show who the well-organized and purposeful capitalists are in St. Louis when it comes to involvement in the civic organizations that attempt to shape the political and cultural climate of that city. But Ratcliff goes one step further, exploiting his unique data on bank loans and mortgages to show that capitalist class consciousness is not smoothly comprehensive and without contradictions. The bank directors he found in the civic groups trying to "save" downtown St. Louis are the same bankers who invest their funds outside of St. Louis, and especially outside of neighborhoods where people of low and moderate incomes reside.

A different kind of data was utilized by Eric Lichten to study the financial crisis that enveloped New York City in the mid-1970s. It allows him to highlight the way in which class conflict enters into the power equation. Through a careful sifting of govenment reports and his perceptive interviews with business, trade union, and government officials in the city, he shows how the demands of city workers and poor people constrained the hand of capitalists until the situation had reached a crisis point. It was only then, and with the help of state and federal levels of power, that the corporate leaders were able to contain elected officials and trade union leaders, and impose fiscal austerity at the expense of the working class in general.

The essay by Irvine Alpert and Ann Markusen moves us to the final third of the book and a consideration of power at the national level in America. Their essay picks up where Ostrander left off, with an explicit discussion of class consciousness. This time, however, the concern is with the consciousness of the academic experts employed by the policy-oriented think tanks financed and directed by members of the national corporate community. Alpert and Markusen explain how such experts end up working to solve problems of corporate capitalism even while they think of themselves as independent and neutral professionals. They address themselves directly to the instrumentalist-structuralist dichotomy, believing the insights into professional consciousness afforded to them as observers at the Brookings Institution and Resources for the Future allow them to bridge some of the gaps between the two sides of this argument.

The essays by Michael Useem, on the one hand, and Harold Salzman and G. William Domhoff, on the other, take us into the question of direct involvement in government by corporate leaders. Useem is able to utilize statistical techniques of a clear and straightforward nature to show just which business people are likely to become involved in formal governance at the state and national levels. Among many interesting findings, he shows that it is the biggest of big business leaders and those with multiple corporate directorships and memberships in national policy organizations who are most likely to serve on federal advisory committees and as trustees of major universities.

If Useem tells us which businesspeople participate in governance, Salzman and Domhoff try to establish the degree to which businesspeople are appointed to positions in the executive branch of the federal government for 1970. As the introduction to their essay informs us, this is one of the oldest and most contested issues in power structure research. It got its start in claims by Mills in *The Power Elite*, and it has been the subject of controversy ever since, with pluralists denying that these appointments are extensive and structural Marxists denying any significance to the appointments, whatever their extent. Meanwhile, say Salzman and Domhoff, there is a great deal of interchange of personnel between the corporate community and the executive branch, which raises a problem for those who say that capitalist governments function best when there are no capitalists in them.

In the end, we are brought back to the old question of what implications should be drawn from position-holding in civic groups and government. That is why we have saved the essay by Nancy DiTomaso for last. By responding to the critics of the positional method so frequently employed in power structure research, she provides the theoretical basis for the empirical findings that have been presented in several of the earlier essays, and especially that by Salzman and Domhoff. A sociologist very familiar with the instrumentalist-structuralist debate, DiTomaso approaches the problem from a fresh angle by drawing out the lessons for power structure research that are contained in the detailed literature of organizational sociology, a field largely ignored by power structure researchers in the past. It is a welcome turn of events to see this more conventional counterpart of power structure research provide new perspectives to disputants within the power structure fraternity.

There is no telling what new critiques will guide power structure research in the 1980s, but we can be sure that power is too charged and difficult a topic for controversy to subside. Wherever the next controversies may lead, let us hope they are ultimately as productive as the arguments of the first three decades have been in inspiring the fine and original contributions that we bring together in this volume as our way of kicking off a fourth decade of important and exciting research.

It has been my pleasure to coordinate this effort and to work with the individual authors. As with a previous volume I edited on power structure research (Domhoff, 1975), this work was undertaken for the benefit of *The Insurgent Sociologist*, an alternative social science journal which publishes radical and Marxian scholarship encompassing a range of concerns that extends well beyond power structure research. Housed editorially in the Department of Sociology at the University of Oregon in Eugene, its existence has contributed greatly to the development of both power structure research and Marxian scholarship. The individual authors and I are happy that our efforts in this book will make *The Insurgent Sociologist* even more widely known and will help to support its encouragement of insurgent scholars committed to what C. Wright Mills called intellectual craftsmanship.

REFERENCES

BALBUS, I. (1971) "Ruling elite theory vs. Marxist class analysis." Monthly Review 23: 36-46.

DAHL, R. (1968) "A critique of the ruling elite model," in G. W. Domhoff and H. Ballard (eds.) C. Wright Mills and The Power Elite. Boston: Beacon Press.

_____ (1961) Who governs? New Haven, CT: Yale Univ. Press.

DOMHOFF, G. W. (1975) "New directions in power structure research." Insurgent Sociologist 5, 3.

ESPING-ANDERSON, G., R. FRIEDLAND, and E. WRIGHT, (1976) "Modes of class struggle and the capitalist state." Kapitalstate 4-5: 186-220.

GILLAM, R. (1975) "C. Wright Mills and the politics of truth: the power elite revisited." American Scholar 28, 4: 461-479.

GOLD, D., C. LO, and E. WRIGHT (1975) "Recent developments in Marxist theories of the capitalist state." Monthly Review 27: 29-43.

HUNTER, F. (1953) Community Power Structure. Chapel Hill: Univ. of North Carolina Press.

MILLS, C.W. (1956). The Power Elite. New York: Oxford Univ. Press.

MILIBAND, R. (1973) "Poulantzas and the capitalist state." New Left Review 62.

_____ (1970)"The capitalist state—reply to Nicos Poulantzas." New Left Review 59.

_____ (1969) The State in Capitalist Society. New York: Basic Books.

_____ (1968). "C. Wright Mills," in G. W. Domhoff and H. Ballard (eds.) C. Wright Mills and The Power Elite. Boston: Beacon Press.

O'CONNOR, J. (1973) The Fiscal Crisis of the State. New York: St. Martin's Press.

OFFE, C. (1974) "Structural problems of the capitalist state," in K. von Breyme (ed.) German Political Studies. Beverly Hills: Sage Publications.

POULANTZAS, N. (1976) "The capitalist state: a reply to Miliband and Laclau." New Left Review 95: 63-83.

_____ (1969) "The problem of the capitalist state." New Left Review 58: 67-78.

1

THE FAMILY OFFICE: COORDINATING MECHANISM OF THE RULING CLASS

Marvin G. Dunn

Power structure researchers have uncovered a number of facets of class and power in the United States by focusing their studies on the social organizations of the upper (or capitalist) class. Seeking to demonstrate that the major capitalists are a ruling class which influences all aspects of American society, their studies show how private schools, social clubs, retreats, and policy groups function to maintain class cohesion and consciousness (e.g., Mills, 1956; Baltzell, 1958; Hunter, 1959; Domhoff, 1974; Shoup, 1975). These and other theorists also have argued that big businesspeople and their descendants may still control, as well as own, the large corporations that dominate the economy (e.g., Burch, 1972; Dunn, 1974; Zeitlin, 1974; Sonquist and Koenig, 1975).

In recent years yet another organization has come to the attention of power structure researchers that may operate to facilitate class cohesion and corporate control. This relatively unknown form of organization—the "family office"—may prove to be one of the more important means available to wealthy families for maintaining their social and economic position in society. After reviewing the scanty information previously available on family offices, this essay will provide a detailed look at a family office through a study of the Weyerhaeuser family. As will be shown, this family office links members of the family together, not only through kinship connections, but also through the structure of economic, charitable, and political activities that are coordinated out of it.

It is my contention that the structure of family wealth and power is not only an historical mechanism of class maintenance, as Daniel Bell (1962) and Talcott Parsons (1960) claim, but a contemporary aspect of corporate capitalism. The kinship group provides the structure and secrecy to perpetuate power relations originating in upper-class families and extending to other institutional structures. The fusion of property and kinship, thought to be a vestige of earlier stages of capitalism, may actually be a major contributor to intergenerational continuity in the class structure. Rather than having been broken up, the upper-class family and its mechanisms of control and cohesion have taken on new organizational forms. This fusion is represented by shared economic interests and kinship bonds. It is best described as a "kinecon group," a concept developed to replace the notion of family capitalism by sociologists Maurice Zeitlin, Richard Ratcliff, and Lynda Ann Ewen on the basis of detailed studies of the ownership and control of corporations and land in Chile in the twentieth century. They define a "kinecon group" as *a complex kinship unit in which economic interests and kinship bonds are inextricably intertwined*" (Zeitlin et al., 1974: 109; italics in original). Continuing, they explain the concept in more detail:

> The concept of the kinecon group is meant to be class specific: where shares of large corporations have become the typical and decisive form of capital ownership, and the relationship between specific ownership interests and corporate control becomes historically problematic, the concept of the kinecon group applies. The corporation is the legal unit of ownership of large-scale productive property. The set of interrelated kin who control the corporation through their combined ownership interests and strategic representation in management constitute the kinecon group [Zeitlin et al., 1974:110].

The concept of a kinecon group has not been applied as yet in the United States. However, the existence of family offices, and in particular the information on the Weyerhaeuser office, provides a means for exploring its utility in this country.

EARLIER EVIDENCE ON FAMILY OFFICES

Although our knowledge of family offices is sketchy, there is enough information available from the business press, family biographies, and government records to conclude that their existence is widespread. Summarizing much of what is known, Shelby White (1978) writes that "To a large extent, the wealthy families of America have managed their money by setting up private offices, which then take care of the family finances from cradle to grave: activating trusts, dispensing allowances to the younger generations, helping obtain divorces for older family members, and, ultimately, managing their estates." She proceeds to describe family offices in the following terms, suggesting their role as a cohesive force in holding large upper-class families together:

> But most of all, family offices have served as *a unifying force,* keeping the money intact as the families have moved out of the entrepreneurial, risk-taking businesses that formed the basis of the wealth. Without a central office, the fortune would lose its power as it was dispersed over generations. Though each member of a family might be worth several million dollars, it is the *collective use of the money* that gives the offices the leverage to buy companies, create tax shelters and invest in oil drilling, real estate and the myriad of other ventures favored by the very rich [White, 1978:9].

Not all family offices consist of a single kin unit. Cramer-Rosenthal & Co., for example, is a partnership that manages the money of three wealthy families "with a collective net worth of $250 million" (White, 1978: 20). In addition to managing investments that include ten do-it-yourself car washes, the office bought a house in Granada which all relatives can use and purchased two hundred cases of a fine French wine, Mouton Lafite, for the personal consumption of family members.

The Phipps family, heirs of a Pittsburgh steel baron, provide an example of a long-standing kinship group using an office to organize its large holdings. Many details concerning the functioning of the office became known because one of the founder's grandsons, Esmond Phipps, brought suit against the rest of the family and the office for allegedly mismanaging a family holding company and family trusts. Journalist Richard Smith (1960: 164-165) described the office as the administrative heart of the Phipps family empire:

> It operates as a private bank, lending as much as $5 million a year; as an investment service, running individual portfolios estimated to total $250 million; as a personal-service company, paying $2 million worth of family bills. Even today the Office's batteries of I.B.M. machines are still toting up Esmond's monthly bills. And from the headquarters at 800 Second Avenue flows the monthly freshet of checks that pay for his club dues (Meadow Brook, Piping Rock), the rental of his Madison Avenue office, the bills for his chess lessons, his tennis lessons, his $50,000 orchid greenhouse (he grows orchids commercially), his gun collection, his watch collection, his collection

of crystalline gold, and ironically, the bills—$720,000 so far—for the suit itself.

The Phipps office has the outward appearance of a family holding company, but according to Smith it is more important and diverse than that. In addition to paying personal bills—for farms, racing stables, and yachts—the office oversees the investment of the Phipps' millions. Investments are channeled through the family holding company, Bessemer Securities Corporation. In 1960, shares in Bessemer were held by thirty-eight family trusts.

According to White (1978), the Phipps office began managing the money of a few nonfamily members in the late 1960s, and now has under its management over $1 billion in assets—70% of it Phipps money. Nonfamily members do not participate in major new investments, but utilize the investment advisory and estate- and tax-planning services. None of the active officers are any longer members of the Phipps family, but family members serve on the board and set the general policy guidelines. A few members of the family no longer use the office's services.

A more prominent family which uses a family office is the Mellon family of Pittsburgh. Family member William Mellon (1948), in a privately printed book, wrote that the formation of T. Mellon & Sons in 1946 was to provide a way to solidify the family and coordinate its activities. The organization of a family office, he said,

> will permit a systematic coordination and action of various responsibilities of us all. This is a more formal society than we used to have. One function of this organization will be to carry on studies of the potentials of investments under consideration [1948: 559].

In 1971 the Mellons established Richard K. Mellon & Sons as a new family office to replace T. Mellon & Sons. New York *Times* (January 19, 1971) quoted Mrs. Richard K. Mellon as saying, "Richard K. Mellon & Sons [is] the sole spokesman for our family in all business matters and in the administration of our charitable programs." A biography of the Mellon family today (Koskoff, 1978) claims the family is diverse politically and in life style. There is only one heir involved in business, but the family has men representing it on various corporate boards and foundations. These representatives of the family operate "out of 'the thirty-ninth floor,' as the Mellon's family offices on that floor of the Mellon Bank Building are known in business and philanthropic circles" (Koskoff, 1978: 477). What power the Mellons have in controlling corporations, political giving, and philanthropic activities is "centralized on the thirty-ninth floor." A diversity of occupations, life styles, and social interests suggests that the family is not operating as a social unit, but the family office continues to represent an "unseen but powerful gravitational force" (Koskoff, 1978: 559).

Recent assessments of who controls Gulf Oil have concluded that Gulf is under Mellon family control (Koskoff, 1978; Burch, 1972). Koskoff put the percentage of family ownership at 21% in 1972, while Burch listed 25% for five years earlier. A recent crisis at Gulf illustrates how the Mellon family exercises its power through its stockholdings and representation on the board, for it is generally agreed that in 1976 the Mellon interests on the board of Gulf played a leading role in ousting Gulf's chairman and several other officers after government investigators discovered a secret company slush fund used for illegal campaign contributions and bribes to foreign officials. "The Mellon forces warned the Gulf chairman that they had the votes to oust him if he refused to resign" (Wall Street *Journal,* January 15, 1976). The Mellon family, with 15% of Gulf stock according to *Newsweek* (January 26, 1976), was successful in dismissing the chairman and several other top managers involved in the illegal activity. Examples such as this illustrate that wealthy families which own seemingly small percentages of corporate stock can influence these corporations, especially at critical junctures. The family office is one mechanism such families have developed for this purpose.

The most famous and powerful family known to use a family office is the Rockefeller family descended from John D. Rockefeller, Jr. Although it had been described in family biographies in the past, its importance in coordinating the economic and political activities of the family only became fully understood in the mid-1970s through congressional testimony (Domhoff and Schwartz, 1974) and an unauthorized family history (Collier and Horowitz, 1976). The office, now called Rockefeller Family and Associates, is located on the fifty-sixth floor of the Rockefeller Center in New York. It is often referred to as Room 5600, but it actually occupies three entire floors of the building. Its scale of operation appears larger than that of other known family offices. Writing in *The New Yorker* several years ago, E.J. Kahn referred to Room 5600 as "the center of the overlapping, if not interlocking, activities of the Rockefeller family" (Kahn, 1965: 40).

Rockefeller Family and Associates (RFA) may differ from other family offices not only in size but in organization. J. Richardson Dilworth, the head of the office, said in his statement before the House Committee on the Judiciary during the hearings on Nelson Rockefeller's nomination for Vice President that RFA "is not a legal entity or organization, but simply a name to describe the 84 descendants of John D. Rockefeller, Jr. who are the office, and the group of people with various specialties who furnish certain services to those members of the Rockefeller family" (U.S. House of Representatives, 1974a: 844).

In his description of the office, Dilworth went on to say:

> In addition to family members, the office consists of 154 staff people who provide accounting, investment, legal, philanthropic, public relations and tax services to these multiple employers. The office also maintains a library, files, messenger and travel services, and has a cafeteria as well as a small purchasing and maintenance group to service its requirements. In addition, individual members of the family employ other people both within the office and elsewhere [1974a: 844].

However, the findings of Domhoff and Schwartz (1974) suggested that the office was much more than that, employing business experts who sit on corporate boards as representatives of Rockefeller family interests. At the same time, some of these men were members of boards for other reasons, demonstrating how complicated it is to sort out the reasons for board membership. For example, George Hinman, a special counsel to the Rockefeller office, was on the IBM board because of a long association between his family and the Watson family, the founders of IBM.

The Rockefeller office also was shown to be used for a questionable political attack on former Supreme Court Justice Arthur Goldberg when he ran for governor of New York against Nelson Rockefeller in 1970. After a legal adviser to Nelson Rockefeller suggested the possibility of financing a book by Victor Lasky attacking the personal and political life of Goldberg, the matter was referred to Laurence Rockefeller, who turned the details over to Dilworth. Dilworth telephoned an uncle in Philadelphia, who sent one of his junior law partners to Delaware to set up a new "corporation" to finance the writing and distribution of the book. The purchase of large quantities of the book was paid for out of the family office account of Laurence Rockefeller. When the book was distributed in New York in 1970, the backers of the project could not be traced, but the story was revealed in 1974 when the FBI and the House Judiciary Committee examined the records of Rockefeller Family and Associates as part of the confirmation hearings of Nelson Rockefeller as Vice President (Lundberg, 1975: 76-79; U.S. House of Representatives, 1974a).

Although this review of available information on family offices suggests their importance in maintaining the economic and political power of wealthy families, there have been no systematic studies of them. Thus, this work on the Weyerhaeusers and their family office provides an opportunity for substantiating and enlarging upon what has been learned to date. The discovery of the Weyerhaeuser office occurred in the context of a more general study of this family as a means of shedding light on the influence of upper-class families in American life.

To that end, a complete family tree was developed from the founder, Frederick Weyerhaeuser (1834-1914), to the fifth generation, who range up to 36 years in age. In addition, everything that has been written about family members and their activities was assembled, and interviews were conducted with nine members of the family and several executives of family-related corporations. As the research progressed, it became apparent that the Weyerhaeusers (many of whom are not named Weyerhaeuser, of course) have a family office and an annual family meeting which play a central role in maintaining family cohesion and economic power. Before describing this organization and its functions, however, it will be useful to trace briefly the history of the Weyerhaeuser family and its companies.

THE WEYERHAEUSER FAMILY

As noted, the Weyerhaeuser family legacy originated with Frederick Weyerhaeuser, a German immigrant who settled in Rock Island, Illinois, and got his start in the lumber business shortly before the Civil War. Weyerhaeuser's involvement with corporations began in 1860 when he took over the assets of a bankrupt lumberyard for which he had been working. He did so with the aid of his brother-in-law, F. C. Denkmann, whose descendants have remained close to the Weyerhaeuser interests to the present day. Incorporating their business as Weyerhaeuser & Denkmann, the two brothers-in-law began operating a sawmill along the Mississippi River in central Illinois.

The family nature of the initial enterprise was soon to expand in two directions. The first involved the sons of the partners. The second was to encompass a number of families from other firms who in their early years were competitors of the Weyerhaeuser & Denkmann Company. This latter was done by organizing a number of other family firms into larger economic units. By convincing them to pool their resources, Frederick Weyerhaeuser made associates out of his former competitors.

Combining the interests of lumbermen on the Mississippi and its tributaries was only the beginning of the Weyerhaeuser empire. By the 1880s the lumbermen organized into various companies by Weyerhaeuser became known as the Weyerhaeuser "syndicate." *Fortune* wrote in 1934 that Weyerhaeuser "was shrewd enough to make associates of competitors and to avoid the lime-light" (1934: 170). Although he never held a majority of the stock in any of these enterprises, *Fortune* had little doubt that "Weyerhaeuser ran the businesses" (1934: 173).

By the end of the 1880s, Frederick Weyerhaeuser and his associates had exhausted most of the white pine in Wisconsin. In 1890, they began buying land on the upper Mississippi in Minnesota, and the Weyerhaeuser empire moved its center of operations from Wisconsin to Minnesota. A year later Frederick moved his family to St. Paul and shortly after arriving bought a house next door to a famous railroad baron, James J. Hill. Hill became a close personal friend and later sold the Weyerhaeuser interests 900,000 acres of choice timberland in the state of Washington for $6 an acre. As he had done three decades earlier, Weyerhaeuser again turned to the lumbermen of the upper Mississippi to raise the money for the new venture. On February 8, 1900, the Weyerhaeuser Timber Company was incorporated after one of the largest land transactions in the country's history.

By the time of Weyerhaeuser's death in 1914, his four sons had joined him in the ownership and management of numerous firms in the timber industry. Within less than a generation the business operations of the Weyerhaeuser family had grown from a small lumberyard to an interest in nearly fifty firms. These companies were interrelated by stockownership and director interlocks involving not only the Weyerhaeusers but many of the earlier Weyerhaeuser associate families. Like families in other industries, the Weyerhaeusers had built their fortune on an expanding economy, industrialization, and monopoly interests.

Fifteen years after Frederick's death the Weyerhaeuser empire had expanded to almost one hundred companies, including the Weyerhaeuser Timber Company, Potlatch Forest, Boise-Payette, Humbird Lumber, Northwest Paper, Wood Conversion, and General Timber Service. Frederick's sons and grandsons, after prep school and Yale or Harvard, had taken over the management and direction of these firms. Stockownership continued to be concentrated within the family. *Fortune* claimed in the aforementioned 1934 article that the Weyerhaeuser family owned about 22% of the stock in these various enterprises at that time. Frederick's youngest son, Frederick Edward (1872-1945), became the overseer and coordinator of the family's corporate interests. In this position he sat on all the major boards of the Weyerhaeuser interests. Under his direction the sons had set up a "central governing agency. . . to coordinate the loosely organized syndicate and affiliated companies" (Salo, 1945: 56). General Timber Service, as it was called, acted as a holding company for the six major companies. It was responsible for handling public relations, advertising, and accounting for the various Weyerhaeuser firms. Along with the Weyerhaeuser Sales Company, General Timber was managed and coordinated through the offices in St. Paul.

The leader of the third generation was Frederick King Weyerhaeuser (1895-1978), who came to maturity in the 1930s and 1940s. He gradually assumed the responsibilities that Frederick Edward Weyerhaeuser, his uncle, had taken on in the preceding generation. He was not only the leader of the family but during his career was also involved with many of the Weyerhaeuser firms, serving as president and/or chairman of the board of many of them. From the 1950s to the early 1970s Frederick King Weyerhaeuser was the patriarch of the family. He retired from the board of Rock Island Corporation, a family holding company, in the 1970s. His sole duty became the telling of the family history at the family meeting.

Through three generations the kinship group remained fairly cohesive and stable. Cousins in the third generation played together and went to school together. As they became active in the family's businesses, they gravitated to the two main centers of the family's operations, St. Paul, Minnesota, and Tacoma, Washington. Here they shared corporate directorates and church and club memberships. At the Minnesota Club, for example, they had their own table, where they often met with business leaders in other fields to transact business.

During the 1950s the family allegedly engaged in what a *Fortune* article (Freedgood, 1959) called "the grand corporate divorcement." This "divorcement" was said to signal the breakup by the Weyerhaeuser family of tightly knit interlocking directorates. The validity of this claim will be assessed after the family office has been discussed.

The fourth generation of the Weyerhaeuser family had a greater diversity of business and social connections. In size alone, the family increased from ten nuclear units to more than twenty-five. By the time the majority of the fourth generation was in college, about 1950, the extended kin group consisted of 63 living members. In less than a generation this would more than double.

The diversity was represented by two changes. First, not every member of this generation continued in the family businesses. This was particularly true of individuals who married into the family. They branched out into other investments, their own businesses (a helicopter company, for example), and careers in teaching and law. Second, individuals who married into the family often came from different socioeconomic backgrounds and had weaker links to upper-class institutions. These changes, however, are not very pronounced or prominent in this generation. As will be shown shortly, their involvement in major family businesses and charities remains considerable, and they have coordinated many of their activities through the family office.

There are over eighty members in the fifth generation, nearly half of whom have reached college age and beyond. Although some attended the Eastern private schools which graduated their parents, many are going to local private schools in St. Paul, Minnesota, Tacoma, Washington, and other cities. Some shunned private schools for public high schools. At the college level, more of this generation attended or are attending small liberal arts colleges rather than the major Eastern schools of which their parents are often alumni. Members of the fifth generation have enrolled in such private colleges as Lake Forest, University of Puget Sound, University of Denver, University of Pacific, Lewis and Clark College, Whitworth College, and Tulane. One member attended Stanford for two years, then dropped out to start an import wine business that subsequently failed.

A few members of the fifth generation appear to be headed for roles in family businesses. John Titcomb and George H. Weyerhaeuser, Jr., for example, worked summers for the Weyerhaeuser Company while in law school and at Yale. Several other young Weyerhaeusers say they plan on entering family businesses. However, some members of this generation have gone into business for themselves, taught school, tried farming, built log cabins with their boy friends, and run off to Hawaii with a professional baseball player.

Although it is too early to determine the ultimate careers of the fifth generation, their present diversity raises the possibility that the family has become too large to maintain its cohesiveness. Such a possibility brings us to a consideration of the role of the family office.

THE WEYERHAEUSER FAMILY OFFICE

In an article on "The House of Weyerhaeuser," *Fortune* (1934: 65) described the family office:

In every house moves the ghost of its founder. In the house of Weyerhaeuser the presence is almost overwhelming. On the twenty-first floor of St. Paul's new, tall First National Bank Building are large offices in which heavy old-fashioned furniture and walls hung with photographs of men long dead give a strangely real air of antiquity. Thick, brown carpet muffles the careless tread of younger men than the two Weyerhaeuser brothers, R.M. and F.E., who work there. Yet neither of them is old—sixty-three and sixty-one—and F.E.'s smile is as youthful as R.M.'s genial bark. The atmosphere is given by the feeling that neither of them is ever quite alone; that each feels himself always in the presence of one who lived long enough to dominate their lives into maturity; that no decision is reached up there without a visit to the Directors' room across the hall and a long look at a portrait done in gloomy oils that a small brass plaque identifies as FREDERICK WEYERHAEUSER (1834-1914).

Over four decades later, the family office still occupies the twenty-first floor of the First National Bank Building in St. Paul. The halls are still dominated by pictures of old logging scenes. Other hallways and offices are filled with pictures of various male members of the family. Completely filling one wall is a picture of Frederick Weyerhaeuser's four sons sitting on a sofa that is overshadowed by a picture of their father. Several rooms contain framed pictures of the "family tree." Picturing six generations of Weyerhaeusers, the family tree in one office is enclosed in a 3 × 4 foot frame. The framed genealogy, "Weyerhaeuser Family Tree: 1857-1970," contains small pictures of Frederick and Sarah Elizabeth Weyerhaeuser in the upper left-hand corner. In this same office, on a wall adjacent to the Weyerhaeuser genealogy, hangs the family tree of the Denkmanns. Behind the door are charts of the Laird-Norton and Musser families, both long-time family associates. The rest of the office is filled with 8½ × 11-inch pictures of numerous Weyerhaeuser associates from various family groupings that have been involved in Weyerhaeuser ventures. The "thick, brown carpet" has been replaced by an even thicker carpet that makes walking difficult. The office has undergone several name changes and reorganizations during the past seventy years. In several interviews, I was told the reasons for the name changes and reorganizations had been to reduce the tax burden, but no one would elaborate on these reasons.

F. Weyerhaeuser and Company, incorporated in 1901, was responsible for servicing the family for a number of years, although in its early years it also managed several operating companies (Hidy et al., 1963: 172). Until the 1940s, the second generation, with Rudolph Michael Weyerhaeuser (1868-1946) as president and his brother, Frederick Edward Weyerhaeuser (1872-1945), as secretary-treasurer, had the primary responsibility for this family office.

The assistant secretary and assistant treasurer at that time, Charles J. McGough, had worked out of the St. Paul office since before Frederick Weyerhaeuser's death in 1914. An accountant by training, McGough was initially involved not only in family affairs, but also in a variety of corporations coordinated out of the office. In the 1930s, for example, he worked out a proposed merger of the Weyerhaeuser interests in the Inland Empire (Hidy et al., 1963: 522-523).

In the 1950s McGough was listed in the *Polk's St. Paul City Directory* merely as an accountant at F. Weyerhaeuser and Company. However, according to my interviews, it was to McGough that members of the family addressed their questions about gift taxes, trusts, investments, philanthropic giving, and a host of other matters. During the 1950s he appeared as the key employee at the office. He died in 1963, leaving an estate totaling more than three-quarters of a million dollars according to probate records at St. Paul. More than 90% of it was in Weyerhaeuser, Wood Conversion, Potlatch, and Edward Hines Lumber Company stock (Ramsey County, 1963).

Polk's St. Paul City Directory shows that the name of the office had been changed in 1959 to the North East Service Company. The Minnesota Secretary of State's office in St. Paul, however, lists April 14, 1941 as the date of incorporation for North East Service Company (NESC). Frederick Edward Weyerhaeuser, Rudolph Michael Weyerhaeuser, and C.J. McGough are listed as the original directors. Although the precise date NESC began functioning as the family office is not known, in any case it was paying bills, arranging travel plans and accommodations, and planning estates for members of the family by the mid-1950s.

By 1960, Frederick King Weyerhaeuser was listed as president of NESC and Donald Hanson was listed as treasurer, with Gordon Hed as assistant treasurer. A long-time employee of the office, Hed was listed as an accountant with F. Weyerhaeuser and Company in 1955, as was Hanson. Ten years later, Hanson still listed himself in *Polk's* as a treasurer of NESC and Hed was listed as the investment department manager. Joseph Micallef, the present president of the family office, first appears as an employee, a tax manager at NESC, in 1967. The year before he had been employed by Weyerhaeuser as an attorney.

In 1969 the name of the family office was changed to WF Associates, Inc. In 1973, the name was changed again, this time to Fiduciary Counselling, Inc. Joseph S. Micallef became president, Hanson chairman of the board, and Hed vice president and assistant secretary. The office also became the property of its employees rather than of family members. Removing members of the family from an ownership role in the office was done for tax and legal purposes (interview). According to Micallef, the office provides an "advisory service" that is not exclusively a service for the family (interview). But, as a member of the family stated, the principal clients are all members of the Weyerhaeuser family (interview).

Not all members of the family "subscribe" to the services provided by F.C.I., and some members subscribe only to part of the services, such as the tax service. The office provides low-cost services for each family member. As the resource and financial center for family matters, the office informs members of family policy, but each member makes his or her own decisions, according to a member of the fifth generation (interview).

Another example of the help and advice provided by the office is financial counseling for the younger generation. Members of the fifth generation inherit large sums of money when they turn 18 or 21. One member of the fifth generation, for example, received "a large sum" that he did not know was coming. Since his father always had been reluctant to talk about financial matters, his advice and help in planning came from the family office (interview).

The main branch of F.C.I. remains on the twenty-first floor of the First National Bank Building in St. Paul. A smaller branch is located in Tacoma to provide services for members of the family on the West Coast. For a number of years a third branch was maintained in Wilmington, Delaware. This branch was responsible for trusts and holding companies incorporated in Delaware. This office was closed in the early 1940s and this work is now done in the St. Paul office (interview).

F.C.I. employs a staff of twenty-five people in St. Paul and an additional six full-time people in Tacoma. Some of the services provided by the office include: paying bills, determining the "best policy" for home, auto, and life insurance, filing tax returns, managing individual portfolios, helping in estate planning, making travel arrangements, and coordinating political and philanthropic giving (interviews). Investment counselors and lawyers on the staff also refer family members to outside brokers and lawyers.

Most members of the family living in St. Paul have personal offices in the family office. W. John Driscoll, for example, has an office there, which he leases from F.C.I. C. Davis Weyerhaeuser has a similar arrangement in the Tacoma branch of the office. Members of the family attending school in St. Paul have used the office for studying. One member of the fourth generation, for example, used his father-in-law's office when he was attending William Mitchel Law School (interview).

While the office manages trusts, foundation portfolios, and individual portfolios, its staff does not make the major decisions. That task is reserved for members of the family. The annual family meeting provides one structure for discussion and decision-making. It brings together members of the family and involves them in major decisions of common concerns (interviews). The meeting is normally held the same week as the annual shareholders' meetings of Weyerhaeuser companies. In the 1950s, for example, the family meetings were held at the end of a week full of other annual shareholders' meetings of a number of Weyerhaeuser companies. In recent years, the meeting has been held in Tacoma around the time of the annual meeting of the Weyerhaeuser Company. This was the case in 1975 when the company celebrated its seventy-fifth year. A special effort was made to encourage the descendants of the original founders to attend this anniversary meeting. During the meeting it was announced that many of these descedants were present. (The author was present at this meeting.) Talks with various family members after the meeting revealed that about eighty members of the Weyerhaeuser family were in attendance.

The following day they held their annual family meeting. The weekend was taken up with socializing both within the family and with members of other families that have been multigenerational associates of the Weyerhaeusers. Shortly after the stockholders' meeting, members of the Weyerhaeuser family and other families left (by a number of buses) to visit Weyerhaeuser operations in the area. The family office, in conjunction with the company, had organized tours of nearby mills, plants, and logging operations. The staff of the family office had lists of who was on each bus. After the meeting the staff mingled with members of the family, answering their questions, and finalizing their travel plans and dinner arrangements. Other families, the Laird-Nortons for example, also held their family meeting the day after the stockholders' meeting.

Interviews with family members yielded conflicting accounts of the annual meeting in recent years. The differences usually centered on the meeting's importance and on how much of a role the family continues to play in some of the larger companies, especially Weyerhaeuser, Potlatch, and Boise Cascade. Family members who were cautious during the interview tended to downplay the importance of the meetings. The annual meetings are a misnomer, one member informed me. The meetings, he said, consist of the annual meetings of companies in which Weyerhaeusers own 100% of the stock. When asked to list these, he mentioned three: Rock Island, Pine Tree Land, and Mississippi Land Company. The latter had recently been liquidated.

Those who were more cooperative in the interviews were more likely to talk about the yearly meeting, and placed more importance on its role in family continuity and control. "These meetings help greatly," a member of the fourth generation told me, "to maintain family cohesiveness. They are primarily social happenings, but reports are still given on the role in companies in which the family has investments" (interview). Another member of the fourth generation claimed the annual meeting was the mechanism holding the family together. "Each individual is doing something on their own," he said, "but the meeting provides a place to discuss the family's investments. Wealth is what keeps the family together, the bond. The ability to keep companies together is this common ownership. . . . If I own stock and my cousins own stock in common we have a reason for getting together. . . .

The holding force is the family's ability to get together every year. The common bond is the companies."

Members of the fifth generation were often more willing to talk, but often did not know as much as I did about family activities. One member from this generation told of the chicken barbecues and baseball games at these yearly gatherings, but said they also discussed directorships in various corporations when an opening was available.

In recent years much of the discussion in these business meetings has centered on Weyerhaeuser and Potlatch. Every year a member of management from one of these companies, usually the president, attends the family meeting. In 1974, the president of Arcata National was asked to give a brief presentation and answer questions that family members had about Arcata's recent activities. The person from management and the key personnel from the family office were the only nonfamily members in attendance (interview).

Another major activity of the meetings concerns the Weyerhaeuser foundations. The boards of various foundations meet and make recommendations to the rest of the family. The area of philanthropic giving is delegated to the women. They do not play any role in discussions of "business," whether that business means deciding which member of the family will replace a retiring family director, or involves a new investment (interview).

In addition to historical sketches, prayers, welcoming addresses, business reports, and discussion, each yearly meeting usually focuses on problems facing the family. In 1974, for example, the younger generation met before the meeting to discuss their common problems. Previous generations had grown up together, played as children, and knew each other well. Many in the fifth generation do not know each other this intimately. This was one of the problems that two of the older members of the fifth generation felt needed to be addressed by the fifth generation. In calling members of this generation together they proposed to discuss three additional problems this generation had in common: (1) a feeling that F.C.I. was less a tool for them than for the adults; (2) their feelings about the inheritance of large sums of money; and (3) their feelings that because of their name they were treated differently. These concerns and problems are identical to issues dealt with by the Rockefeller cousins in recent meetings (Collier and Horowitz, 1976).

In spite of the fact that they did not know each other too well, most members of the fifth generation felt they had certain responsibilities and family ties. In addition to discussing these problems, they asked the heads of the various Weyerhaeuser companies to come before them and answer questions. This took two days. Either at this meeting or at the regular family meeting, the younger generation asked questions about the companies' environmental practices, hiring of women and minorities, and overseas operations. These actions also are similar to those taken at meetings held by the youngest generation of the Rockefeller kin (Collier and Horowitz, 1976).

A problem associated with many family businesses is finding capable and qualified family members to manage the firm. This and several related problems are usually discussed at the annual family meeting. In 1974, for example, a sign-up sheet was circulated to determine who was interested in working for one of the Weyerhaeuser interests. Only eight people out of a potential thirty in the fifth generation who were between eighteen and thirty-six signed the list (interview).

This information on the Weyerhaeuser family office and the annual family meeting suggests that the Weyerhaeuser family fortune has remained coordinated at least through its first four generations. It now will be shown how this coordination manifests itself in the control of major corporations, in the utilization of holding companies, and in the coordination of philanthropic and political contributions.

THE CONTROL OF CORPORATIONS

The dominant view in American social science is that there has been a separation in the ownership and control of large corporations. The "break-up" of family capitalism purportedly has led to an upper class with dividend wealth and a managerial class with considerable power. Sociologist Maurice Zeitlin (1974: 1075), a skeptic about this claim, summarizes it well:

> The prevailing view is that the diffusion of ownership in the large corporation among numerous stock owners has resulted in the separation of ownership and control, and, by severing the connection between the family and private property in the means of production, has torn up the roots of the old class structure and political economy of capitalism. A new class of functionaries of capital, or confreries of economic "elites," in control of the new forms of productive property, appear: nonowning corporate managers displace their capitalist predecessors.

As noted, it has been claimed that the Weyerhaeusers lost control of all but the Weyerhaeuser Company during the late 1950s (Freedgood, 1959). However, the author did not look closely at the ownership and control patterns of these companies in terms of coordinated stock ownership and interlocking directorates among members of the extended Weyerhaeuser kinship group. Our information on the Weyerhaeuser family tree and the role of its family office provides an opportunity to reconsider this question.

For the general purpose of determining family control of a corporation, I would propose the following criteria. First, members of the same kinship group must own a combined total of 10% or more of the common stock. This is a highly conservative figure, for control is often defined by control of 5% or more of the common stock. Second, either of the following two conditions also must be met: (1) It must be shown that this investment is coordinated. (2) It must be shown that family members are involved in the company as managers or as directors.

In the case of the Weyerhaeuser kinship group, the evidence for coordination already has been presented. Thus, we can turn to ownership, management, and directorship information on the four major timber corporations that have emerged from the mergers of former Weyerhaeuser companies— Weyerhaeuser Company, Boise-Cascade, Potlatch, and Arcata National.

In 1975 Weyerhaeuser Company, the largest of these firms, was ranked 78 in the *Fortune* listing. Two members of the Weyerhaeuser family, C. Davis Weyerhaeuser and George H. Weyerhaeuser, were on the board of directors. Between them they owned directly or indirectly less than 1% of the shares of outstanding common stock. But when their holdings are added to the stock held in various family foundations, the other stock held by some 180 family members, and the stock these members held in trusts and holding companies, the family owned approximately 15% of the stock in the Weyerhaeuser Company (interview). In addition, George H. Weyerhaeuser is president and chief executive officer of the company, and his brother-in-law, Howard Meadowcroft, is the assistant to the president. In this capacity, Meadowcroft, the husband of George's youngest sister, serves as a liaison between George, other directors, and the family (interview). There are also three or four members of the fifth generation in lower-level management positions.

Boise-Cascade is the only company with historical links to the family which can no longer be considered under family control. Only one member of the Weyerhaeuser family, Edward R. Titcomb, sat on the board of directors in 1975. Although his tenure has been longer than any other director (since 1952), he owns less than two-tenths of one percent of the stock. With the family's combined interests accounting for only 2–3%, Boise-Cascade is the company least integrated into the family's interests, and by our criteria not under Weyerhaeuser control.

Potlatch, in 1975, continued to have the strongest links to the family. Four members of the family, Frederick W. Davis, George F. Jewett, Jr., John J.

Pascoe, and Frederick T. Weyerhaeuser, sat on the board. Adding the holdings of all family members, trusts, foundations, and holding companies, the family held 35-40% of Potlatch's stock (interview). Ten years before, "some 102 members of the Weyerhaeuser family" were said publicly to hold 52% of the outstanding common stock (Potlatch, 1965: 3).

By 1975 Arcata National had slipped into the second 500 in the *Fortune* ranking. Three members of the family, John J. Pascoe, Albert J. Moorman, and C. Davis Weyerhaeuser, were on Arcata's board. Together they owned 7.32% of the outstanding common stock (Arcata National, 1975). When the stock held in trusts and individual accounts by other family members is tallied, it could total close to 50%. The only approximation family members would reveal in interviews was that the family owned "a lot" of Arcata stock (interview).

Several smaller companies, Conwed (formerly Wood Conversion), COMSHARE (a computer software company), Dietzgen (precision drafting instruments), Rodman Industries, and Comerco, are owned by the family or by one or two members. With the exception of Conwed and COMSHARE, they are all closely held and assumed to be under family control.

In addition, all of these nine companies except Weyerhaeuser itself have direct interlocks with Rock Island Company, which is the family holding company. Rock Island and the other family holding company will be the topic of the next section. For now, it can be concluded that Weyerhaeuser family involvement in several major corporations meets our three criteria for family control, and establishes the Weyerhaesers as a major "kinecon group."

HOLDING COMPANIES

The holding company is another unit in a maze of interconnected corporations, foundations, trusts, personal holdings, and family offices that can coordinate a network of family wealth. Coordinated and managed by the family office, the holding company is often the central link in the network of corporate control. Lundberg (1968) claims the key to "superwealth" is family holdings. Such holdings, or "generic fortunes" as he calls them, usually revolve around a combination of institutional forms which includes one or more holding companies.

The Rock Island Corporation is a former operating company that has become a major holding company for the Weyerhaeuser family. One of the original companies founded by Frederick Weyerhaeuser in Rock Island,

Illinois, it should not be confused with the famous railroad holding company of the same name. All members of the Weyerhaeuser family have a "stock interest—investment" in Rock Island. Today its board consists chiefly of members of the Weyerhaeuser family from the fourth generation. Two members of the fifth generation—Rod Titcomb and his third cousin, Dan Davis—are serving a two-year apprenticeship of sorts on the board (interview). The only board member who is not a member of the family is Joseph S. Micallef, head of Fiduciary Counselling—the family office.

Through Rock Island Corporation the family shares in a number of common investments. In addition to the stock holdings already discussed, the family has investments in a number of other ventures. The Dietzgen Corporation is the only operating company still owned by Rock Island. The others were bought by a member of the fourth generation, Edward R. Titcomb, when Rock Island wanted to convert its holdings to cash. In the late 1960s several members of the family became involved in real estate and hotel investments in Hawaii. The family has recently divested itself of these investments, but it still retains real estate elsewhere, including a recreational land development and orange groves in Florida (interview). Other investments include a 50% interest in the Minnesota North Stars, a professional hockey team, by members of the family living in St. Paul.

Whether these investments are coordinated through Rock Island could not be determined. The exact structure of these investments and the relationship between holding companies and investments remain unknown. While it is clear that not all family members buy into every venture in which the family engages, Rock Island does handle investments, especially stocks and bonds, for family members (interview). It is the job of family member W. John Driscoll, president of Rock Island, to find profitable investments for the family.

Many wealthy families have become involved in what is known as "venture capital," the investment in new and sometimes risky ventures. One such venture capital spin-off for the Weyerhaeusers has been COMSHARE, Inc. "The Company is engaged in the business of providing remote processing computer services utilizing technology commonly known as timesharing" (COMSHARE, 1975: 1). The proxy statement for COMSHARE provides additional help in piecing together one of the mechanisms of internal coordination. Two members of the Weyerhaeuser family, Stanley R. Day and W. John Driscoll, are on the board of directors. The proxy statement, however, not only provides information on the stock holdings of these two directors, but also maps out the relationship between this corporation, another family holding company, and two "nominee partnerships." Under the heading

"Principal Shareholders" we read:

> The Common Stock is the only voting security of the Company. Bliss &
> Company and Hanson & Company, St. Paul, Minnesota, own 217,842 and
> 105,771 shares of Common Stock of the Company respectively, of record.
> Bliss & Company and Hanson & Company are nominee partnerships for
> various members of the Weyerhaeuser Family. The shares owned of record by
> Bliss & Company constitute 16.19% of the outstanding shares of Common
> Stock of the Company as of September 18, 1974, the record date. The "Wey-
> erhaeuser Family" as used in this Proxy Statement means certain of the
> descendants (and their spouses) of Frederick Weyerhaeuser, who died in 1914
> and who was one of the founders of Weyerhaeuser Company, a forest products
> company located in Tacoma, Washington. Stanley R. Day and W. John Dris-
> coll, Directors of the Company, and their wives are members of the Wey-
> erhaeuser Family. Members of the Weyerhaeuser Family own beneficially an
> aggregate of 346,513 shares of Common Stock of the Company, constituting
> 25.76% of the outstanding Common Stock of the Company as of September
> 18, 1974. No member of the Weyerhaeuser Family owns beneficially more
> than 10% of the outstanding Common Stock of the Company [COMSHARE,
> 1975].

And under a footnote in reference to Driscoll's holdings we find the following:

> In addition, Mr. Driscoll is an officer, director and owns 3.0515% of the stock
> of Green Valley Company, a corporate holding company, which owns benefi-
> cially 113,646 shares of Common Stock of the Company. These shares are
> held of record in the name of Bliss & Company. All of the capital stock of
> Green Valley Company is owned by members of the Weyerhaeuser Family.
> Mr. Driscoll is a co-trustee of six trusts which own an aggregate of 53,734
> shares of Common Stock of the Company, which are held in the name of Bliss
> & Company or Hanson & Company. Mr. Driscoll disclaims any beneficial
> interest in such shares. The shares in these trusts include the shares owned
> beneficially by Mr. Driscoll's mother. All of the shares of Common Stock
> described in this footnote as being owned of record by Bliss & Company or by
> Hanson & Company are included in the shares referred to under the caption
> "Principal Shareholders" in this Proxy Statement [COMSHARE, 1975].

The Green Valley Company mentioned in these legalistic-sounding documents is another family holding company. Members of the Weyerhaeuser
family own 100% of its capital stock. Like Rock Island, Green Valley is
another former operating company. Further complicating matters, Green
Valley holds 80% of the capital stock of Rock Island. This "arrangement,"
according to one member of the fourth generation, provides certain tax
advantages. It gives the companies liquid assets and the ability to carry over

losses and gains (Weisenberger, 1965: 95-98).

The stock of Green Valley and Rock Island, the two major holding companies, is held directly and indirectly by family members. As the proxy statement reports, W. John Driscoll owns slightly more than 3% of Green Valley's stock. Through a variety of family foundations and trusts set up for individual family members, the family owns the rest of Rock Island's and Green Valley's stock. These holding companies in turn own stock in COM-SHARE, Potlatch, Boise-Cascade, and the Weyerhaeuser Company. These holding companies, however, as agents of corporate control, do not seem to be central elements in the Weyerhaeuser network. It appears that the Weyerhaeuser holding companies are more important as devices for investment and for reducing taxes than for corporate control. But when combined with their holdings in trusts, foundations, and personal accounts, the holding companies do form part of a mechanism enabling the family to maintain control over a number of timber corporations and other firms.

FOUNDATIONS

Like the other components in this network overseen from the family office, charitable foundations afford the Weyerhaeuser family with another device for maintaining family cohesiveness and societal influence. Fifteen foundations can be identified as family foundations. The criteria for classifying a foundation as a Weyerhaeuser family foundation are (1) if a majority of the foundation's board consists of members of the family or of employees from the family office, or (2) if the foundation's books are kept at the office. Using *The Foundation Directory* and the IRS-990-AR forms on each foundation provided by the Foundation Center, we can identify the Weyerhaeuser family foundations, as shown in Table 1.1.

The boards of the family foundations are filled exclusively by members of the family or employees of the family office, except for the Black Foundation and three foundations established by C. Davis Weyerhaeuser. These latter three foundations, the Stewardship, C. Davis Weyerhaeuser Religious Trust, and CDW Corporation, all have C. Davis Weyerhaeuser and his brother-in-law, Clarence A. Black, on the board of trustees. The Black family is not a part of the Weyerhaeuser kinship group, but is related to the Weyerhaeusers through C. Davis's marriage to Annette Black. The Black Foundation is included as a Weyerhaeuser foundation because (1) the books are kept at Fiduciary Counselling, Inc., and (2) Frank Underwood, an employee of F.C.I. in Tacoma, is an officer of the foundation. This is a good

Table 1.1   Weyerhaeuser Family Foundations

Foundation	Assets	(Date)
Black	119,684	(1971)
CDW Corporation	74,398	(1973)
Davis (Edwin and Catherine)	3,506,213	(1973)
Driscoll	975,607	(1972)
Jewett (G.F.)	13,627,847	(1972)
Meadowdale	20,967	(1972)
Rodman	66,615	(1970)
Stewardship	7,597,289	(1972)
Titcomb[a]	237,308	(1972)
Weyerhaeuser		
C. Davis Religious Trust	11,790,526	(1973)
Charles A. Memorial	18,435	(1972)
F.K. and Vivian	61,073	(1972)
Frederick and Margaret L.	15,000	(1971)
Weyerhaeuser Foundation	3,422,617	(1972)
Woodbridge	55,647	(1972)
	Total $41,589,226[b]	

a. This foundation lists an address other than the Family Office.
b. The total is only an indication of the assets of these foundations. There are discrepancies among the reports of different sources, due primarily to differences between market values and book or acquisition values of stock held.

example of the interrelatedness of kin groupings among upper-class families.

Of the fifteen Weyerhaeuser family foundations, only one bridges all nuclear units and encompasses the whole kinship group. This is the Weyerhaeuser Foundation. It has the largest board of trustees and the largest number of officers. By studying each nuclear unit in the third generation, we found that each has representation on the board of trustees. In addition to the eleven members of the family on the board, Joseph S. Micallef serves as the assistant treasurer of the Weyerhaeuser Foundation.

This one foundation, then, serves as an important link between all the subunits within the larger kin group. Like the office out of which this foundation is managed, and the annual meeting which makes the philanthropic decisions, this foundation is a key aspect of the family's internal coordination.

Although these foundations serve as an important internal mechanism uniting the nuclear kin groups, their source of power lies in their connections to external institutions. Family foundations often serve as conduits which channel giving to charitable, religious, and educational institutions. These foundations often list assets of less than $100,000 but receive over $200,000 a year in gifts. These gifts come from family members and their trusts and holding companies, all of which make tax-deductible gifts from their income. Warren Weaver (1967: 43) describes foundations of this type:

The foundation acts for the family as a reservoir into which they can put, as a *contribution to capital,* a maximum deductible gift of 20 percent of current income in any one year. The foundation, under existing statutes, must expend into income annually, but that income is the earnings on the capital gifts it has received, not the gifts themselves.

Because these foundations receive yearly gifts two or three times larger than their assets, the assets of family foundations are not a good indicator of their importance or potential as givers. Most of the Weyerhaeuser family foundations with assets of less than $100,000 follow this pattern. The Rodman Foundation, for example, had assets of only $27,451 in 1972. However, in 1973 the foundation received gifts totaling $29,000—$7,000 in cash from E.R. Titcomb, and the rest in quarterly installments from the 1968 Irrevocable Trust of Edward R. Titcomb. In 1973 the foundation distributed $30,359. The Charles A. Weyerhaeuser Memorial Foundation listed $4,073 in assets in 1972, yet received $106,878 in contributions. The year before, this foundation received gifts totaling $212,976. The F.K. and Vivian O'Gara Weyerhaeuser Foundation, with assets of $60,787 in 1970, reported that it received $182,250 in gifts. In 1971, the Frederick and Margaret L. Weyerhaeuser Foundation listed assets of $15,000, but received $157,319 from the trusts of Margaret L. and Frederick T. Weyerhaeuser.

Space does not permit a detailed presentation of the findings on the beneficiaries of Weyerhaeuser foundation grants. In general, however, an analysis of information available on the smaller foundations for the years 1970-1972, and the Weyerhaeuser Foundation for 1950-1970, suggests that they go to educational and religious organizations in which the Weyerhaeusers are involved as alumni, members, or directors. For example, in 1970 the Stewardship Foundation gave $2,220,500 to the endowment of Fuller Theological Seminary, where C. Davis Weyerhaeuser was chairman of the board of trustees. In 1973, the same foundation gave 40% of its $255,200 in grants to an evangelical Protestant group, Young Life Campaign, of which C. Davis Weyerhaeuser is reported to be one of the founders (interview).

Weyerhaeuser foundation monies also go to organizations related to forestry. The Weyerhaeuser Foundation gave nearly 10% cf its contributions to such organizations over a twenty-year period. Two groups received the bulk of these contributions, the Yale University School of Forestry and The Forest History Society. The latter is a small educational and research organization dedicated to preserving original sources, writing biographies, and collecting oral histories from men and companies of historical interest in forest-related activities.

The several hundreds of thousands of dollars these foundations give each year, combined with the substantial number of trusteeships that Weyerhaeuser family members hold in many of the recipient organizations and institutions, give the family considerable influence in a variety of noncorporate areas of American society.

CAMPAIGN CONTRIBUTIONS

We have seen how the Weyerhaeuser family office is used to perpetuate wealth and power through the management of common corporate investments, trusts, holding companies, and foundations. In the area of campaign contributions the office plays an equally central role—collecting, channeling, and distributing money. An examination of the money flowing to political candidates reveals how the family office serves as a conduit for campaign contributions and how the sources of campaign money are hidden from the public. Money flows from individuals—both family members and corporate officials—through various political funds in the family office to various candidates. The use of these funds and their coordination in the family office is important in understanding the family's involvement in the political process.

In recent years the family and the Weyerhaeuser Company have used three funds for channeling money to political candidates. Money is not given to the candidate directly but passes into either the Tacoma Fund, the Hanson Fund, or the W.J. Driscoll Special Fund. The Tacoma Fund is a Weyerhaeuser Company fund. The Hanson Fund is primarly a family fund, but is often used by officers and directors of the Company, or by family members of Weyerhaeuser associates. The W.J. Driscoll Fund is mainly a family fund. Figure 1.1 shows how the flow of Weyerhaeuser political contributions can be mapped out.

Both the Hanson Fund and the Driscoll Fund are housed at the Weyerhaeuser family office. The treasurer of the Hanson Fund is Gordon E. Hed, long-time employee of the family office, and former personal secretary of Frederick King Weyerhaeuser. The Fund itself is in all probability named after Donald N. Hanson, another long-time employee of the office, and the person for whom one of the family's nominee partnerships for stock holdings is named.

Campaign contributions are collected from family members by the staff at the family office. In 1974, for example, the Hanson Fund received money from the W.J. Driscoll Fund as well as directly from family members.

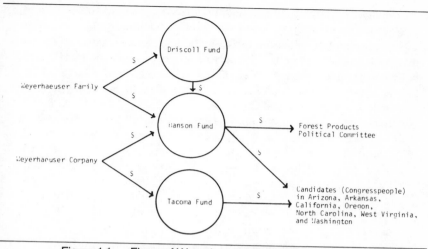

Figure 1.1   Flows of Weyerhaeuser Political Contributions

Weyerhaeuser family members giving directly to the Hanson Fund that year included Carl A. Weyerhaeuser and his daughter, Elizabeth W. Bentink-Smith. Weyerhaeuser Company directors giving to the fund in 1974 included John H. Hauberg, John M. Musser, and Edmund Hayes, who is retired. Hauberg is a member of the Denkmann family. His sister, Catherine H. Sweeny, also gave to the Hanson Fund (U.S. House of Representatives, 1974b).

The Hanson Fund in turn distributed money to the Forest Products Political Committee, which in turn contributed to candidates in West Virginia, Oregon, North Carolina, and Washington. The Hanson Fund contributed directly to candidates in Arizona, Arkansas, California, Oregon, and West Virginia. These are all states in which the Weyerhaeuser Company has operations or plants, or in which a member of the family lives.

The office not only houses the funds and serves as a conduit, but in all probability coordinates political contributions on advice from the family. Information of the family's campaign contributions in 1972 provides evidence to suggest a coordinated effort by members of the Weyerhaeuser family in their political giving. Evidence for coordinated political giving comes from several observations drawn from the contributions of twenty-six family members listed in the U.S. General Accounting Office report (1973): (1) contributions were made on the same day by family members living throughout the United States; (2) these contributions were for the same amount or for multiples of that amount; and (3) the contributions were to the same committee. This suggests that the task of coordination is carried out by a person at the family office, since the funds are housed there.

The pattern of contributions to the W. Driscoll Special Fund is especially revealing. In 1972, 22 of the 25 family members who gave political contributions contributed some $11,700 to the W. Driscoll Special Fund. (The fund is named after W. John Driscoll, the president of the family holding companies.) On June 27 and 28, 1972, for example, 13 individual family members contributed to this particular fund—nearly all contributed $180 or multiples of $180. Frederick T. Weyerhaeuser, his second cousin, John P. Weyerhaeuser III, and another cousin, William B. Weyerhaeuser, made contributions of exactly $180; Rudolph W. Driscoll and his mother each contributed $720, or four times $180; Carl A. Weyerhaeuser and his cousin, C. Davis Weyerhaeuser, each gave $1080, or six times $180. Other family members gave to the Driscoll Fund during a two-week period in July.

Not everyone gave in multiples of $180, although those that did not came close enough (e.g., $770 rather than $720, $460 rather than $360, and $620 rather than $720) to cause us to suspect a mistake in the reporting. Whether this is what happened cannot be determined from the report (U.S. General Accounting Office, 1973). What is more convincing, though, is that only members of the fourth generation gave $180; members of the third generation usually gave more, generally a multiple of $180. Carl A. Weyerhaeuser, C. Davis Weyerhaeuser, Catherine M. Davis, and George F. Jewett, Jr., for example, all members of the third generation, follow this pattern. Gifts for exactly the same amount and given on the same day, and the pattern of generational differences, strongly suggest that these contributions were coordinated.

Two additional dates are worth noting because they lend additional evidence to the thesis of coordination. On July 25, three members of the Weyerhaeusers, Catherine M. Davis, Sara Maud W. Sivertsen, and Frederick K. Weyerhaeuser each gave $1,563.65 to the Minnesota Republican Finance Committee, while W. John Driscoll gave $3,563.65 to the same committee. On September 21, five family members made contributions totaling $31,250 to three different media committees—the Media, Radio, and TV Committees to Re-Elect the President. Once again this is suggestive of family coordination.

Many of the individuals involved in these contributions live in various cities around the country. In the case of the Driscoll Fund, for example, individual family members living in Pasadena, St. Paul, Tacoma, Milton (Mass.), Englewood (Colo.), Santa Fe, Kirkland (Wash.), Atherton (Calif.), Chevy Chase, Ross (Calif.), Wayzata (Minn.), Denver, Haverford

(Penn.), and Spokane all made contributions to this family political fund. This dispersion around the country, in addition to exact amounts and the same dates, suggests there is some way of coordinating the process. It thus appears that the family office actually writes the checks to these committees. It would be a difficult task to coordinate the giving of thirteen individuals to the Driscoll Fund in any other way. It also would be next to impossible for five individuals to give the same amount on the same day to the media committees without some device for coordinating their actions.

CONCLUSION

This study has examined the ways in which one major capitalist family uses a family office to maintain a cohesive family unit through successive generations. It also has looked at how the family continues to exercise control over large corporations and how the family exerts political, cultural, and religious influence. This study has shown how the office functions to perpetuate internal and external coordination. Internal coordination manifests itself through the strengthening of kinship bonds between family members. This is accomplished by the office in its management of trusts and foundations. Both trusts and foundations have stock portfolios which enable the office to provide links between the generations and to link different nuclear units of the larger kin group together. In addition to common economic interests (joint stock holdings), trusts and foundations provide added linkages through shared trusteeships and common foundation boards. Internal coordination thus serves to strengthen family cohesiveness.

Through the family office the family is linked to other institutions in society, such as corporations, political parties, and the institutions to which foundations give. Thus, the family office serves to provide external coordination between the family and social institutions. In addition to strengthening kinship solidarity, investments in common economic interests provide the potential for corporate control. The pooling of political gifts likewise provides the potential for a great deal of influence on the political process. The family's influence on civic, cultural, and religious life is enhanced by combining its financial giving through foundations.

The connections among kinship, class, corporations, and the political process uncovered here are relatively unknown. Additional studies of family offices might contribute to understanding the network of organizations linked to wealthy families. We need to develop more case studies of upper-class kinship groups to determine the extensiveness of family offices. Coordinated political funds, shared foundation directorates, a common address where foundation books are kept, and kinship connections on corporate boards all point to evidence of a family office.

Additional theoretical work is also needed to integrate the findings on family offices into a more comprehensive analysis of the structure of power in America. It might be that "kinecon groups" are more extensive than we realize, and that a form of family capitalism has survived.

REFERENCES

Arcata National Corporation (1975) Proxy statement. Menlo Park, CA: Arcata National Corporation.

BALTZELL, E.D. (1958) Philadelphia Gentlemen. Chicago: Quadrangle.

BELL, D. (1962) The End of Ideology. New York: Free Press.

BURCH, P.H., Jr. (1972) The Managerial Revolution Reassessed: Family Control in America's Large Corporation. Lexington, MA: D.C. Heath.

COLLIER, P. and D. HOROWITZ (1976) The Rockefellers: An American Dynasty. New York: Holt, Rinehart & Winston.

COMSHARE Incorporated (1974-1975) Proxy statement. Ann Arbor, MI: COMSHARE Incorporated.

DOMHOFF, G.W. (1974) The Bohemian Grove and Other Retreats: A Study in Ruling Class Cohesiveness. New York: Harper & Row.

——————— and C.L. SCHWARTZ (1974) Testimony and report entitled "Probing the Rockefeller fortune," pp. 717-772 in U.S. Congress, House, Hearings before the Committee on the Judiciary, 93 Cong., 2d Sess., Nomination of Nelson A. Rockefeller to be Vice President of the United States. Washington, DC: U.S. Government Printing Office.

DUNN, M.G. (1974) "The Weyerhaeuser family tree uprooted: a genealogical and historical narrative." Presented at the Annual Meeting of the Pacific Sociological Association, San Jose, California.

Fortune (1934) "Bunyan in broadcloth: the house of Weyerhaeuser." 9 (April): 62-75.

Foundation Center (1975) The Foundation Directory. Fifth Edition. New York: Foundation Center.

FREEDGOOD, S. (1959) "Weyerhaeuser timber: out of the woods." Fortune 60 (July): 93-96ff.

HIDY, R.W., F.E. HILL and A. NEVINS (1963) Timber and Men: The Weyerhaeuser Story. New York: Macmillan.

HUNTER, F. (1959) Top Leadership, U.S.A. Chapel Hill, NC: Univ. of North Carolina Press.

KAHN, E.J., Jr. (1965) "Resources and responsibilities." The New Yorker (January 16): 40-41.

KOSKOFF, D.E. (1978) The Mellons: The Chronicle of America's Richest Family. New York: Thomas Y. Crowell.

LUNDBERG, F. (1975) The Rockefeller Syndrome. New York: Lyle Stuart.

——————— (1968) The Rich and the Super-Rich: A Study in the Power of Money Today. New York: Lyle Stuart.

MELLON, W.L. (1948) Judge Mellon's Sons. Privately printed.

MILLS, C.W. (1956) The Power Elite. New York: Oxford Univ. Press.

Moody's Investors Service (1950-1975) Moody's Industrial Manual. New York: Moody's Investors Service.

PARSONS, T. (1960) "The institutional framework of economic development," pp. 98-131 in Structure and Process in Modern Societies. New York: Free Press.

Polk, R.L. & Co. (1950-1975) Polk's St. Paul City Directory. St. Paul, MN: R.L. Polk & Co.

Potlatch Corporation (1965) Form 10-K Annual Report (Securities and Exchange Commission). San Francisco: Potlatch Corporation.

Ramsey County (1963) "Estate of Charles McGough." Probate Court. File No. 109505. State of Minnesota.

SALO, S.J. (1945) Timber Concentration in the Pacific Northwest. Ph.D. dissertation, Columbia University.

SHOUP, L.H. (1975) "Shaping the postwar world: the Council on Foreign Relations and United States war aims during World War Two." Insurgent Sociologist 5, 3 (Spring): 9-52.

SMITH, R.A. (1960) "The heir who turned on the house of Phipps." Fortune 62 (October): 168-175ff.; 62 (November): 162-165ff.

SONQUIST, J. and T. KOENIG (1975) "Interlocking directorates in the top U.S. corporations: a graph theory approach." Insurgent Sociologist 5, 3 (Spring): 196-230.

Standard and Poor's (1950-1976) Poor's Register of Corporations, Executives, and Directors. New York: Standard and Poor's Corporation.

U.S. General Accounting Office (1973) Federal Election Campaign Act of 1971: Alphabetical Listing of 1972 Presidential Campaign Receipts. Washington, DC: U.S. Government Printing Office.

U.S. House of Representatives (1974a) Nomination of Nelson A. Rockefeller to be Vice President of the United States. Hearings before the Committee on the Judiciary, 93 Cong., 2d Sess. Washington, DC: U.S. Government Printing Office.

————— (1974b) Report of Receipts and Expenditures for a Committee. Office of the Clerk. Washington, DC: U.S. Government Printing Office.

WEAVER, W. (1967) U.S. Philanthropic Foundations. New York: Harper & Row.

Weisenberger, A. & Co. (1965) Investment Companies 1965. 25th annual edition. New York: Arthur Weisenberger & Co.

Weyerhaeuser Foundation (1972) Report for the Years 1950 through 1970. St. Paul, MN: Weyerhaeuser Foundation.

WHITE, S. (1978) "Cradle to grave: family offices manage money for the very rich." Barron's (March 20): 9ff.

ZEITLIN, M. (1974) "Corporate ownership and control: the large corporation and the capitalist class." American Journal of Sociology 79 (March): 1073-1119.

————— , L.A. EWEN, and R.E. RATCLIFF (1974) "'New princes for old? the large corporation and the capitalist class in Chile." American Journal of Sociology 80 (July):87-123.

2

AMERICAN JEWS: IN OR OUT OF THE UPPER CLASS?

Richard L. Zweigenhaft

INTRODUCTION

Although American Jews have been very successful economically, and are overrepresented among scientists and scholars, numerous studies have shown that they have been excluded from the highest levels of power in America, that pinnacle atop the social structure referred to by Mills (1956) as "the power elite," by Baltzell (1964) as "the Protestant establishment," and by Domhoff (1970) as "the higher circles." These writers, and others, have demonstrated convincingly that, as of the late 1960s, Jews were for the most part excluded from the national upper class (see Lundberg, 1968: 327-287).

The upper class, though by no means in the forefront of social change, is not completely static in terms of membership. In fact, as Marx pointed out (and non-Marxists like Baltzell, Lundberg and Domhoff agree), "the more a ruling class is able to assimilate the most prominent men of the dominated classes, the more stable and dangerous its rule" (Baltzell, 1964: 3). In America, the upper class has assimilated Jews in varying ways and to varying degrees over time. The purpose of this chapter is to consider this process, first from an historical perspective, and then by looking at the

AUTHOR'S NOTE: The author would like to thank Letitia Johnson for her careful work as a research assistant for the first study described in this chapter and Harold Salzman and Barbara Wright for their computer assistance for the third study.

current interaction between upper-class American Jews and upper-class American gentiles. To what extent have Jews, in the past and in the present, become a part of the national upper class? Are there, in the way this process has taken place, patterns which shed light on the broader (sociological) issue of class in America, and on the narrower (psychological) issue of the self-image of those who have successfully attained membership in the upper class? These are the questions we hope to explore in this paper.

UPPER-CLASS GENTILES AND JEWS PRIOR TO WORLD WAR II

Jews have not always been excluded from the upper class in America. There have been three major waves of Jewish immigration, each leading to a different relationship between Jews and the upper class.

The earliest Jewish settlers, Sephardic Jews who were descendants of Jews who had been expelled from Spain and Portugal in the fifteeneth century, arrived in New Amsterdam in 1654. By 1790, the time of the first census, there were about two thousand Jews living in American colonies (Baltzell, 1964: 55, Handlin, 1954). Because there were so few of them, and because they were so widely dispersed throughout the colonies, they had a great deal of interaction with non-Jews. They were, for the most part, successful merchants, and are described by Manners (1972: 63) in the following way:

> By combining a proud adherence to their faith, an ineluctable gift for achiev-
> ing affluence and an impressively grand manner, the Sephardim were first
> among equals in the new democracy for which they had fought in the Revolu-
> tionary War. (Of course a few were loyal to King George III, and they packed
> up and went to England to live among the British upper class, where it was
> supposed they were happier with their own kind.) They were the elite, among
> the founders of such Establishment institutions as the New York Stock Ex-
> change, Columbia University, New York University, the American Medical
> Association, and the Boston Athenaeum.

Despite their "proud adherence to their faith," there was among the Sephardic Jews a high frequency of intermarriage and extensive assimilation. This was caused in part by the shortage of Jewish women, and in part by the absence of rabbis. Baltzell (1964: 55) writes that "This, then, was the classic period of aristocratic assimilation, and even today there are leading families within the old-stock and Protestant upper class, some of whose ancestors were prominent Jews during the Colonial period."

The second major wave of Jewish immigration, in the midnineteenth century, brought German Jews to every section of America. They came in numbers large enough to create Jewish communities, and, unlike their Sephardic predecessors, they came with rabbis. As of 1880 every state had a Jewish community, though Jews were not yet clustered in urban areas. For example, in 1880 New York City's population was only 3% Jewish—by 1920 it was 30% and by 1960 it was 40% (Baltzell, 1964: 56). These German Jews were typically middle-class entrepeneurs. Whatever their occupation in the "old country" (many were foreign traders and stockbrokers), most had to start from scratch when they came to America. Birmingham (1967) and Supple (1957) have recounted how many Jewish immigrants of this era, including Joseph Seligman, Simon and Meyer Guggenheim, and Henry Lehman, started as peddlers. By the 1870s a good number had become extremely wealthy. In fact, historian John Higham (1975: 144) tells us that, "Proportionally speaking, in no other immigrant group have so many men ever risen so rapidly from rags to riches."

Like the Sephardim who preceded them, the wealthiest German Jews were not excluded from the most prestigious clubs, and many interacted with and were accepted socially by "the best" gentile society. Indeed, many Jews were influential in founding the very clubs that helped set the upper class apart from the rest of society. Just as sugar merchant Moses Lazarus, a descendant of Sephardic Jews, was a founder of New York's Knickerbocker Club in 1871, investment banker Joseph Seligman helped found the Union League in 1863. Baltzell (1964: 56) writes: "Even as late as the 1870s, when young Louis D. Brandeis was welcomed into the best Boston society, Jews still belonged to the best clubs in many cities, and a leading society journal could feature the news of a fashionable 'Hebrew Wedding' in New York's Orthodox Thirty-fourth Street Synagogue."

During this period of German Jewish immigration, what could be considered a national Jewish upper class developed. Many members of this group (such as the Guggenheims, Lehmans, Schiffs, Seligmans, and Warburgs) ended up living in New York and have been popularized in Birmingham's *Our Crowd* (1967). But influential and wealthy German Jews lived outside New York as well, and were for the most part accepted into predominantly gentile upper-class society. There were, for example, "the Gimbels and Brentanos in Vincennes, Indiana; Adolph Gluck of Dodge City, Kansas; the Rosenwalds of Chicago; the Rosewaters of Omaha, Nebraska; the Michaelsons of Virginia City, Nevada; the Spiegelbergs of Santa Fe, New Mexico; the Seasongoods of Cincinnati, Ohio" (Manners, 1972: 65). These Jewish-American immigrants wanted to be more like other Americans and less like immigrants, and made vigorous efforts to assimilate into American culture. Some were "assimilated completely through marriage or conversion and others through membership in exclusive clubs and associations" (Baltzell, 1964: 58).

Higham (1975: 139) points out the important distinction between behavior and attitudes. Jews were not, for the most part, discriminated against during this period, but the images held of Jews by many were not wholly favorable. He puts it in the following context:

> The image of Scotsmen as stiff-necked and penurious and the image of Englishmen as snobs have not handicapped members of either of these groups in America. Similarly, the Jews in early-nineteenth-century America got along very well with their non-Jewish neighbors although American conceptions of Jews in the abstract at no time lacked the unfavorable elements embedded in European tradition.

In the 1880s, Eastern European Jews began to arrive in America in great numbers, and the comfortable relationship between upper-class Jews and gentiles changed. Between 1881 and the passage of the American Immigration Act in 1924, 2,798,046 Jews came to the United States from Russia alone; this was the largest exodus of Jews "since the one from Egypt" (Birmingham, 1967: 289). By 1907, about 90,000 Jews, mostly from Russia and Poland, were arriving in New York City every year (Manners, 1972: 51). By 1930, there were four million American Jews, and 80% of them were of Eastern European origin. Unlike the Sephardic and German Jews who arrived before them, most of whom had been middle-class and self-employed, this third wave of Jewish immigrants consisted primarily of wage workers. They were, in Birmingham's (1967: 289; see also Rischin, 1962: 94) words, "ragged, dirt-poor, culturally energetic, toughened by years of torment, idealistic, and socialistic." They had little in common with those Jews who had preceded them except their shared religion, and even that was not without significant differences. As Glazer and Moynihan (1963: 139) point out in *Beyond the Melting Pot*, "In practice, tone, and theology, the Reform Judaism of the German Jews diverged from the Orthodoxy of the immigrants as much as the beliefs and practices of Southern Baptists differ from those of New England Unitarians." The heavy influx of lower-class Jews, densely populated in urban areas along the east coast, was accompanied by increasingly frequent episodes of anti-semitism. One could speculate that the anti-semitism more than anything else ultimately brought the Jews of different backgrounds closer together (Rollins, 1973).

The first widely publicized anti-semitic incident actually occurred in

1877, a few years before the heavy influx of Eastern European Jews began. Joseph Seligman was refused accommodation at the Grand Union Hotel in Saratoga. Saratoga was, at that time, "the queen of American resorts," and the Grand Union Hotel was by far the most elegant hotel in Saratoga; it was the kind of place that people took their valets, personal maids, laundresses and even chefs, and settled in for a long stay (Birmingham, 1967: 143). When Seligman was informed that the hotel had adopted a new policy which did not allow it to accept "Israelites," he wrote a scathing letter to the owner of the hotel and released it to the newspapers. The issue received a great deal of coverage in the press, with many expressing shock and outrage that this could happen in America. But happen it did, and it soon began to happen elsewhere. Other resorts asserted their exclusivity by advertising "No Jews Accepted," "Hebrews Need Not Apply," or "Hebrews Will Knock Vainly for Admission" (Birmingham, 1967: 147; Manners, 1972: 56; Rischin, 1962: 261).

The exclusion of Jews from resorts was followed by their exclusion from certain social clubs. In 1893, the Union League Club of New York refused to admit Theodore Seligman, the son of one of the club's founders (and the nephew of Joseph), even though his membership was staunchly supported by such dignified members as Joseph Choate and Elihu Root. By the turn of the century, Higham (1975: 151) informs us that "Jewish penetration into the most elite circles in the East had become almost impossibly difficult." And by 1920, as public a figure as Henry Ford was embarking on a viciously anti-semitic campaign in which he and his newspaper, the *Dearborn Independent*, argued that Jews or their gentile "fronts" (like President Taft!) controlled every aspect of American life (Manners, 1972: 298). In 1922, A.A. Lowell, the President of Harvard University, urged the college to adopt a quota system to solve "the Jewish problem." A similar stance by the President of Columbia University, Nicholas Murray Butler, cut the proportion of Jews at Columbia from 40% to 20% within two years (Baltzell, 1964: 210-211).

Not surprisingly, the rather abrupt appearance of overt anti-semitism at just about the same time that tens of thousands of Eastern European Jews arrived in America led to a hostile reception of the new immigrants by many established American Jews. As Esther Panitz (1963: 105) writes, "With but few exceptions, from 1870 to 1890, America's representative Jews were not eager to welcome their kin from abroad." She goes on:

Though American Jews had been subjected to instances of anti-Semitic bias, they were still free to attempt to scale the ladder of economic and social acceptability. But they were most fearful lest the alien customs and manners of their immigrant relatives imperil their ascent. Numerous studies have by now quoted oft-repeated judgments by America's established Jewry, concerning the allegedly uncivilized modes of life deemed endemic to their East-European kin. It would be pointless to reiterate these many contentions, some of them founded on reality, others based on prejudices. But all of them, including the view that the East-European Jewish immigrant was capable only of petit bourgeois transactions, stemmed from the American Jews' fear of a loss of status [1963: 118].

There were some elite social clubs for German Jews prior to the onset of overt anti-semitism in the 1880s. For example, New York's Harmonie Club, founded in 1852, was one of the oldest social clubs in the city. Some of the more influential German Jews in New York were members of the Harmonie Club as well as predominately gentile clubs. Birmingham (1967: 141) writes that in the early 1870s Joseph Seligman, "the leading financier in New York . . . grew to care less for the Harmonie, and began to spend more time at the Union League Club, whose membership he sometimes seemed to prefer." When upper-class German Jews were no longer accepted in upper-class gentile social clubs, they formed more of their own fashionable clubs—and didn't accept Eastern European Jews. In fact, their efforts at exclusion involved more than just clubs. As Baltzell (1964: 61) points out:

> In much the same way as their gentile peers, they were forming their own exclusive clubs and neighborhoods as well as a series of exclusive summer colonies along the Jersey shore. They also built in the manner of the Episcopalian gentry, new Reform synagogues, uptown, out in the suburbs and down at the shore. What was happening, in other words, was that both the old-stock gentile and Jewish upper classes, once organized along familistic and communal lines, were now becoming more formal and associational.

Though many of these institutions maintained their exclusion of Eastern European Jews well into the 1930s, by the beginning of World War II most had absorbed Jews of Eastern European origin who had become rich and influential. In an article published early in 1946, Solomon Bloom (1946: 7) had this to say about the relationship between Eastern and Western Jews:

> The clash between Eastern and Western Jews has lost its former intensity. The events of the last decade, the fear of a common danger, have brought about a strong rapprochement. The Eastern Jew is losing his self-consciousness and his sense of neglect, the Western is shedding his traditional attitude of exclusiveness. East and West meet, and they are perforce becoming one. Slowly.

UPPER-CLASS GENTILES AND JEWS SINCE WORLD WAR II

Since World War II there have been periodic investigations of the degree to which Jews have been kept out of upper-class WASP institutions. Lundberg, in *The Rich and the Super-Rich,* published in 1968, cites a number of studies which demonstrate the glaring underrepresentation of Jews at the higher levels of corporate management. For example, although Jews make up about 8% of those who have college degrees in the United States, less than one half of one percent of the total executive personnel in American industrial companies are Jewish. Similarly, another study found that less than half of one percent of the 2000 managers at U.S. Steel were Jewish. Lundberg concludes:

> The facts are established as well in a number of careful special studies, national and local. Even in cities with large Jewish populations, like New York and Philadelphia, where frequency in the population might be expected to be reflected at least locally in management ranks, the percentage of Jewish participation is negligible [1968: 363].

More recently, Irving Howe (1976: 611) made the same point in *World of Our Fathers,* claiming that the research has shown that very few Jews occupy "position of genuine power within the corporate economy."

Lundberg (1968: 340-352) points out that the leading social clubs (like the Links and Knickerbocker Clubs of New York) continue to exclude Jews, though "the well-known middle-level clubs" (like the Century Association and the Manhattan Club) have accepted a few Jewish members. Baltzell (1964: 357) also documents the continued exclusion of Jews from social clubs, referring to such "caste policies" as "among the sorriest symbols of discrimination in America." Furthermore, he argues that it is the policies of these clubs that lead the corporations to bar some of their most qualified people from top positions; without access to the clubs, where important business deals may be conducted over lunch or dinner, these men would be less able to perform effectively in the corporate world. The club, says Baltzell (1964: 362), is the tail that wags the corporate dog.

Yet Baltzell asserts that there are Jews within the American elite (even though they may not be accepted into certain clubs). He uses the theory of the "triple melting pot," in which third- and fourth-generation Jews, Protestants and Catholics are "Americanized" within their religious communities. Each of the three major religious communities incudes a number of different classes, and with upward mobility through these classes comes assimilation. Just as a middle-class Methodist might join a suburban Presbyterian church as part of his rise to the Protestant upper class, so might an Orthodox East European Jew join a conservative synagogue uptown, or a reform synagogue in the suburbs (Baltzell, 1964: 53-54; see also Kennedy, 1944 and 1952, and Herberg, 1955).

Baltzell asserts that things are different at the very top of the class hierarchy. There the triple melting pot becomes a single melting pot. That is, at the highest levels of the class system, religious differences between Protestants, Catholics, and Jews become so minimal as to be meaningless. In short, as Baltzell (1964: 62-63) says, "class tends to replace religion."

Domhoff's work, more recent than Baltzell's, also indicates the possibility of changing patterns within the upper class. He, however, is not convinced that Jews have yet become a part of the national upper class (or, at least, part of the highest of the higher circles). In *Who Rules America?* (1967: 52), he refers to "a small, parallel Jewish upper class which may or may not be more fully assimilated into the national upper class in the next several decades." More recently, in *Fat Cats and Democrats* (1972), he suggests that Jews are in the power elite, but still on the fringes. In that book Domhoff documents how Jewish businessmen from New York and Texas oilmen dominated fund-raising for the Democratic party through the early 1970s. He refers to these fat cats as "the Jewish-Cowboy clique," and says this about their role in the national upper class:

> The Jewish-Cowboy group is the major fringe group in an overwhelmingly Anglo-Saxon power elite rooted in commercial banking, insurance, public utilities, railroads, and manufacturing—precisely the areas from which people of Jewish background are almost completely excluded. Even where the Jews and Cowboys are highly visible, as in investment banking, oil, and real estate, they are decidedly minor leaguers compared to the even wealthier gentiles [1972: 54].

In a more recently published study, Domhoff compared the corporate connections of various social clubs and policy planning groups. When he compared the corporate connections of a 1965 membership list of New York's Links Club, "one of the best-known big business clubs in the country," and a 1968 membership list of the Harmonie Club, "the oldest and perhaps most prestigious Jewish men's club in the nation," he found a clear pattern that

> puts the lie once again to any claim that Jews may have a "grip" on banking or any other sector of big business in this country. The Links Club has 113 connections to the top 25 banks; the Harmonie Club has five. The Links Club has 79 connections to the top 25 industrials; the Harmonie Club has three. The situation is similar for other sectors of the big-business community. There are

wealthy Jews in the United States, but they are a small minority who are clearly secondary to the gentile majority that really make the decisions that anti-semites and ultra-conservatives do not like [1975: 180].

In addition to the work of social analysts like Lundberg, Baltzell, and Domhoff, there also have been a number of articles, books, and dissertations written about specific local Jewish communities which shed light on the nature of the interactions between upper-class Jews and gentiles since World War II. For example, in his three-part series in the Los Angeles *Times* on the "Jews of Los Angeles," Robert Scheer (1978) demonstrates how closely the interactions between wealthy gentiles and Jews paralleled the national pattern that has been described in this paper. German Jewish merchants, many of whom started as peddlers, were central to the economic life of Los Angeles in the second half of the nineteenth century. They were well accepted socially, and when the elite California Club was formed in 1888, at least 12 of the 125 founding members were Jewish. With the national wave of anti-semitism that began in the 1890s, however, Jews were no longer accepted into the highest circles of power, including the very clubs they had helped to found. No additional Jews were allowed in, and as the founding Jewish members died off, these clubs became off limits to Jews (except as guests). In 1920, the wealthier members of the Jewish community, excluded from the California Club and the Los Angeles Country Club, started their own country club, the Hillcrest Country Club.

At the time Scheer did his interviews for the articles, the California Club "had yet to admit a Jewish member who [did] not happen to be secretary of defense." Harold Brown, the lone Jewish member, former president of the California Institute of Technology, and secretary of defense under Jimmy Carter, fits snugly into the top of Baltzell's melting pot theory by being extremely well-assimilated. Accepted into the California Club only when it became clear he would be named secretary of defense, Brown was described to Scheer by one prominent member of the Los Angeles Jewish community as an "'ice-cold Jew' because he appears to shun Jewish identification."

When Solomon Sutker did his dissertation research in the late 1940s on the Atlanta Jewish community, he found that at the time there were three Jewish Clubs. "A major reason for the existence of these Jewish social clubs," he wrote (1958: 262) "lies in the fact that the Jewish population is excluded from the other major social clubs of the city." The flap that surrounded the revelation that two of Jimmy Carter's appointees, Griffin Bell and Bert Lance, were members of the exclusive and restricted Piedmont Driving Club demonstrated that in the ensuing twenty-five years things had not changed on this score. Atlanta's Piedmont Driving Club, founded in

1887, has continued its "informal but apparently ironclad restrictions against Jews and blacks" (*Washington Post*, 1976). For many years, it was traditional for the mayor of Atlanta to become an honorary member of the club. This tradition was halted abruptly in 1969 when Sam Massell, a Jew, was elected mayor. (No attempt was made four years later to reintroduce the tradition when a Protestant was elected mayor. That Protestant, Maynard Jackson, was also black).

My research (Zweigenhaft, 1978) on another southern city, Greensboro, North Carolina, provided a rare exception to some aspects of the pattern depicted thus far in this chapter. In Greensboro, Jews not only helped to found the most elite country club, but they are still overrepresented at this country club, at the downtown dining club, and on boards of directors of the Greensboro corporations listed in Dun and Bradstreet's *Million Dollar Directory*. There is evidence that in earlier times only Jews of German descent were acceptable at the country club, and there is evidence of considerable assimilation on the part of many of the foremost Jewish families.

The most important Jews to come to Greensboro were Ceasar and Moses Cone. They came to the city in the 1890s to sell groceries to mill villages, and ended up owning Cone Mills, at one time the world's leading producer of denim, corduroy, and flannelette. These Jewish Cones were influential enough to be employing a good segment of the population of Greensboro in 1909, the year the country club was started. Since that time many of the Cone children have married Protestants (especially Episcopalians), and only three of Ceasar's seventeen grandchildren were raised Jews (Moses Cone had no children).

The overrepresentation of Greensboro Jews in the most prestigious clubs seems to be an aberration caused by the unusually important role played by Jews in the city's economic history. In a comparison study with nearby Winston-Salem (a town similar in size and population, but one whose wealthiest and most influential residents have always been gentiles involved in the tobacco industry), it was found that there were no Jewish members in the two most prestigious country clubs, and no Jewish members of the downtown dining club (Zweigenhaft, 1979). Though journalist Harry Golden (1955: 6) touts the South, and specifically the Carolinas, as "the most favorable 'atmosphere' the Jewish people have known in the modern world," he sees the country club pattern of Winston-Salem more typical than that of Greensboro. He writes (1974: 176) "This remains the pattern throughout the South. The Jews are excluded from the social country clubs and the downtown city clubs."

In addition to Los Angeles, Atlanta, Greensboro, and Winston-Salem, academicians and journalists have also written about the Jewish communities in other cities since World War II. Few have dealt with the issue being addressed here at any depth, though a number have touched on it in passing. For example, Elaine Maas's (1973: 188) dissertation on the Jews of Houston mentions that "Jews are not considered part of the city's top elite society. Jewish women do not belong to the Junior League, and, with few exceptions, Jews do not belong to the better Gentile country clubs." She concludes that in Houston, "although many Jews have attained relative wealth, the real power remains in the hands of WASPS." Similarly, Frank Petrusak and Steven Steinert (1976) report in their article on the Jews of Charleston, South Carolina, that 83% of their Jewish respondents disagreed with the statement that "Jews are accepted in social circles."

Some of the studies that have been done in greatest depth have been performed on unidentified cities. For example, Kramer and Leventman's *Children of the Gilded Ghetto* (1961) provides a detailed study of the Jewish community of "North City—a Midwestern American city." Similarly, Sklare and Greenblum's *Jewish Identity on the Suburban Frontier* (1967) describes in detail another Midwestern setting: "Lakeville . . . a suburb of 'Lake City,' one of the leading industrial and commercial centers of the nation." Both books describe relationships between upper-class Jews and Gentiles (and between German and East European Jews) that correspond with the patterns depicted thus far in this chapter.

These studies, performed at different times, using different methods, focusing as they do on a varied but nonrandom group of communities, provide only a piecemeal image of the extent to which Jews and gentiles have come to interact at the national level of social and economic power in America. Therefore, the remainder of this chapter will be an attempt to provide a systematic up-to-date consideration of the relationship between prominent American Jews and upper-class gentiles at the top of the economic structure. Do national samples indicate increased presence of Jews among America's corporate and social elite? If so, is there evidence, as we found earlier in Greensboro, for Baltzell's theory of the "triple melting pot"? At the highest level of the class structure, does class identification increase, and does ethnic identification decline?

THE AMERICAN JEWISH COMMITTEE

The first study to be described is based on an investigation of the corporate and social connections of the members of the American Jewish Committee's Board of Governors over the past 28 years. From its inception over 70 years ago, the American Jewish Committee has been considered one of the most prominent and prestigious national organizations of American Jews. As such, it would seem likely that members of the American Jewish Committee would be among the first Jews to be accepted into the national gentile upper class.

The Committee began with 50 members in 1906 and gradually increased to almost 400 members by 1944. In that year, responding to what some members of the Committee felt were wide-spread misconceptions about the nature of the AJC, a "chapter plan" was adopted. Thirty-eight chapters were organized throughout the country, and within five years there were 18,000 AJC members. Cohen (1972: 338) describes the "average member of the Committee's executive in 1950" in the following way:

> The average member of the Committee's executive in 1950 was a man in his early sixties, affluent, respected in his business or profession, and involved more in civic than in specifically Jewish affairs. He was American-born, usually of old German stock, Reform in his synagogue affiliation, and non-Zionist. Of above-average academic training, he was a moderate or conservative on political issues and has joined the Committee primarily out of a sense of noblesse oblige. The Committee deliberately sought out Jews of East European background—but only those who had "arrived" in terms of social status and wealth; AJC remained an exclusive club.

Although the AJC grew to 26,400 members by 1956, four years later there were only 27,800. Concern over the minimal growth, plus increasing discomfort about the continuing image of the AJC as elitist, led the Committee to hire outside consultants to help it assess its image. As a result of this self-analysis, a new image was projected by the Committee and by its Public Relations Department, leading to more new members (46,200 by 1966) and, according to Cohen (1972: 559), a new "type" of AJC member:

> Compared to his 1950 counterpart, the average active member in the late 1960s was younger, less wealthy, more liberal in his politics, and not necessarily Reform in religious conviction. He came to the Committee out of a deep interest in national and world affairs, rather than for reasons of noblesse oblige. Like his predecessor, his civic affiliations were more pronounced than his organizational Jewish ties.

Despite attempts in the 1960s to alter its image, the AJC continues to be the single Jewish group national in scope whose members seem most likely to enter the higher echelons of power in America. In order to keep our focus on a group of manageable size, it was decided to look at the social, educational and corporate connections of the AJC's Board of Governors, which is a smaller "executive" committee within the larger National Executive Committee of the even larger American Jewish Committee. It was not assumed that AJC members were in any way a random sample of Jews who may have entered the national upper class. Rather it was assumed that they, as a definable group of relatively consistent size and make-up over a thirty-year period, would provide a useful window into the patterns of upper-class assimilation.

Membership lists of the AJC's Board of Governors were obtained for 1952, 1967-1968, 1976, and 1978. Over this 26-year period, the Board of Governors ranged from 61 members (in 1952) to 143 members (in 1978). The names on all four lists were looked up in the following sources: *Who's Who in America, Who's Who in the East, Who's Who in the West, Who's Who in the Midwest, Who's Who in the South and Southwest,* and *Standard and Poor's Register of Corporations, Directors and Executives.* In each case, the year of the publication corresponded to the year of the list; thus, for example, the names on the 1967 Board of Governors list were looked up in the 1967 volumes of the above sources and the names on the 1976 Board of Governors list were looked up in the 1976 volumes of these sources. In addition, for the three lists after 1965, all names were looked up in *Who's Who in World Jewry* (1965 and 1972) and in the *Biographical Directories Masters Index* (1975-1976). Any listings in the Masters Index which had not previously been looked up in the appropriate source (e.g., *Who's Who in American Politics, Who's Who in American Art*).

For each individual, the following information was recorded: year of birth; college attended; children's names; membership on one of six policy groups (Council on Foreign Relations, Committee for Economic Development, Conference Board, Business Council, Brookings Institution, and American Assembly); corporate directorships; and social clubs. In addition, for each person that we found from the 1951 and 1967 lists, we looked up his (or, rarely her) name in the same source for each successive year in order to determine individual changes over time. If, for example, a member of the AJC Board of Governors in 1967 was listed in the 1967 *Who's Who in America,* and was admitted to a formerly all-WASP social club in 1973, we hoped to find this by seeing him list the new club in the 1974 or 1975 *Who's Who in America.*

CORPORATE DIRECTORSHIPS

Our investigation of the corporate directorships of the AJC's Board of Governors over the past 26 years indicates, first of all, that during this period from 33% to 71% of the AJC Board located in our search were directors of corporations employing more than 100 people (see Table 2.1). The Board of

Table 2.1   Corporate Directorships of AJC Board
of Governors

	1952	1967	1976	1978
No. on Board of Governors	61	109	135	143
No. found in our search	24	65	69	66
No. on corporate boards of corporations employing more than 100 people	9	27	49	22
No. on boards of *Fortune* 500 or 50s		6	9	7
No. on more than one *Fortune* 500 or 50s		0	3	1
No. on boards of *Fortune* 1000 or 50s			14	12
No. on more than one *Fortune* 1000 or 50s			4	2

Governors does, then, draw substantially from the corporate world. But relatively few of those we located sit on boards of corporations large enough to be included in *Fortune* magazine's ranking of the 500 (or, as of 1970, the 1000) leading corporations. As Table 2.1 indicates, there was an increase in membership on boards of major corporations from 1952 to 1967, and from 1967 to 1976, but a slight decline from 1976 to 1978. A closer look reveals that in 1967 there were six men on boards of the *Fortune* 500, or on the boards of *Fortune's* top fifty commercial banks, life insurance companies, merchandising companies, transportation companies or utilities (the top "Fifty's"); none of these six men was on more than one such board.

Nine years later, in 1976, there were nine of our sampled AJC members on such boards (three were repeaters from the 1967 list of six), and three of these nine were on more than one such board. Clearly the most prominent of the interlocking directors was Max Fisher who, in addition to his membership on the Board of Governors of the AJC, sat on the boards of Dayco Corporation (Fortune No. 411), Fruehauf (Fortune No. 186), Manufacturer's National Bank (the twenty-eighth largest bank that year), Owens-Illinois (Fortune No. 88), and United Brands (Fortune No. 94).

By 1978, though Fisher was still on the Board of Governors, and it had added new members with corporate directorships on the boards of Tosco (Fortune No. 227) and Witco Chemical Company (Fortune No. 331), it had lost members who had been on various boards, and there was a notable decrease in corporate directorships. Only seven men, two fewer than in 1976, sat on boards of *Fortune's* 500 largest industrials or the various "Fifty" lists. Only one (Max Fisher) held multiple directorships. The addition of the second 500 leading industrials, which *Fortune* began in 1970, allows for a slightly more expansive comparison between 1976 and 1978. Again, the pattern shows a slight decrease: only 12 of our 1978 sample are on boards of *Fortune* 1000, as opposed to 14 in 1976, and only two in 1978, as opposed to four in 1976, are on more than one *Fortune* 1000 or "Fifty's" Board. Furthermore, it should be noted that the most precipitous drop was in the broader, less elite, category of companies employing more than 100 people. Whereas 49 members of the 1976 AJC Board sat on such boards, there were only 22 from the 1978 Board. This finding suggests the decline in corporate board membership may have been more than "slight."

The pattern, then, from the early 1950s into the mid-1970s, is one of slow but gradual increase in Jewish participation on boards of directors of major industries. This pattern, however, does not persist from 1976 to 1978. The reason for the drop from 1976 to 1978 is not clear at this time. Although it could indicate a reversal of the more general pattern found over thirty years, it could just as well indicate increasing difficulty on the part of the AJC in drawing from the ranks of corporate power. The third study to be reported in this chapter, which investigates the corporate and social connections of Jewish trustees of charitable foundations, will shed further light on this question.

CLUBS

Those members of the 1952, 1967, 1976, and 1978 AJC Board of Governors who we located in our various sources listed a total of 110 clubs to which they belong. Not one of these 110 clubs appears on Domhoff's (1970: 21-22) list of social clubs which indicate membership in the national upper class. Nor are there any AJC Board members who listed membership in any of the seven clubs rated by Ferdinand Lundberg (1968: 340) as the most important clubs in New York City (The Links, The Knickerbocker Club, The Metropolitan Club, Racquet and Tennis Club, The Brook, The Union, and The Union League).

Most of the 110 clubs on our list had only one or two AJC Board Members from one of the years investigated. Twelve clubs had three or more members in any one of the four years investigated; only four of those clubs are predominantly gentile clubs. The club with the largest representation over the years was the Harmonic Club of New York, the oldest and most prestigious of Jewish men's clubs. In sum, there is *no evidence* in these data that AJC members have been accepted into the clubs at the top.

EDUCATION

The undergraduate colleges attended by the four AJC Boards of Governors are presented in Table 2.2. Though we were able to locate a smaller percentage of AJC members for 1952 than for any other year, all but one of them attended college. In fact, over half attended Ivy League schools, and slightly under half attended either Columbia or CCNY.

Table 2.2   Undergraduate Colleges Attended by AJC
Board Members

	1952	1967	1976	1978
Total No. of members	65	109	135	143
No. found in our search	23	65	69	66
No. who attended college	22	59	65	63
Percentage found who attended college	96%	91%	94%	95%
No. who attended:				
Harvard	4	7	7	6
Yale	0	3	5	4
Princeton	0	0	0	0
Columbia	7	9	5	6
Other Ivy	1	10	8	6
Other "Outstanding Eastern Schools"	1	6	5	2
State Schools and Big Ten	1	14	19	20
Other	8	10	16	19
	22	59	65	63

It is notable that the percentage of AJC Board members found in our sources who attended Ivy League schools decreased over time, from 49% in 1967 to 38% in 1976 and 1978. If this decline indicates that the AJC is drawing fewer members from those schools traditionally linked to the upper class, then again, as with the data on corporate directorships, we may speculate that there has been a decline in the prestige of the AJC. Also notable is the absence of Princetonians on our four lists of AJC Board members.

POLICY GROUPS

Domhoff (1970, 1979) has suggested that certain policy groups serve the interests of the power elite. Although it is beyond the scope of this chapter to discuss how that process works, we did record whether the members of the four AJC Boards were also members of what Domhoff calls "the Big Four of the policy network": The Council on Foreign Relations (CFR), Committee for Economic Development (CED), the Conference Board, and the Business Council. From two to six AJC members were in the Council on Foreign Relations in each of the four years. A single Board member was on the Committee for Economic Development in 1967. None listed membership on the Conference Board or the Business Council for any year.

CONCLUSIONS

The AJC data, then, suggest some clear patterns for our attempt to understand the degree and manner of Jewish acceptance into the predominantly WASP upper class. Our data on corporate directorships indicate gradually increasing involvement on corporate boards of major American industries over a twenty-five-year period. There is, however, a drop-off from 1976 to 1978 that calls for further investigation; it may call into question the nature of the AJC Board of Governors and its ability to recruit from the higher corporate levels, or it may indicate increasing difficulty in Jewish access to the highest levels of economic power. There is no evidence in these data of significant breakthroughs in terms of membership in the most exclusive social clubs. Our data indicate that AJC Board members are (and for those that we found data on, have always been) well-educated, are represented on the Council of Foreign Relations but, with one exception in 1967, not on the other major policy groups.

Before we can accept these tentative patterns as final conclusions, or consider their implications, it is necessary to look at two additional studies that we have done.

A SURVEY OF UPPER-CLASS CLUBS

In order to gain a clearer impression of the presence or absence of Jews in upper-class social clubs, we mailed a cover letter and a brief questionnaire to the directors of the twenty-five regional offices of the American Jewish Committee (AJC) and the directors of the nineteen regional offices of the American Jewish Congress (AJCong). The questionnaire asked the respondent to indicate "the most exclusive predominately Gentile clubs" in his or her geographical area, whether or not these clubs have Jewish members, and, if so, approximately how many and when they were first accepted. The respondents were also asked if they would be willing to answer additional questions by phone.

Fourteen of the twenty-five questionnaires mailed to the AJC were returned, either by the directors themselves or by others they asked to do so; all but one indicated willingness to participate in a follow-up interview by phone. Only four of the nineteen questionnaires mailed to the AJCong were returned. Our suspicion that the AJC would be more involved in and aware of upper-class club membership than the AJCong was supported by the higher frequency of responses on the part of the AJC. In fact, one of the four AJCong respondents sent back her questionnaire with an accompanying note indicating that she had obtained her information from the regional director of the AJC in her city.

A few of the respondents expressed the belief that Jewish membership in social clubs had increased significantly in their cities, and in the country, over the past few years. One wrote: "It is my distinct impression that there has been a major change in club patterns in this country in the past six or so years relative to Jews." Another wrote of the clubs in his city that, "Most, these days, have at least a few Jews." Though this was the pattern for some of the cities included in our sample—that is, that most of the clubs have at least a few Jewish members—it was certainly not the pattern for all, or even most of the cities described by our respondents. Of the fourteen cities, only Cincinnati and Los Angeles were portrayed as having Jewish members in each of the top social clubs included, and in both of these cases, the number of Jewish members was quite small. More often, the barrier has been broken in some but not all clubs. For example, in Pittsburgh the Duquesne Club and the Pittsburgh Athletic Association began to accept Jewish members about three or four years ago, but the Pittsburgh Golf Club, Fox Chapel Country Club, and the nearby Rolling Rock Club have yet to accept Jewish members. As our respondent put it, "The breaking of the Duquesne Club and the PAA was considered significant, as much business is done there. There is much less concern about the others."

Eleven of the social clubs Domhoff included among his list of social indicators of the upper class were included on the list we developed from the responses to our questionnaires. Our respondents indicated there are between six and fifteen Jewish members of the Chicago Club, at least six Jewish members in the Detroit Club, one to three Jewish members in Los Angeles's California Club, and six to eight Jewish members in Seattle's Rainier Club. The Chicago Club has had Jewish members at least since the mid-1960s; the other three clubs first accepted Jewish members in the 1970s—the Detroit Club in 1970-1971, the Rainier Club "within the past six years," and the California Club in the past two to three years. In contrast, our various respondents indicated that they were aware of no Jewish members of the following clubs which were also on Domhoff's list: Atlanta's Piedmont Driving Club, Chicago's Casino Club, Houston's Eagle Lake, Milwaukee's Milwaukee Club, Philadelphia's Philadelphia Club, Pittsburgh's Rolling Rock, and St. Louis's St. Louis Country Club.

In those clubs which have accepted Jewish members in recent years, who are the people getting in? Our phone interviews indicate that the new club members are likely to be lawyers, realtors, and owners of sizable family businesses who have considerable contact with the gentile community. That they are less likely to be upper-level executives of large corporations seems to be a reflection of the fact that there are so few Jews in such positions. They are, as one put it, "not the kind of people you'd find in shul on a Saturday morning," and, if indeed they are members of a congregation, it's almost definitely the more elite reform temple rather than the conservative synagogue. As one of our respondents said of the Jews in the Chicago Club, "they're either not perceived as Jews, or they are German Jews who have been in Chicago for four to five generations." Though they don't hide their Jewishness (one man was referred to as "seeing himself as the Jewish ambassador to the non-Jewish community"), and are likely to contribute enormous amounts of money to Jewish causes, "their definition of religion becomes increasingly cultural."

The evidence indicates, then, that in some clubs, in some cities, some Jews are getting in, although these do not tend to be the most prestigious clubs. Those who join the clubs do not deny their Jewishness, but they are unlikely to be involved with the spiritual side of Judaism. Their Jewish involvement is often indicated by their fund-raising activities, and their presentation of themselves as Jews is seen by our respondents as "cultural" rather than "religious." Thus, there is some evidence of increasing Jewish membership in some upper-class clubs, and some indication that those who become members have less identification with the Jewish community. This brings us to the results of the third study.

JEWISH TRUSTEES OF FOUNDATIONS

In this third study, we looked at the corporate and social connections of Jews who were trustees of charitable foundations. Our "population" for this study consisted of those individuals listed in the *Trustees of Wealth,* a "who's who" of contemporary American philanthropy. The book lists biographical information, including corporate directorships and club memberships, for the trustees and major donors in, as the editor puts it, "the philanthropic world." The editor (Brodsky, 1975) candidly acknowledges the value of such information, "because so much giving depends on contacts—who knows whom." And although it is doubtful that she had power structure research in mind when she wrote her preface, it states quite clearly the importance of corporate and social contacts in an analysis of the way power works in the United States. Jean Brodsky (1975) writes:

> The information contained on these pages can lead you and your institution to the discovery of contacts with funding sources that might otherwise go undiscovered and unutilized. Perhaps a member of your board went to the same school as a foundation trustee, belongs to the same country club, or in some other way has a connection. *Trustees of Wealth* is a tool that can start the process of people-to-people planning rolling.

From this population, a sample was drawn of those individuals whom we could assume to be Jewish. Specifically, all individuals were studied whose biographical sketches included membership in a clearly Jewish organization (such as the United Jewish Appeal, the Federation of Jewish Philanthropies, the National Jewish Welfare Board, and, of course, the American Jewish Committee), a social club known to be exclusively, or nearly exclusively, Jewish (such as New York's Harmonie Club, Chicago's Standard Club, or Los Angeles's Hillcrest Country Club), or who listed ongoing formal affiliations with Brandeis University, Albert Einstein Medical College or the American Friends of Hebrew University. Their directorships, club memberships, and civic and religious organizational memberships were recorded and entered into a computer data bank, as were their memberships on policy-planning groups such as the Council of Foreign Relations.

In addition to the above data, we determined which of the 227 Jewish trustees sat on boards of directors of companies listed in *Fortune's* 1000 leading industrials or on the boards of companies listed in *Fortune's* various lists of "Fifty's" (banks, utilities, etc.). We started by looking to see if the corporate directorships listed in *Trustees of Wealth* for each person were for companies included on *Fortune's* various lists for 1976 (*Trustees of Wealth* was published in December 1975). To confirm that the individual was indeed a director of the company listed, we cross-checked using *Standard and Poor's* and *Dun and Bradstreet* for the years 1974-1976. In a few cases, through such cross-checking, we found additional directorships not listed in *Trustees of Wealth;* these were included. In those few cases where we could not confirm a directorship through *Standard and Poor's* or *Dun and Bradstreet,* it was not included in the data.

We were interested in finding out which Jewish trustees of foundations with which kinds and combinations of club, civic and religious memberships, were most likely to sit on one or more boards of America's largest corporations. In addition, since for this study the American Jewish Committee was one of many possible Jewish affiliations, it served as a way of assessing the relative entry into the upper class by members of the AJC, as opposed to other wealthy Jews who are not members of the AJC.

A summary of the data can be seen in Table 2.3, which includes only those associations and clubs with five or more Jewish trustees as members. As is readily seen, a much higher percentage of the club members sit on major boards than do the association members. Whereas only 19.2% of all individuals listing a Jewish association in the *Trustees of Wealth* sit on at least one *Fortune* board, and only 5.2% sit on two or more such boards, 40.4% of the club members sit on at least one of these boards, and 27.6% sit on two or more.

There was, however, overlap in the above analysis. That is, many of the same individuals were members of more than one association or club. When we looked separately at those fifty-one people who belonged to at least one club, but no associations, and those thirty-seven who belonged to at least one club and one or more associations, we found very similar differences to those just described: 41.2% of the former group sat on at least one *Fortune* board, but only 16.2% of the latter were on at least one such board. Similarly, 29.4% of those with club memberships but no Jewish association affiliations sat on two or more *Fortune* boards, but only 5.4% of those listing both a club and at least one association were on two or more *Fortune* boards. Further, when we looked at the corporate directorships of the forty-four Jewish trustees who listed membership on two or more clubs, we found that 43.2% sat on at least one *Fortune* board, and 27.3% sat on two or more.

Table 2.3   *Fortune* Board Representation of Jewish
Trustees of Wealth Who List Memberships in Jewish
Associations or Clubs

Associations	N	One or More Fortune Boards	Percentage	Two or More Fortune Boards	Percentage
Council of Jewish Federations and Welfare Board	6	4	66.7	0	0
American Friends of Hebrew Univ.	5	3	60.0	2	40
Albert Einstein Medical College	11	5	45.4	2	18.2
United Jewish Appeal	13	4	30.8	1	7.7
Jewish Community Centers	7	2	28.6	0	0
Brandeis Univ.	15	4	26.7	0	0
Anti-Defamation League	6	1	16.7	0	0
Federation of Jewish Philanths.	22	2	9.1	1	4.5
National Jewish Welfare Board	13	1	7.7	1	7.7
American Jewish Committee	13	0	0	0	0
Hebrew Union College	9	0	0	0	0
National Conf. Christians and Jews	6	0	0	0	0
American Jewish Congress	5	0	0	0	0
Jewish Federation	5	0	0	0	0
	135	26	19.2	7	5.2

Continued on page 68

Clubs	N	Fortune Boards	Percentage	Fortune Boards	Percentage
Commercial	9	6	66.7	2	22.2
Recess	5	3	60.0	3	60.0
Executive	7	4	57.1	3	42.8
Mid-Am	7	4	57.1	3	42.8
Harvard	10	5	50.0	1	10.1
Tavern	6	3	50.0	2	33.3
Lake Shore Cntry	9	4	44.4	3	33.3
Economics	7	3	42.8	3	42.8
Century Cntry	12	5	41.6	5	41.6
Century Assoc	5	2	40.0	0	0
Concordia	5	2	40.0	1	20.0
Midday	11	4	36.4	4	36.4
Standard	32	10	31.2	7	21.9
Hillcrest	7	2	28.6	1	14.3
Harmonie	24	6	25.0	5	20.8
	156	63	40.4	43	27.6

Thus, it is clear that Jews who have entered the world of corporate power at the level of the companies included on *Fortune's* lists are more likely to be recognized as Jews through club memberships than through memberships in Jewish associations.

A closer look at the Jewish organizations, and their rankings (based on the percentage of Jewish trustees who sit on *Fortune* boards), as shown in Table 2.3, sheds further light on the patterns of Jewish representation on boards of major corporations. It is noteworthy that three of the six top associations are primarily academic in nature: the American Friends of Hebrew University, Albert Einstein Medical College, and Brandeis University. These data suggest, as did our respondents in the second study, that Jews involved in the highest level of corporate power, if they are in Jewish organizations at all, are more likely to be involved in those which focus on the "cultural" rather than the religious aspects of Judaism.

These findings also help place the American Jewish Committee in the broader context of the many affiliations available to wealthy Jews. Though there can be no doubt, as has been stressed throughout the chapter, that the AJC is a highly prestigious organization, our findings suggest that Jews in the highest levels of corporate power are less likely to list membership in the AJC than to list affiliation with various other Jewish social clubs or Jewish associations.

Our data on associations are based on small samples, and are not meant to be definitive in ranking the economic prestige of the various associations. It is quite possible that an in-depth investigation of all members of the associations listed in Table 2.3 would lead to a higher ranking for the AJC. We were unable to do that. But we did look up the 135 members of the AJC's 1976 Board of Governors in *Trustees of Wealth* and found that only seven of the twenty-one who appeared listed their AJC membership. None of the seven who listed AJC membership was on *Fortune* boards. In contrast, four of the fourteen who did not list their AJC affiliation were on *Fortune* boards, and three of these four were on two or more such boards. Surprisingly, six of the fourteen who did not list their AJC affiliation had provided no information that enabled us to identify them as Jewish when we drew our sample from the *Trustees of Wealth*.

The AJC's Board of Governors, then, includes some members who wield immense corporate power, but they are the very AJC members least likely to indicate their AJC affiliation in a biographic source-book like the *Trustees of Wealth*. However, even with four *Fortune* board members among the twenty-seven Jewish trustees whom we now know to have been in the AJC in 1976, the AJC does not move to the top of the list in Table 2.3. The AJC, with 14.8% *Fortune* board representation, would be listed under the Anti-Defamation League (16.7%), but above the Federation of Jewish Philanthropies (9.1%). These data bring to mind the words of Lew Wasserman, chairman of MCA, thought by many to be "the most powerful Jew in Los Angeles." When Robert Scheer (1978) asked him about the AJC's criticism of MCA for producing "Jesus Christ Superstar," a musical that the AJC claimed resurrects the idea of Jews as the killers of Christ, Wasserman replied: "This bugaboo about the American Jewish Committee speaking for all the Jews in America, well, I know one Jew they don't speak for—they don't speak for Lew Wasserman."

A closer look at the club memberships of the Jewish trustees also is informative on the question of Jewish identification. Three of the clubs included on Domhoff's list of upper-class indicators have a total of six Jewish trustees as members. Three trustees are in the Chicago Club, two are in New York's Piping Rock, and one is in the Links, described by Baltzell (1964: 371) as "the New York rendezvous of the national corporate establishment." These six men list an average of eight club memberships. Five of the six sit on *Fortune* boards, and three are on three or more such boards. But only one lists a membership in a Jewish civic or religious association—the National Jewish Welfare Board. As we found in our second study, then, a few Jews are becoming members of gentile clubs in some cities, including the most exclusive clubs in America. However, those who are members of the most prestigious of these clubs appear very unlikely to identify themselves as members of Jewish civic and religious organizations.

CONCLUSION

Some American Jews are involved in directing the most powerful corporations in the country. A relatively small number of these are now members of prestigious clubs which formerly did not admit Jews as members. Using the standard definitions of upper-class membership, the data described in these three studies indicate that there are some, but not many, Jews in the American upper class. However, those that we have identified as having moved furthest into America's economic and social elite are unlikely to be involved in overtly Jewish organizations, though they are likely to be members of Jewish clubs. We do not know if they *feel* less Jewish, or if they think of themselves as less Jewish, but we do know that the way they present themselves to the outside world through their biographical sketches does not include emphasis on, or in some cases, even acknowledgement of, their Jewishness.

Our data reveal that Jews are once again being assimilated, however slowly, into the upper class, as were the Sephardic and German Jews prior to the 1880s. As Baltzell's (1964) class-replaces-religion theory would expect, our data also suggest that as this assimilation occurs, they are less likely to be involved with Jewish religious and civic organizations. Perhaps the grandchildren of Greenboro's Ceasar Cone, fourteen of seventeen of whom were raised as gentiles, suggest the future course for the offspring of successful Jewish businessmen.

REFERENCES

BALTZELL, E. (1964) The Protestant Establishment: Aristocracy and Caste in America. New York: Vintage.

BIRMINGHAM, S. (1967) Our Crowd: The Great Jewish Families of New York. New York: Harper & Row.

BLOOM, S. (1946) "The saga of America's 'Russian' Jews." Commentary 1, 4: 1-7.

BRODSKY, J. [ed.] (1975) Trustees of Wealth. Washington, DC: Taft Information Services.

COHEN, N. (1972) Not Free to Desist: The American Jewish Committee, 1906-1966. Philadelphia: Jewish Publication Society.

DOMHOFF, G. W. (1979) The Powers That Be: Processes of Ruling Class Domination in America. New York: Vintage.

————— (1975) "Social clubs, policy-planning groups, and corporations: a network study of ruling-class cohesiveness." Insurgent Sociologist 5, 3: 173-184.

————— (1972) Fat Cats and Democrats. Englewood Cliffs, NJ: Prentice-Hall.

————— (1970) The Higher Circles: The Governing Class in America. New York: Random House.

————— (1967) Who Rules America? Englewood Cliffs, NJ: Prentice-Hall.

FELDSTEIN, S. (1978) The Land That I Show You: Three Centuries of Jewish Life in America. Garden City, NY: Anchor.

GLANZ, R. (1969) "The rise of the Jewish club in America." Jewish Social Studies 31, 2: 82-89.

GLAZER, N. and D. MOYNIHAN (1963) Beyond The Melting Pot. Cambridge, MA: Harvard Univ. Press.

GOLDEN, H. (1974) Our Southern Landsman. New York: Putnam.

——————— (1955) Jewish Roots in the Carolinas: A Pattern of American Philo-Semitism. Greensboro, NC: Deal Printing.

HANDLIN, O. (1954) Adventure in Freedom: Three Hundred Years of Jewish Life in America. New York: McGraw-Hill.

HERBERG, W. (1955) Protestant-Catholic-Jew. New York: Doubleday.

HIGHAM, J. (1975) Send These to Me: Jews and Other Immigrants in Urban America. New York: Atheneum.

HOWE, I. (1976) World of Our Fathers. New York: Harcourt, Brace, Jovanovich.

KENNEDY, R.J. (1952) "Single or triple melting-pot? intermarriage in New Haven, 1870-1950." American Journal of Sociology 58, 1: 56-59.

——————— (1944) "Single or triple melting-pot? intermarriage trends in New Haven, 1790-1940." American Journal of Sociology 49, 4: 331-339.

KRAMER, J. and S. LEVENTMAN (1961) Children of the Gilded Ghetto. New Haven, CT: Yale Univ. Press.

LUNDBERG, F. (1968) The Rich and the Super-Rich. New York: Bantam.

MAAS, E. (1973) "The Jews of Houston: an ethnographic study." Ph.D. dissertation, Rice University.

MANNERS, A. (1972) Poor Cousins. New York: Coward, McCann & Geohegan.

MILLS, C. (1956) The Power Elite. New York: Oxford Univ. Press.

MORRIS, T. (1971) Better Than You: Social Discrimination Against Minorities in America. New York: Institute of Human Relations Press.

PANITZ, E. (1963) "The polarity of American Jewish attitudes towards immigration (1870-1891)." American Jewish Historical Quarterly (December): 105-118.

PETRUSAK, F. and S. STEINERT (1976) "The Jews of Charleston: some old wine in new bottles." Jewish Social Studies 38: 337-346.

RISCHIN, M. (1962) The Promised City. Cambridge, MA: Harvard Univ. Press.

ROLLINS, J.H. (1973) "Reference identification of youth of differing ethnicity." Journal of Personality and Social Psychology 26: 221-231.

SCHEER, R. (1978) "Jews in L.A." Los Angeles Times (January 29-31).

SINGER, D. (1978) "An uneasy alliance: Jews and Blacks in the United States, 1945-1953." Contemporary Jewry 4, 2.

SKLARE, M. and J. GREENBLUM (1967) Jewish Identity on the Suburban Frontier. New York: Basic Books.

SLAWSON, J. and L. BLOOMGARTEN (1965) The Unequal Treatment of Equals. New York: Institute of Human Relations.

SUPPLE, B. (1957) "A business elite: German-Jewish financiers in nineteenth century New York." Business History Review 31, 2: 143-78.

SUTKER, S. (1958) "The role of social clubs in the Atlanta Jewish community," in Marshall Sklare (ed.) The Jews: Social Patterns of an American Group. New York: Free Press.

Washington Post (1976). December 29: A1.

ZWEIGENHAFT, R. (1979) "Two cities in Carolina: a comparative study of Jews in the upper class." Jewish Social Studies 41: 291-300.

_____ (1978) "The Jews of Greensboro: in or out of the upper class?" Contemporary Jewry 4, 2: 60-76.

3

UPPER-CLASS WOMEN: CLASS CONSCIOUSNESS AS CONDUCT AND MEANING

Susan A. Ostrander

INTRODUCTION

Fundamental to American popular ideology is the belief that social class is not of much importance in everyday life. Moreover, academic studies of class consciousness often state that this anticlass ideology is accurate. They conclude that Americans are not particularly "class conscious" and do not consistently behave or define their lives in class-related ways (e.g., Mayer and Buckley, 1970; Rothman, 1978; Hurst, 1979). This ideology and its scientific supports contribute to a lack of interest among policy-makers and the general populace in the issue of class inequality. Since classes are not perceived as important or real, strategies to bring about an equalitarian class structure and eliminate class privilege are seen as unnecessary and receive little attention among those who would benefit most from these changes.

My study of women of the upper class led me to conclude that current academic theorizing about class consciousness is inadequate and accounts in part for the failure of social scientists to explore the reality of class. The aim of this chapter, then, is to critique existing conceptualizations of class consciousness, and to consider an alternative formulation of class consciousness using data from interviews with women of the upper class as empirical illustrations. Upper-class women are a particularly useful group for an exploration into class consciousness, since the upper class in general and the women of this class in particular are thought to be the most class-conscious segment of the American population (Warner and Lunt, 1941; Mills, 1956; Domhoff, 1970; Seider, 1974). My formulation of class consciousness was dictated by my data and later clarified theoretically by further delving into the relevant sociological literature. The conceptualization of class consciousness I will propose is neo-Marxian in the sense of other recent efforts to bring together the insights of phenomenology and Marxism (see, for example, Lichtman, 1970; Sallach, 1973; Piccone, 1973; Dallmayr, 1973).

I will begin with a brief review of the methodology and major findings of my larger study on upper-class women. I will then examine the formulations of class consciousness used by both non-Marxists and traditional Marxists, and work toward a neo-Marxian perspective that views class consciousness in terms of activity and meaning in everyday life. Evidence for this new formulation will be provided from my interviews.

THE STUDY OF UPPER-CLASS WOMEN

In-depth focused interviews were conducted with thirty-eight upper-class women from a large Midwestern city. The strategy of data collection and analysis, to be explained in the following paragraphs, conformed to the "inductive methods of discovery" outlined by Glaser and Strauss (1967) and Bogdan and Taylor (1976). Respondents were obtained through referral and checked against objective criteria of upper-class membership established by previous studies. A brief review of each of these features of the methodology and sampling procedures is in order and is suggestive of some aspects of the findings.

A focused interview has been defined by sociologists Robert Merton and Patricia Kendall (1946) as one where there is a certain aspect of a subject's experience about which the interviewer wishes to know. This aspect is defined by the researcher in the formulation of the research question. In this study, the aspect I wished to know about was how the activities of the women of the upper class contributed to maintaining the power and privilege of this class, and thus to maintaining the class structure. A focused interview is a partially structured form of questioning in contrast to the unstructured non-focused interview where a wide range of the interviewee's concerns are pursued as they arise spontaneously in open and lengthy conversation (Becker and Geer, 1957).

In the focused interview, as in the nonfocused, nondirective questioning is of particular importance early in the data-gathering process. Since the goal of the discovery method is to generate theory from the data in an inductive way rather than to test preset hypotheses from existing theory, an established set of questions used throughout the study is not appropriate. Instead, questions are continuously revised, expanded, and refocused as new issues and better ways of asking about old ones emerge. As tentative hypotheses are formulated in early interviews, they are checked out, specified, reformulated, and checked again in later interviews. Simultaneous collection and analysis of the data is thus inherent to the discovery process. Validity of information is established in part by a conscious search for negative instances, for respondents who differ from the others in experience and point of view. The extent to which a subject spontaneously volunteers specific information in response to an open and general question as opposed to a structured and particular one is also considered as an indication of validity (Becker, 1958). Another indicator of validity is the element of surprise on the part of the researcher. All these validity criteria were evident in the data presented here, as will be pointed out throughout.

The sample of respondents was obtained by asking each woman at the conclusion of the interview if she would suggest "another woman of your social group, with a background like yours, who might be willing to talk to me." The initial respondent who set off this "snowball" method was located largely by accident, though she met the objective criteria I had established. A colleague who knew of my study and had worked with this woman on a community project suggested that I contact her. She was immediately enthusiastic about my interest in "learning about the role of women in some of the old and influential families in the city." She offered to refer me to the oldest "grande dames" who would give me further entrée. She said, "It's important for you to go in the right order. You have to start at the top." I had so little difficulty gaining the consent of my subjects to be interviewed and taped that my experience leads me to conclude that upper-class persons are more accessible than has been previously thought, and I urge my fellow social scientists to be less hesitant in approaching them. To the extent that we do not study the upper class with the same frequency that we study others, we contribute to the elusive sense of power and ability to intimidate that helps to maintain the class structure.

My first respondent and the others in my sample, in addition to being defined by each other as class equals, met the standards for upper-class membership set in the sociological literature (Baltzell, 1958; Dahl, 1961; Domhoff, 1970). That is, respondents belonged to the distinctly upper-class clubs in the city and to the Junior League. They and their children attended the private secondary schools that have been found to be characteristic of their class, and the majority had graduated from Smith, Vassar, and Welles-ley. The women and their families were listed in the *Social Register* for their city. Respondents lived in the very wealthiest areas in the city. Husbands, for the most part, were employed in the top echelons of business. Many were either presidents or board chairmen of their firms, and half headed presti-gious old firms established by their own family two or three generations earlier. Husbands not in business were in medicine or law. The women studied thus combined the family-of-origin descendants of the first families of the city, and the family-of-marriage links to the top of the city's oldest and most prestigious firms.

The major findings of the larger study (Ostrander, 1976, 1977, 1979) were in the areas of how the family roles and community roles of these women contributed to maintaining the position of the upper class, what meaning the women themselves gave to these roles, and the degree of convergence between the social consequences and the personal meaning of the roles. One of the specific major findings, reported above in the discus-sion of the sample, was that the subjective and objective definitions of class peers were the same, that is, the women my subjects referred me to as their social equals were members of the upper class as it is defined and measured by social scientists. Another major finding was the importance of the role of the mother in maximizing children's achievement in a class context. The subservience of the upper-class wife in her relationship with her husband also was a striking pattern. This subservience was in clear contrast to another major finding, the influential role of these women in the community as members of the boards of academic, cultural, and human service organiza-tions.

As will be reported in my reformulation of the concept of class con-sciousness, the personal reasons the women gave for their community work were the very ones which could be said to have the greatest consequences for maintaining the position of the upper class. Most striking was the willing-ness of subjects to state spontaneously the political function of volunteer work as staving off an extension of the public sector. The women viewed their work on civic boards as an effort to keep decision-making private as a positive holding action against what they saw as anti-American ideologies. They were aware that their economic position made it possible for them to maintain this private hold on public affairs, and that their position as an economic elite excluded the participation of persons not of this group from community decision-making in anything like representative numbers. None of the women cited a desire or intention to solve community problems as a motive for volunteer work. Instances of these major findings will be cited later in the chapter as they relate specifically to my concern with formulating a new view of class consciousness. Before doing that, however, I will discuss how class consciousness is currently defined by non-Marxists and traditional Marxists, using my data to critique or support these conceptualizations.

CURRENT VIEWS OF CLASS CONSCIOUSNESS

Class consciousness is often defined by sociologists in subjective or psychological terms, seeking to establish whether persons can locate themselves and others in the stratification hierarchy. This perspective reflects a concern with status as opposed to class; that is, with social prestige rather than with economic power. This has occurred to such an extent in American sociology that the terms position and status are often used synonymously (e.g., Davis and Merton in Biddle and Thomas, 1966; Chinoy, 1968; Rothman, 1978), and class is often defined in terms of one's relative location on a continuum of social levels (e.g., Warner, 1949; Mayer and Buckley, 1970).

Richard Centers provided an example of the psychological approach to class and class consciousness, though few sociologists today would agree with the degree of psychological reductionism he used to define an objective class structure out of existence. Centers claimed that social classes are by definition "psycho-social groupings . . . subjective in character and dependent on class consciousness" (1949: 135). In other words, if people are not willing and able to articulate the existence of social classes, and to locate themselves properly in this hierarchy, then social classes do not exist. Social scientists who use this approach to studying class ask people to what class they belong. Sometimes specific class categories—upper, middle, working, or lower—are provided for respondents to characterize themselves. Such efforts usually search for correlations between the class consciousness of respondents and other attitudes, particularly political ones (Centers, 1949; Hodge and Treiman, 1968; Rinehart and Okrahu, 1974; Guest, 1974).

As noted, few sociologists today would go as far into subjectivity as Centers and others of his time did, and there have been many critiques of the use of what British sociologist Runciman (1970) called self-rated class as a measure of class consciousness. However, a search of current sociological journals demonstrated that the tendency to equate class identification of individuals with at least some form of class consciousness is still very much with us. Schreiber and Nygreen, for example, suggest that, "We can attempt to sort out the 'class conscious' respondents . . . by the use of the screening question, 'Do you ever think of yourself as being in one of these (middle or working) classes?'" (1970: 354). Rinehart and Okrahu (1974) conducted a study of class consciousness in Canada, using the question, "If you were to use one of these names for your social class, which would you say you belong to?" The choices were upper, upper middle, lower middle, working, and lower. Guest (1974) used the leading question, "Most people say they belong to either the middle class or the working class. Do you ever think of yourself as being in one of these classes?" Several authors, in an attempt to develop points on a continuum of class consciousness, place self-identification at the minimal point (Morris and Murphy, 1966; Laumann, 1976), implying that it is necessary that self-placement exist before other forms of class consciousness need even be considered. If an individual is not willing or able at the very least to verbally place him- or herself in a social class in response to an interviewer's question, then "higher" forms of class consciousness seem to be ruled out. For example, one author who urges the study of how important class is to people, as opposed to simply whether they can place themselves in a class, nonetheless begins with the tradition of Centers when he asserts that "willingness or ability to designate where [individuals] feel they belong in the system of stratification is a necessary condition of class consciousness" (Lewis, 1965: 172).

Research centered around this social psychological notion of class often comes to seemingly contradictory conclusions. Class is reported as of not much importance to people, but objective class membership is highly correlated, often in the same studies, with political attitudes. It appears that, although people may deny the existence and importance of class when directly asked, class does make a difference in their attitudes. How can we explain this discrepancy? One obvious direction is to reconsider our view of class consciousness as measured by class identification. Empirical data derived from interviews with upper-class respondents sensitized me to the idea that it is not valid to view class consciousness as related to willingness to place oneself in a particular class or to willingness to articulate the existence of a class structure in society. The respondent who initially sensitized me to this idea was a negative instance of it; that is, she expressed herself clearly about the existence of a class hierarchy and her own position in it. In the context of telling me the advantages of her own particular life style, she said,

> We're not supposed to have layers [in our society]. I'm embarrassed to admit to you that we do, and that I feel superior at my social level. I like being part of the upper crust.

This comment came after a two-hour interview and was followed shortly by a rather curt dismissal. It appeared to me that she had acknowledged something she felt she should not have—that classes exist in American society, that she belonged to the one at the top, and that she liked it just fine. Other respondents, who I would consider to be highly class conscious in ways I will relate later in this chapter, were far more on guard about the existence of a class structure and their place in it. When asked directly about whether they would consider themselves upper class, respondents rejected the use of this term with comments like:

> I hate [the term] upper class. It's so *non*-upper class to use it. I just call it "all of us," those of us who are wellborn.

> I wouldn't classify anyone as upper class, just as productive, worthwhile people.

> I'd prefer to think of it as established, of a certain economic group or social status.

> I hate to use the word "class." We're responsible, fortunate people, old families, the people who have something.

One woman directly and spontaneously denied being class conscious. She said, "There may be some people who are class conscious, but I don't feel that way." This woman probably did not use the term class conscious in the way social scientists use it, but she did appear to be saying that being upper class was not of much importance to her—a verbalization that her behavior denied by that fact that she had been so personally affected by her class membership that she had moved over twenty miles outside the city limits to escape what she saw as the demands placed on her for community service because of her prominent family name and family wealth.

I would not want to declare these respondents as not class conscious based on their rejection of upper-class self-identification. This is because, as sociologist Avery Guest has suggested, the willingness of individuals to place themselves in social classes is itself a "recognition of inequities in the American system" (1974: 509). Such open acknowledgment of class inequality is not in the interests of those in society who accumulate privilege as a consequence of this inequity. It also seems possible that persons in positions of powerlessness could deny the existence of objective structural inequalities as a defense against personal despair. It might be therefore that, especially among the privileged and powerful, *not* being willing to place oneself in a particular social class, or to acknowledge that such classes exist, is a *more* class-conscious response than a willingness to do so. As sociologist Anthony Giddens has stated it, "class awareness may take the form of a denial of the existence or reality of classes" (1975: 111). I believe, then, that verbal measures of self-placement and awareness of class structure are too fraught with ideological overtones to be accurate indicators of class consciousness or the importance of class itself. I conclude that what is needed is a definition and measurement of the concept more realistically based in the meaning and behavior of everyday life.

Another non-Marxian orientation toward the study of class and class consciousness has its origins in the work of Max Weber. Weber (1946) made the distinction between class as an economic dimension of inequalities of power, status, or prestige as a social dimension, and party as a political dimension. Several current studies in the sociological literature stress the importance of recognizing these multiple dimensions of structured inequality. Laumann and Senter (1976), for example, caution against confusing class consciousness with status consciousness. Landecker (1963) suggests that class consciousness varies according to what he calls "class crystallization," that is, the empirical correlation of different measures of rank in the stratification hierarchy. He says this crystallization varies throughout the class system, from a core of those clearly identifiable as members of particular classes, until the "core shades off into a less and less structured fringe" (Landecker, 1963: 219). He proposes a typology of class consciousness that is broken down into status consciousness (personal allegiance to one's class as friends), structure consciousness (awareness of the existence of class in the community and of class boundaries), and interest consciousness (recognition of class interests and the need of class conflict). He suggests some means for empirical measurement of these theoretical categories, and cautions that "findings representing one category of the proposed scheme should not be generalized to variables in other categories" (Landecker, 1963: 229). Morris and Murphy (1966) also seek to develop a paradigm for the study of class consciousness. They view class consciousness as one dimension of a continuum of stratum consciousness, to be seen as part of a developing process. They advocate an indirect measure of genuine class consciousness, stating "[If] members of labor unions or those in unskilled occupations favor economic reforms, while those in managerial or professional occupations do not, this is prima facie evidence of class consciousness . . . . [Subjects should be] asked to supply information on objective status (occupation, education, income) and then asked for political attitudes about economic and political issues" (Morris and Murphy, 1966: 304).

What I have characterized as a Weberian approach to the study of class consciousness has much to offer. What is perhaps most interesting about the works cited is the apparent lack of attention that has been paid to them in contemporary studies of class consciousness, though some recent texts in stratification cite them (e.g., Beeghley, 1978). I find Morris and Murphy's empirical referent approach particularly appealing. However, I believe that the Weberian perspective, at least as it tends to be applied in American sociology, puts too much emphasis on multidimensionality and thus detracts from a clear recognition of the fundamental realities of inequality as I see them in contemporary industrial society. The stratification hierarchy from this view is often seen as a gradated continuum, without rigid boundaries, with no real impenetrable barriers to social mobility, and no deep antagonisms or conflicts (e.g., Rinehart and Okrahu, 1974).

The traditional Marxian view of class consciousness, unlike the two perspectives I have discussed so far, defines class consciousness ultimately in terms of class-based political action directed toward fundamental change in the economic structure of capitalism. For a Marxist, class consciousness develops in stages under certain empirically specified structural conditions related to the nature of capitalist production and conflicts between capitalists and workers. It is a revolutionary consciousness which, by definition, can only be a characteristic of a revolutionary class. For the orthodox Marxist, a class is not really a class until such consciousness is present. It is therefore something of a Marxist inelegance to speak of class consciousness as a characteristic of the ruling class. Only the working class or proletariat can be class conscious, since only the proletariat can develop a revolutionary consciousness. The ruling class has rather a bourgeois ideology, formulated for the purpose of maintaining the power and position of the ruling class and preventing the occurrence of the socialist revolution. To quote Georg Lukacs, an early Marxist writer on the subject, working-class consciousness is "the sense . . . of the historical role of the class" (1971: 73). The late contemporary Marxist sociologist Charles Anderson stated that class consciousness "includes not only a psychological awareness of common and conflicting class interest, but also an understanding and comprehension of the changes required to alter the course of society in the direction of objective class interests" (Anderson, 1974: 135). In this view there are three components of class consciousness: (1) an awareness of one's own class interest and identification; (2) an understanding of the inherent conflict of interest with other classes; and (3) a willingness to engage in political struggle to realize class interest.

These three components, specified by sociologist C. Wright Mills (1951), considered by some to be a Marxist, were initially useful in my study. Allow my data to demonstrate its utility. Indicative of the solidarity component, for example, was the consistent use of a class terminology among the women I interviewed to refer to what they considered to be their class equals. Acceptable persons were referred to almost universally by my respondents as "congenial" or "compatible." There was a very clear sense of "we-ness," of a sense of belonging and consciousness of kind, of class cohesiveness. Respondents typically made comments like:

> A feeling of camaraderie is important. That's difficult to get as a group gets more heterogeneous.

> Your social life is the people you choose, a certain group, those you would have in your home, people who are congenial. That implies social behavior.

> When it comes to [social clubs], I'm the worst snob you know. People have a right to choose their own friends. I work with people on boards that I wouldn't have in my house.

> If I go out to the club to relax, I don't want people around I don't care about. I like having people like me around—people who are quiet and conservative, nice to their children, who don't run around with other people's wives, who are interested in the community. I find the homogeneity very pleasant.

> The members [of the Junior League] do have a certain caliber. I would hate to see just anybody get in. Manners are still important and a little breeding, a little polish. It's in one's carriage, a way of speaking, well-bred.

> The people who are members [of the social club] are friends before they become members. They like to do similar things in a similar way, and that's important for a private club.

In addition to the clear sense of commonality and solidarity evident in these statements, the women of the upper class with whom I spoke also were clear about the differences between themselves and others, although this did not always express itself specifically in terms of conflict of interest. One evidence of awareness of class differences is the distinct sense of moral superiority expressed in the statements quoted above. This sense of being better than persons of other classes was evident not only in regard to personal morality but also in commitment to work. One woman said in regard to the difference between paid workers and volunteers like herself:

> The paid workers stop working at a certain time and won't lift a finger after that. The volunteer will work all night if we have a project to get done. That comes from education and commitment. Maybe this is where family background comes in. We've been brought up to do more than is expected of us. There are many people who won't lift a finger to help. They'll take their forty-five minutes for lunch no matter what's happening.

Another indication of the sense of class difference that my subjects felt was in the distinction they made between the functions of paid professionals in the organizations on whose boards these women served, and themselves. The initial question in regard to distinction of function was intended simply to delineate the function of the board member and volunteer as compared to paid professionals. My subjects answered in terms of their desire to "represent the broader community" in contrast to the "narrower" focus of the paid professional. At first I thought my subjects meant that they represented the citizenry, the general populace. I soon found that this type of representation was referred to by my subjects as "client" or "consumer" participation, and that they were opposed to it. The "community" that upper-class women represent is that group which provides the money they say makes possible the running of these organizations, the people they define as important. In other words, they represent themselves, the upper class. They draw a firm line between themselves and both the paid professionals and the consumers, and often recognize that their interests are quite different. Let these women speak for themselves:

> We in the community are sensitive to reactions from the point of view of public relations and finance. Volunteers have this broader perspective which is different from that of professionals.

> The generalist comes from the community and she can help the professional see what is possible in the general community—often, of course, in the area of financing programs.

> I do represent a segment of the community. Sometimes I represent old [city]. Sometimes I represent the Junior League.

> Sometimes the professionals don't understand what's financially feasible or feasible in terms of the community. Consumers also often lack a basic understanding, perhaps due to their own financial limitations. They also want to throw away what's being done and put the money somewhere else. From what I've seen, most of the consumers who have been on boards don't contribute much. I think they're in over their heads.

> Boards are basically tuned in to the money aspect. They exercise a veto power over policies. The professional has a narrower perspective than community board members. There is a lack of knowledge about business, and the wealthy person has more access to power than the professional. [Professionals] aren't making the decisions. The wealthy in the community are. The people who run United Way, for example, are businessmen. They're the only ones who can get the money. Consumers can't do it and neither can paid professionals. How can they speak up to top executives? It just doesn't work out. They need wealthy citizens who represent money, as I do.

It may be stretching a point to call such distinctions between board members, professionals, and consumers the recognition of class conflict. However, put in the context of the stated holding-action function of the upper-class woman's work in the community, this argument is more convincing. As the last quote above illustrates, these women are aware and articulate about the wealth and power of the upper class. They are also clear and articulate about the societal consequences of this power, and the benefits to them as those who are in control. As several women put it:

> There must always be people to do volunteer work. If you have a society where no one is willing, then you may as well have communism where it's all done by the government.

> [If there were no volunteers] you'd have to go into government funds. That's socialism. The more we can keep independent and under private control, the better it is.

In my view, what this last respondent meant was that private control was upper-class control, and that better meant better for her and her class. In this context, the recognition of class differences can be seen as a recognition of class conflict and the need to take political action to defend one's own collective interest. The women I spoke with defined their work on community boards in terms of such political action.

Thus, a revised Marxian concept, extending the notion of class consciousness to the upper class, seems to me both theoretically and empirically useful as a starting point. However, like the non-Marxian definitions, it too emphasizes subjective terms like awareness, understanding, and willingness, rather than concentrating on actual activity. It gives us few clues about how to assess the existence of class consciousness in concrete action in everyday life. It is to this issue that I will address myself shortly.

Although I found a revised Marxian concept of class consciousness to be a useful starting point, my interviews led me to have certain concerns with a more literal or orthodox Marxian definition. These concerns refer, first, to the notion of class consciousness as a revolutionary socialist consciousness; second, to the attributing of true class consciousness only to the proletariat or working class; and, third, to the notion that a class is not really a class until it becomes fully conscious in the literal Marxist sense. In regard to the first concern, rather than defining class consciousness in terms of political action for or against the transition from capitalism to socialism, I consider it more useful in terms of both theory and practice to define political action in a broader sense. Realistically, the issues of capitalism and socialism are hardly at the center of political debate in twentieth-century America. A broader conceptualization of political action seems to me theoretically more useful in describing and understanding current realities of class in American society.

It seems to me more fruitful to define action in the sense of activity or conduct in the most general sense, leaving the very important question of whether or not such action is explicitly political (as it was for the upper-class women considered here) as an empirical question.

In regard to the second concern about more orthodox Marxist definitions of class consciousness, I think it is useful to apply the term to actions of the upper class as well as to other classes, rather than defining the consciousness of the ruling class as "bourgeois ideology." There is no question that the women with whom I spoke have a class ideology in the sense that sociologist Karl Mannheim conceived it: a set of beliefs serving to perpetuate the status quo (Mannheim, 1952). But what these women have is far more than a set of beliefs. They have a way of life, centered on the meaning of class. They have a clearly defined and explicitly conscious set of behaviors and collective actions, passed on from one generation to the next and absorbed by rising members of other classes that they select to assimilate into the power and position of their class. If it is an ideology, it is an ideology that lives in everyday activities, and I believe this emphasis is lost by focusing on ideology as subjective belief as compared to objective action. Another aspect of this concern derives from the role of social scientist committed to seeking empirical evidence of the existence of various attitudes and behaviors among subjects. One cannot assume that the consciousness of the working class is in fact one favoring structural change, though I believe it would be in their best interest. Nor can one assume that the consciousness of the ruling class is necessarily opposed to such change, though it would seem so logically. People do take positions counter to their self-interest, a feature a Marxist would term false consciousness. One woman I spoke with, for example, though hardly a proponent of basic societal change, recognized that "social problems" could be eliminated only through the use of public tax funds. In the context of a digression about an extremely costly painting recently purchased by the local art museum and whether this money could have been better spent elsewhere, this woman said, "I can't see what private money can do. I favor all these problems being solved by public funds through taxes." When I asked if this did not mean that she herself would have to pay a good deal more in taxes, she answered good-naturedly and without a moment's hesitation, "It certainly would!" In short, I find it more valid from the point of view of a social researcher to leave the matter of whether the proletariat has a revolutionary consciousness, and the ruling class a status-quo-oriented one, as empirical questions. It seems conceptually more useful to use the term class consciousness for both phenomena, and to examine the particular form that consciousness takes.

My third concern with a more orthodox Marxist position is in regard to the notion that "a class fully deserves the name of 'class' only if its members are conscious of class interests and feel solidarity" (Ossowski, 1963:140), and are well on their way to revolutionary consciousness. At first reading, this position seems not unlike that taken by Centers and the others who define class consciousness in terms of self-placement. If class is not real in the minds of society's members, then class is not objectively real either. The difference is in the meaning of the term "conscious," which to a Marxist means not just awareness, but a predisposition to political action directed toward fundamental change in economic structure. I would prefer to avoid the dichotomous question of whether classes are or are not real as determined by measures of class consciousness and concentrate rather on the question of how and when people see the world from a class perspective and under what conditions they are willing to engage in class action. This is a perspective represented by sociologists Maurice Zeitlin (1967) in his study of Cuban workers and John Leggett (1968) in his study of Detroit auto workers. This perspective transforms Marxist assumptions about the reality of class into a set of empirical questions from which theory can be built and around which practice can be developed.

Thus far I have reviewed critically the existing definitions of class consciousness as they appear in recent sociological works representing non-Marxist and Marxist views. I will now attempt to define class consciousness in the context of an integration between Marxism and phenomenology, once again using the interviews with women of the upper class as a starting point.

CLASS CONSCIOUSNESS AS ACTIVITY AND MEANING

To my upper-class respondents, class consciousness expressed itself in the meaning of their objective behavior. By this I mean that in response to general questions about the activities of everyday life, they reported the ways they organized these activities in terms of class-related behaviors and values. Three different illustrations show how the upper-class women I interviewed defined class in meaningful ways that guided their behavior. What I would call class-related actions were reported in response to open-ended questions regarding: (a) personal reasons for community volunteer work; (b) functions of volunteer work for the community; and (c) club memberships and exclusivity.

When I asked my subjects about their personal reasons for doing volunteer work, I expected them to emphasize the personal satisfactions that derived from helping others, the joys of being of service and of contributing to the quality of community life. Not a single subject responded in this way. They answered rather with distinctly class-oriented responses. They said that what it had meant to them personally to be involved in volunteer work was the carrying on of the family tradition of noblesse oblige, and the opportunity to pursue decision-making positions for themselves. I was surprised by the distinctly class-related nature of these responses, and by how powerful the concept of class must be to these women to emphasize this kind of response so exclusively and spontaneously in response to an open-ended question outside any apparent class context. It was these data that first sensitized me to the high degree of congruence between personal meanings and societal consequences among the class-conscious upper class. What they did as individuals, in pursuit of their own self-interest and happiness, was also in the best interests of their class. As they sought positions of power for themselves, so they maintained and enhanced the elite position of the upper class. As they carried on their family's tradition of community service in gratitude for their inherited privileges, so their class privileges were legitimated and maintained. In this way, the objective phenomena of class position and privilege took on personal meaning through class-related behaviors. What class *means* to the women themselves *is* in fact how they *behave* toward and about it—in this case, in regard to volunteer work in the community, with its class-based motivations and consequences.

Typical responses illustrative of the noblesse oblige motive and its class-privilege-legitimating consequences are:

I believe to whom much is given much is expected.

When you have more than your share, you should return what you can to the community.

If you're privileged, you have a certain responsibility.

Those who are able should help the less fortunate.

Typical responses illustrative of the individual women's pursuit of power, with its class position-maintenance consequences are:

You can get higher in volunteerism than you would be able to as a paid employee. You can direct procedures and policy and get involved in the power structure.

The board level is where the decisions are made. I don't want the little jobs.

I like the jobs where I'm running the show.

Responses in regard to the second category of major findings to be discussed here, the function of volunteer work in the community, were given in response to the question, "What would it mean for the community if there were no volunteers like yourself?" I expected that my subjects would answer in terms of their contributions (time, labor, and money) to the various cultural, educational, and human service organizations for which they worked. I expected them to emphasize how the community would be a less desirable place to live were it not for their civic activities. In fact, they emphasized almost solely the financial aspect of their contributions. They believed that the primary function of their work in the community was the provision of money, both their own contributions and their activities raising money from others. The solving of social problems was rarely mentioned; and when it was, the women recognized that their work contributed little in this direction. The comment of a particularly active volunteer was typical. She said: "Most anything we do is just a drop in the bucket." My respondents went on to tell me of the political functions of their financial contributions. Charitable donations were seen as providing an economic base for the exercise of power in the community in terms of (a) maintaining an elite structure of decision-making as to the use of these funds, and (b) serving as a barrier to the expansion of public funds and public decision-making, seen as leading to socialism. These political functions were presented by my subjects both as intended consequences for the structure of society, and as relevant personal motivations for doing community work. For example, a woman who saw upper-class donations as a legitimate basis for elite decision-making said, in response to a question about community representation on the boards of social service agencies:

> After all, the people who contribute most of the funds for these services feel they deserve to have the major say in what's done with their money.

An example of the recognition of private charity as a holding action against socialism came from a woman whose prominent family name has been linked with industry and national politics for generations. She stated, when asked whom she represented on community boards, that she represented "the old families." When I asked her what was the responsibility of those who represented this segment of society, she answered quickly and directly:

> It's our job to keep things from going too far to the left politically—to keep private institutions alive.

"Maintaining private institutions" is the upper-class catchword that my subjects used for elite control (or dominance) and upper-class opposition to leftist ideologies. This maintenance is the primary function of service on boards of cultural, educational, and human service organizations, and of fund-raising activities for these organizations. The upper-class women are explicitly aware of this function, and it is a guiding motive for their activity in the community. What is surprising in retrospect is not so much their own recognition of this primary function and of their own class-interest, but rather the failure of the rest of society to recognize it as clearly.

The final illustration to be considered here is the class-related function of exclusive social clubs. When I asked my subjects why it was important that their clubs be invitational, rather than open to anyone who wishes to join, they spoke of how these clubs served to screen out unacceptable persons from class membership, and to screen in a few individuals deemed acceptable for membership. Indeed, the process of getting into the upper class itself seemed modeled after the way in which persons get into upper-class clubs. Persons considered unacceptable for membership were referred to by my subjects as "everybody" or "just anybody," and persons considered acceptable were those judged to be "congenial," "compatible," or otherwise like themselves. The process through which acceptable persons were assimilated was termed being "sponsored" and "becoming known." The almost universal use of this kind of terminology by my respondents indicates a high degree of consensus regarding the meaning of class exclusivity and the appropriate behavior for maintaining it. Data illustrative of the process through which selected individuals are assimilated into the upper class are as follows:

> Who proposes you for membership makes a big difference, what kind of people they are.

> If you're a new family you have to be sponsored. The owners of my husband's firm are well-known in [this city]. That was enough of a recommendation. They said he was a good candidate and the rest took it on faith.

Thus, part of the meaning of the term class for my respondents was evidenced in what upper-class persons are expected to *do* to maintain the boundaries of class association. This behavior involves participating in invitational social clubs, and taking part in the process of assimilating new members. For nearly all of my respondents this means serving as sponsors so that "new" families can become known and accepted as members of the class.

These three examples drawn from interviews with women of the upper class have served as illustrations of what I consider a useful and objective way of defining and measuring class consciousness. This activity-oriented definition is less subjective and more empirically based than the commonly used subjective definitions of class consciousness reviewed earlier. The term class is shown to have meaning to subjects by the way in which they actually behave toward it and about it. The class structure and one's own relationship to it is defined according to one's activity and how one actually organizes behaviors. This definition does not require that one be willing to identify with a particular class or to explicitly recognize a class structure. It does not make a distinction between class-related activities and status-related activities. It assumes and demonstrates that if class is recognized as a salient object in the social world, then there will be concrete ways of behaving in class-defined ways. These ways of behaving, these forms of social action, will be engaged in by "class-conscious" respondents. Consciousness is the interpretation of a social object as meaningful in conduct, and it is that conduct by which we define and measure consciousness. Meaning and conduct, awareness and behavior, thought and action, are not separate and distinct phenomena—neither to the social scientist nor to people in everyday life. The concept of class takes on meaning for actors as they behave in class-related ways, and it is this behavior that expresses and defines class consciousness.

None of the ways of conceptualizing class consciousness reviewed in the previous section seemed entirely adequate for understanding this phenomenon as I discovered it to exist among my respondents, and I therefore sought an alternative. This alternative developed in large part out of the findings themselves, although as is true with any piece of research, I began with several underlying assumptions.

I began my research with an assumption that a complete understanding of the social life of any group requires consideration of both objective behavior and subjective meaning, that objective and subjective are not dichotomous ways of looking at the world, and that class consciousness is one of the few concepts we have in sociology that attempts to bridge these views. I was interested in the bridging of subjective meaning and objective action in the sense that is meant by those sociologists who call themselves symbolic interactionists. For symbolic interactionists such as George Herbert Mead (1934) and Herbert Blumer (1969), we should understand the meaning of an object in terms of how people act toward it. Actions define an object, in this case class as an object in the social world. There is no separation between meaning and behavior, awareness and practice, subjective and objective. As conversations with my upper-class respondents went on, what these theoretical assumptions led me to was that "class" and "class action" take on meaning in everyday life as people behave in class-defined and -related ways. I believe that the symbolic interactionists' general notion as applied specifically to class consciousness is consistent with the Marxist notion that how we conceptualize the world derives from how we act in it, that "theory" develops out of "practice." As sociologist Giddens states, "In the Marxian view, consciousness . . . constitutes the attribution of meaning which guides conduct, and is inseparable from that conduct" (1975: 113).

The perspective suggested here also seems consistent with the attempts to supplement traditional Marxist views with the insights of phenomenology, a perspective within sociology of which symbolic interactionism is a theoretical example. The origin of phenomenology, as it is applied in sociology, is usually ascribed to philosopher Alfred Schutz. Schutz stated that:

> the goal of social science is to explain social reality as it is experienced by man living his everyday life in the social world [1963: 334].

One of the major emphases of sociologists working within a phenomenological perspective is that the concepts they use in research are discovered in the process of study rather than defined previous to empirical observation. In the case of the concept of class consciousness, rather than beginning with a definition such as awareness of position in the class structure or potential for revolutionary action, the phenomenologist allows one's subject to define the term as it is meaningful to them in their everyday lives. As Schutz put it:

> The thought objects constructed by the social scientist refer to and are founded upon the thought objects constructed by the commonsense thought of man living his everyday life among his fellowmen [1963: 306].

The position of a more phenomenological Marxism suggests that the perspective of Schutz can be useful in reconstituting Marxist concepts so that they deal with present social-historical realities and the experience of everyday life under current conditions (e.g., Piccone, 1973). Authors holding this point of view note the similarities between a Marxist perspective and a phenomenological one. For example, David Sallach wrote in a 1973 issue of *Insurgent Sociologist:*

> Marx and Schutz are similar in their attempt to locate their perspective thought systems in the empirical world. For Schutz this involves a return to "the actor in the social world whose doing and feeling lies at the bottom of the whole system" (Schutz, 1964: 7). Similarly, Marx states (1947: 14), "We do not set out from what men say, imagine, conceive, nor from men as narrated, thought of, imagined, conceived in order to arrive at men in the flesh. We set out from real active men."

Throughout this chapter, in addition to developing a theoretical perspective, I have suggested in the form of examples a methodology for studying class consciousness. Let me briefly consider this methodology more explicitly in the context of two issues: (1) the objective study of subjective meaning; and (2) the changing context of meaning. In regard to the first issue, the term "meaning" carries connotations of mental subjectivity which social scientists who emphasize more material realities find problematic. "Meaning" is often equated with dimensions of awareness, as in the self-identification studies of class consciousness. It should be clear by this point that the definition of meaning as it is used by Schutz, Mead, and Blumer is very different from such inner psychological states of mind. Phenomenologists and symbolic interactionists recognize, however, that providing a basis for the study of meaning as a scientifically observable object in the social world is a primary methodological concern. As Schutz said, "Our main problem is to develop methods in order to deal in an objective way with the subjective meaning of human action" (1963: 342). Since Schutz's writing, much work has been done toward developing objective methods for the study of subjective meaning (e.g., Becker and Greer, 1957; Becker, 1958; Bruyn, 1966; Blumer, 1969). In my own study, the method used involved asking open-ended questions about life activities that my respondents told me were important in their lives, activities about which I had no expectations as to whether their meanings to my respondents were or were not class-related. My respondents answered these questions in terms they used to mean class, as the data presented illustrate. There was no apparent reason for them to answer in these ways, no preset context of class set by the questions themselves. I was thus convinced of the objective relevance of class as a material reality in their social world, and therefore considered their activities to be objectively class conscious. I believe this is a method that can be used by other researchers with other respondents to ascertain the relevance of class in everyday life.

It is also relevant to point out that phenomenological efforts to objectify subjective experience are quite different from attempts to "integrate" subjective awareness and objective behavior by simply considering both and assessing the extent to which they are interrelated empirically. It is not considered useful by those wishing to create a synthesis between Marxism and phenomenology to preserve the division between objective and subjective, to present a dual perspective rather than a truly integrated one where there is no dichotomy between the two (e.g., Dalmayr, 1973). As defined here, meaning *is* action, in the broad sense of behavior or conduct. They are not two sides of a coin, but are rather one and the same. The continuing efforts to specify objective study of subjective experience must pursue a synthesis rather than a duality of the subjective and the objective.

A second methodological issue of concern is that the meaning of a concept or object in the social world, such as social class, depends upon the context within which it occurs. Thus, a particular piece of behavior may be class-related in one social situation and not in another. The context of such behaviors may vary over time and place. This seems consistent with the Marxian notion of class and class consciousness as historical phenomena. As Marxist sociologist Morton Wenger suggests, "For Marx, history develops. [This] means that class consciousness is situational; it has no universal, trans-social or trans-historical content" (Wenger, 1978: 7). From this perspective, the sociologist who wishes to see the social-historical context as one's subjects see it, and to understand its relationship or lack of relationship to class, must become involved enough in this context to know the relevant events and life activities to ask about. It is these events and activities that, if the collectivity we are studying is class conscious, will be defined in class-related terms. We cannot know the relevant events and activities before our immersion in this context, and thus cannot discover the existence or nonexistence of class consciousness.

To deal with changing meanings, the first step in the study of class consciousness, as it is defined here, is to identify the most important areas of social conduct for the particular group of respondents being studied. Important activities must be identified in terms of the actual behavior of respondents. This behavior may or may not be consistent with the respondents' own reports of what they perceive as important. For example, the women I studied often denied that upper-class debut activities for their children were important. They would make statements like:

I think it's passé, and I don't care about it, but it's just something that's done.

And yet, participation in such activities was universal. More to the point, the women insisted on participation even when the children objected and did not want to take part. The reasons for such insistence were class reasons, specifically intraclass marriage and the carrying on of family class tradition, expressed as follows by respondents.

The [debut] is important. It's a way of saying, "Here is my daughter. She is eighteen and ready for marriage."

It's a way of putting the boys and girls together. The private schools separate them so they don't have much opportunity to meet one another.

We do have a family image to maintain. I felt it was an obligation [for my daughter to have the debut].

My mother was one of the women who started [the debutante ball], so I felt the children should do it whether they wanted to or not.

Verbal protestations to the contrary, then, the life events that my upper-class respondents defined by their behavior as important in their social world and as important in a class-meaning context did include exclusive debuts for their children. It may be that in some segments of the upper class, or in future studies of the upper class, such activities will be found to be either unimportant or not to have class-related meanings. It may be that other activities will emerge as important, and these activities may or may not have class meanings; that is, they may or may not be expressive of a conscious upper class.

Activities and their meaning cannot be specified in advance of study and of immersion in the group being studied. If the most important life activities of a social group, those activities which have the highest priorities when choices have to be made, are found not to have meaning for respondents in terms of class, then those activities must be characterized as not indicative of class consciousness. It is therefore the actions with their meanings that reflect class consciousness.

Class consciousness is thus a characteristic not of individuals, but of behaviors in a class context. By this definition, women of the upper class are highly "class conscious" because they behave in ways dictated by the social object of class in everyday life.

REFERENCES

ANDERSON, C.H. (1974) The Political Economy of Social Class. Englewood Cliffs, NJ: Prentice-Hall.

BALTZELL, D. (1958) Philadelphia Gentlemen. New York: Free Press.

BECKER, H. (1958) "Problems of inference and proof in participant observation." American Sociological Review 23: 652-660.

——— and B. GEER (1957) "Participant observation and interviewing: a comparison." Human Organization 16 (Fall): 28-32.

BEEGHLEY, L. (1978) Social Stratification in America. Santa Monica, CA: Goodyear.

BIDDLE, B.J. and E.J. THOMAS (1966) Role theory: Concepts and Research. New York: John Wiley.

BLUMER, H. (1969) Symbolic Interactionism: Perspective and Method. Englewood Cliffs, NJ: Prentice-Hall.

BOGDAN, R. and S.J. TAYLOR (1975) Qualitative Research Methods. New York: John Wiley.

BRUYN, S. (1966) The Human Perspective in Sociology. Englewood Cliffs, NJ: Prentice-Hall.

CENTERS, R. (1949) The Psychology of Social Classes: A Study of Class-Consciousness. Princeton, NJ: Princeton Univ. Press.

CHINOY, E. (1968) Sociological Perspective. New York: Random House.

DAHL, R.A. (1961) Who Governs? Democracy and Power in an American City. New Haven, CT: Yale Univ. Press.

DALLMAYR, F. (1973) "Phenomenology and marxism," in George Psathas (ed.) Phenomenological Sociology. New York: John Wiley.

DOMHOFF, G.W. (1970) "The feminine half of the upper class," in The Higher Circles. New York: Random House.

GIDDENS, A. (1975) The Class Structure of the Advanced Society. New York: Harper & Row.

GLASER, B.G. and A.L. STRAUSS (1967) The Discovery of Grounded Theory. Chicago: Aldine.

GUEST, A.M. (1974) "Class consciousness and American political attitudes." Social Forces 52 (June): 496-510.

HODGE, R.W. and D.J. TREIMAN (1968) "Class identification in the U.S." American Journal of Sociology 73 (March): 535-547.

HURST, C. (1979) The Anatomy of Social Inequality. St. Louis: C.V. Mosby.

LANDECKER, W.S. (1963) "Class crystallization and class consciousness." American Sociological Review 28 (April): 219-229.

LAUMANN, E.O. and R. SENTER (1976) "Subjective social distance, occupational stratification and forms of status and class consciousness." American Journal of Sociology 81 (April): 1304-1338.

LEGGETT, J.C. (1968) Class, Race, and Labor: Working Class Consciousness in Detroit. New York: Oxford Univ. Press.

LEWIS, L.S. (1965) "Class consciousness and the salience of class." Sociology and Social Research 49 (January): 173-182.

LICHTMAN, R. (1970) "Symbolic interactionism and social reality: some Marxist queries." Berkeley Journal of Sociology 15: 75-94.

LUKACS, G. (1971) History and Class Consciousness: Studies in Marxist Dialectics. Cambridge, MA: MIT. (Originally published 1922.)

MANNHEIM, K. (1952) Ideology and Utopia. New York: Harcourt, Brace.

MAYER, K.B. and W. BUCKLEY (1970) Class and Society. New York: Random House.

MEAD, G.H. (1964) On Social Psychology. Edited by Anselm Strauss. Chicago: Univ. of Chicago Press. (Originally published 1934.)

MERTON, R. and P.L. KENDALL (1946) "The focused interview." American Journal of Sociology 51: 541-557.

MILLS, C.W. (1951) White Collar. New York: Oxford Univ. Press.

MORRIS, R.T. and R.J. MURPHY (1966) "A paradigm for the study of class consciousness." Sociology and Social Research 50 (April): 297-313.

OSSOWSKI, S. (1963) Class Structure in the Social Consciousness. New York: Free Press.

OSTRANDER, S.A. (1979) "Upper class women: the feminine side of privilege." Qualitative Sociology (in press).

——— (1977) "Upper class women: community action in the American class structure." Presented at the annual meeting of the American Sociological Association, Chicago.

——— (1976) "Upper class women: A study in social power" (unpublished manuscript).

PICCONE, P. (1973) "Phenomenological Marxism," in Bart Grahl and Paul Piccone (eds.) Towards a New Marxism. St. Louis: Telos Press.

RINEHART, J. and I.O. OKRAHU (1974) "A study of class consciousness." Canadian Review of Sociology and Anthropology 2, (August): 197-213.

ROTHMAN, R.A. (1978) Inequality and stratification in the United States. Englewood Cliffs, NJ: Prentice-Hall.

RUNCIMAN, W.G. (1970) Sociology in Its Place. London: Cambridge Univ. Press.

SALLACH, D. (1973) "Class consciousness and everyday world in the work of Marx and Schutz." Insurgent Sociologist 3 (Summer): 27-39.

SCHREIBER, E.M. and G.I. NYGREEN (1970) "Subjective social class in America." Social Forces 48 (March): 348-356.

SCHUTZ, A. (1963) "Concept and theory formation in the social sciences," in Maurice Natanson (ed.) Philosophy of the Social Sciences. New York: Random House.

SEIDER, M.S. (1974) "American big business ideology: a content analysis of executive speeches." American Sociological Review 39: 802-815.

WARNER, W.L. (1949) What Social Class Is in America. New York: Harper & Row.

———— and P.S. LUNT (1941) The Social Life of a Modern Community. New Haven, CT: Yale Univ. Press.

WEBER, M. (1946) From Max Weber: Essays in Sociology. Edited and translated by H.H. Gerth and C.W. Mills. New York: Oxford Univ. Press.

WENGER, M. (1978) "Toward a viable theory of class consciousness: pre-theoretical issues." Presented at 1978 Annual Meeting of North Central Sociological Association, Cincinnati, Ohio.

ZEITLIN, M. (1967) Revolutionary Politics and the Cuban Working Class. Princeton, NJ: Princeton Univ. Press.

4

CAN CAPITALISTS ORGANIZE THEMSELVES?

J. Allen Whitt

A central issue in the debate concerning the relation between the ruling class and the state has been the question of the extent to which capitalists are capable of organizing themselves politically. Power structure research has been criticized by structural Marxists or those influenced by that perspective on a number of bases (Mollenkopf, 1975: Gold et al., 1975; Esping-Anderson et al., 1976; Block, 1977). A common theme, implicit if not explicit, in these critiques and in other structuralist analyses is the idea that the capitalist class is internally divided by conflicts of interest. These divisions are presumably serious enough to render the class incapable of achieving the degree of class consciousness and political unity required to rule the society in the interests of the capitalist class. Given this lack of class coherence, it is the state which must protect capitalist interests as a whole by insuring that the private accumulation process operates effectively and that the essential legitimacy of the system is preserved. In order to accomplish these tasks, the structuralists argue, the state must have some degree of autonomy from the competing segments of the capitalist class.[1] According to the structuralist view, then, the state is not freed from the requirements of preserving the capitalist system, but it is freed from the narrow, conflicting influences within the class that would undermine its broad, systemic mission.

CAPITALIST CLASS DIVISION:
THE STRUCTURALIST VIEW

Poulantzas (1973) and Offe (1973) explicitly present the vision of an internally divided capitalist class. Poulantzas writes of "the profound division of the bourgeois class into antagonistic fractions, a division which starts from the level of the actual relations of production." Unlike the working class, the capitalist class has no internal mechanisms to generate unity: "on the side of the capitalist class of 'private capitalists' the effect of isolation on socio-economic relations is not compensated by anything, as it is by 'collective labour' on the side of the wage-earning workers" (Poulantzas, 1973: 298). This means that the bourgeoisie "are incapable (*through their own organizational means*) of transforming their specific interest into the political interest." Therefore, it is the state which must provide unity to the class:

> The state plays this role [of political organizer] *only* because the political parties of the bourgeois class and of its fractions are unable to play an autonomous organizational role, let alone one analogous to the role of the working class parties. Hence, the state's essential role emerges more clearly as the factor of the political unity [Poulantzas, 1973: 299; emphasis added].

Offe (1973: 111) also draws a picture of a fractionated and relatively ineffective capitalist class which must be organized by the state:

> The liberation of the class interest from the narrow and short-sighted interests of the necessities of the capitalist class happens—if it happens at all—through the institutionalization of political "counter-power". Not counter-power to capital as a whole, but to the fragmented, stubborn and short-sighted empirical interests of single capital units.

THE NEED FOR EMPIRICAL ASSESSMENT

It makes a great deal of practical and theoretical difference as to whether the capitalist class is, in fact, internally divided. First of all, questions of revolutionary strategy hinge on such matters. Second, and directly relevant to my point here, much of the structuralist theoretical model rests on the premise of a divided bourgeoisie. However, little empirical work that specifically addresses this issue has been done by structuralists. They have generally been more concerned with unraveling the logic of the capitalism system as a whole, and with showing how this logic structures the operation of institutions (such as the state) and gives rise to class conflict. The broad, theoretical mandate that structuralism has set for itself has resulted in a highly abstract and largely translocal focus. The tendency often has been to *deduce* the behavior of the capitalist class from the supposed logic and constraints of the system as a whole. Whatever the merits of this approach—and it certainly does have its merits—it has, especially when combined with distrust of more traditional empirical social research methods, obscured from sufficient analysis the problem of capitalist class cohesion or disunity. Yet, this is a central issue that needs much research and elaboration. It is this issue which this chapter addresses.

We must begin by making a distinction between *economic* competition and *political* competition. That capitalism is based on economic competition is something that few will doubt, even though that competition may be attenuated among the largest economic units in the monopoly stage of capitalism. However, economic competition does not necessarily equate to political competition. Mollenkopf (1975: 252) points out (rightly, I believe) that power structure researchers tend to undervalue the political realm as opposed to the economic, with resulting underestimation of "the constraints inherent in developing large followings, and hence legitimacy, for business-sponsored policies." But it is also possible to err in the other direction by assuming that the task of political organization is so difficult that the capitalist class is relatively ineffective politically. Pluralists, and I believe some structuralists, make this mistake. We need to recognize that *economic* competition does not necessarily imply *political* competition, that politics can indeed be somewhat independent from immediate economic interests. With regard to Poulantzas's work, Bridges (1974: 174) makes much the same point:

> While Poulantzas characterizes the bourgeoisie as individualistic, the case can be made that while they are economically competitive, their political *unity* [emphasis in original] is more relevant to understanding state-class relations than are their divisions.

I wish to present evidence here to show that the ruling class can indeed achieve a degree of political organization. I will argue that capitalists can and do solve crucial problems of coordination and settle disputes by *intraclass* mechanisms, often eliminating the need for these issues to be referred to bourgeois political parties or to the state for resolution.

THE EMPIRICAL RESEARCH

The evidence I will cite has to do with the degree of coordination that major corporate interests were able to attain in an important series of political campaigns. I focus on a series of five electoral campaigns relating to public transportation issues in California between 1962 and 1974. The campaigns revolved around ballot measures that would have diverted some of California's highway trust fund monies to nonhighway transportation uses. These issues were important because they proposed to alter significantly both the physical aspects of transportation and the funding mechanisms to pay for it in that state. Transportation is an essential infrastructural element in the functioning of the corporate economy. The production and circulation of capital requires that commodities and people be moved from place to place efficiently. When significant transportation problems occur, this essential process is endangered. The early history of BART (Bay Area Rapid Transit system) illustrates this point.

During World War II, the San Francisco Bay Area was a prime location of defense manufacturing and military facilities. Stepped-up war production and the influx of thousands of workers produced severe problems in the area, a chief one being transportation. There were massive traffic jams and delays in the movement of materials and people. The situation eventually became so acute that a congressional subcommittee recommended that no further war industries be brought into the Bay Area (Scott, 1959: 244-255). Not surprisingly, the expansion and reorganization of Bay Area transportation became a top priority for big business (mainly through the powerful Bay Area Council) immediately following the war. The business community began to make plans to construct a new mass transit system for the area. Many years later, these plans resulted in BART (DeFreitas, 1972; Zwerling, 1974; Whitt, 1975). Business acted to reshape the area transportation infrastructure in order to maintain and strengthen the accumulation process.

Mollenkopf (1975: 253) uses the example of BART to argue for an essentially structuralist interpretation. He concludes that BART came about because

> the declining central city location advantages threatened central business property values, made more difficult the capital accumulation process, and disrupted the spatial relations certain firms felt necessary for their operations. At a political level, the urban fiscal crisis and the weakening hold on big city politics threatened to undermine the urban aspects of the cold war consensus. In terms of the allocation of resources, suburban sprawl, while it created opportunities for real estate development at the periphery, made commuting to the central city much more difficult, time- and resource-consuming, and costly. BART provided a handy tool for bolstering the economic, political, and fiscal role of the downtown, enhancing the ease of commuting, and thus the central business districts' influence over entire regions.

These structural requirements, in the BART example and similar cases, "make possible and make imperative certain state actions, regardless of who attempts to instigate them" (Mollenkopf, 1975: 253).

I agree with Mollenkopf concerning the reasons why BART was *needed*, but I believe that it makes a great deal of difference *who* instigated the construction of BART. In this case, it was the local component of the ruling class, the local organs of the state having played a reactive and subsidiary role (Whitt, 1975). What is most necessary to grasp, however, is that BART was a part of the larger *pattern* of transportation politics in California. The following analysis of the five related issues will demonstrate the extent to which economically and politically contending segments of the ruling class can achieve compromise, cooperation, and unity even on divisive issues.

In addition to the central role of transportation as an infrastructural element, transportation issues are important for another reason. They illustrate the possibility of ruling-class conflicts of interest of the kind structuralists emphasize. Corporations (and the ruling class which is based on those producers of wealth) in California and elsewhere are not always in agreement as to what *kinds* of transportation system are needed, how they should be *financed*, or *where* they should be built. Potential and actual conflicts of interest exist from the standpoint of individual firms engaged in specific kinds of businesses and operating in specific areas of the city. For example, some companies, such as administrative and financial firms, need to move only people and information, while heavy manufacturing concerns must move bulky raw materials and finished products. Moreover, some corporations are located in central-city areas and some are in the suburbs or beyond. As a result, some prefer more transit service to their own specific areas. Also, certain companies have a direct interest in the actual process of constructing new transit systems; in this regard, there is a clash between the "highway lobby" (oil, auto, tire, insurance, paving and construction companies) and those firms interested in producing new mass transportation systems (aerospace, coach and bus, and electrical and electronics firms, for instance).

These conflicts of interest were clearly present in the California campaigns. The state has a powerful and successful highway lobby, but also a considerable and increasingly powerful mass transit interest group, particularly well-represented in segments of the state's high-technology aerospace, electronics, and defense companies (Simmons, 1968). These transportation issues were rendered even more complex by a firm's location: centrally located companies often tended to favor the construction of high-density new subway systems, like BART, which were believed to promote central-city access by workers and customers and would supposedly increase central-city and near-station land values. On the other hand, suburban and exurban companies were more likely to favor extension of peripheral highways.

So far, the picture I have sketched is one with which structuralists (and pluralists) would likely agree: there are numerous conflicts of interest which divide the corporate community. Both of these groups, however, would then go one step further and say that the corporate community is therefore *politically* divided. In reality this is a fateful step, and we should look carefully before we take it. Does the existence of conflicts of interest imply the political division of a *class*? Now let us examine the evidence.

The empirical question to be addressed here is: How did the business community deal with these actual and potential conflicts over this important infrastructural issue of urban transportation? Were they able to deal effectively with these problems *within* the business community, achieving compromise or resolution of conflicts of interest, and attaining general political coordination? I present the following evidence to show that they were able to do these things. Let us begin with a look at the earliest of the five electoral campaigns to be analyzed, the construction of San Francisco's BART system.

BART Campaign. The construction of the expensive and technologically sophisticated BART system was officially authorized by Bay Area voters in a bond election in 1962. However, for many years before that election, the chief force pushing for the establishment of a rail rapid transit system in the Bay Area was the Bay Area Council (BAC). This is an organization of the largest corporations in the Bay Area, headquartered mainly in downtown San Francisco. The role of the BAC is confirmed by interview data, media accounts, by statements from the BAC itself, by previous research and by campaign contributions (Zwerling, 1974). The BAC companies were early advocates of such a system, were instrumental in getting the California Legislature to create the San Francisco Bay Area Rapid Transit District in 1957, and took a very active part in organizing and financing the 1962 bond campaign for BART. The bonds to construct the system were to be paid for by local property taxes. As can be seen in Table 4.1, over $200,000 was contributed in support of the BART campaign, the sum coming almost exclusively from the BAC companies. Executives from downtown banks and financial institutions played particularly active roles in organizing the pro-BART electoral campaign. The system was sold to voters by using symbolic appeals: BART would dramatically reduce traffic congestion on major traffic routes, such as the San Francisco-Oakland Bay Bridge, and would alleviate air pollution. However, BART planning documents, interviews with business leaders, and publications of business groups after the election make it clear that the main business supporters of BART were more concerned with the system's presumed ability to promote centralized growth and property development in the heart of San Francisco than they were with reducing traffic congestion or air pollution. In spite of the public claims that BART would reduce local dependence on the automobile, there was no organized opposition to BART by the California highway lobby. In fact, at least one major oil company gave money for BART.

Los Angeles Campaign of 1968. Six years after the successful BART campaign in Northern California, Los Angeles attempted to build a similar rapid transit system. The Proposition A campaign of 1968 (Table 4.1) proposed to construct a combination rail and bus system that would be financed out of an increase in the local sales tax. Formally organized by the Southern California Rapid Transit District (SCRTD), the pattern of actual support was essentially the same as in San Francisco: large businesses near the central area of Los Angeles were the main source of organizational and financial support for the plan. Fourteen percent of the contributions came from heavy construction labor unions and from individuals, but approximately 86% came from business. Of this latter sum industrial corporations gave 28.3%, insurance companies 12.6%, oil companies 10.9%, construction, engineering and architectural firms 9.8%, and banks 6.4%. This time a very small amount of money was contributed against the measure. It came from a car dealer, a rental agency, a public relations firm, an individual, and a cement company. In this case, the measure failed at the polls.

Proposition 18. The next important transportation issue to be decided by California voters was, unlike the two earlier ones, a statewide issue. Proposition 18 on the November 1970 California ballot proposed that up to 25% of the state highway trust fund could, upon approval by voters in local areas, be used to support public transit systems such as BART. The national and state highway trust funds are said to be jealously guarded by highway-auto interests, and this campaign was no exception (Kelley, 1971; Leavitt, 1970). The California highway lobby gave $348,000 to (successfully) defeat Proposition 18. Leading contributors were: oil companies (75.1%), automobile clubs (12.9%), highway equipment and construction companies (7.9%), and trucking and taxi companies (1.8%). On the other hand, virtually all of the small amount of money in support of Proposition 18 came from individual contributions. Only two California businesses, Kaiser Industries and Rohr Corporation, both with direct mass transit interests, gave small amounts for Proposition 18. The median contribution for Proposition 18 was $5; the median contribution against was $500. Although public transit systems like BART (and like the system proposed for Los Angeles two years earlier) would have benefited from the passage of the measure, the companies that had supported these systems in San Francisco and Los Angeles did not contribute for Proposition 18.

Proposition 5. Four years after Proposition 18 went down to defeat, a similar measure (Proposition 5 of 1974) was again presented to California voters. Proposition 5 was somewhat milder than Proposition 18, permitting an initial 5% of the fund to be diverted should local voters so decide, going up to a maximum of 25% after a few years. This time a startling thing happened: there was almost a complete *reversal* of the previous pattern of business opposition that had been revealed in the Proposition 18 campaign. There was no public opposition to Proposition 5 by the highway lobby, and there was support for the measure by large businesses in urban centers (mostly Los Angeles). Contributions came mainly from one oil company (49%), from insurance companies (15%), other industries (6.5%), and banks (5%). This was in striking contrast to political positions only four years before. The measure passed this time.

Los Angeles Campaign of 1974. The final campaign studied was Proposition A of 1974, another version of the unsuccessful Los Angeles campaign of 1968 to create a BART-like system. Again, there was a familiar pattern of support: central-city businesses were the leaders in giving more than half a million dollars in support of the creation of the system. This time there was no money in opposition. As in the case of the earlier (1968) transit campaign in Los Angeles, the Los Angeles electorate turned down the proposal. Pro-transit money was not able to overcome Los Angeles voters' desire to avoid higher local taxes and presumably their desire to maintain their automobile-centered way of life. In each of the other three campaigns (BART, Proposition 18, and Proposition 5), however, the side that contributed the greater sums of money was successful.

COMMENTS ON FINDINGS

Table 4.1 summarizes these five campaigns. Concerning them, I wish to call attention to three points. First, the great bulk of the money to support or oppose each of these five measures came not from citizens' groups but from the corporate world. In that sense, they were more *corporate* campaigns than they were popular campaigns. Second, the pattern of the contributions is striking. Even though there is good reason to expect that, for each issue,

Table 4.1   Summary of California Transit Elections

Issue	Date	Area	Proposal	Financing	Contributions		Outcome
					For	Against	
BART	Nov. 1962	Bay Area	rail	$792 million bond issue to be financed out of property taxes	$203,000 from business	none	passed
Prop. A	Nov. 1968	L. A.	rail and bus	$2.5 billion bond issue to be financed by sales tax	$458,000 with 86% from business	$25,000 from five contributions	failed
Prop. 18	Nov. 1970	CA	divert 25% of highway funds	none required	$18,000 in small contributions	$348,000 from highway lobby	failed
Prop. 5	June 1974	CA	divert 5-25% of highway funds	none required	$203,000 with 99% from business	$1,700 from auto club	passed
Prop. A	Nov. 1974	L. A.	rail and bus	sales tax to match federal funds	$563,000 with 94% from business	none	failed

some companies would favor it and some would oppose it, the money in every case is virtually *all on one side or the other of the issue*. In other words, the *business community did not oppose other segments of the business community.*

Neither the liberal competitive model of capitalism put forth by pluralists, the intraclass conflict model suggested by structural Marxists, nor the simple interest position of individual firms would have allowed us to predict this result. Some sort of higher ordering principle seemed to override more narrow single-firm interests. The desire for ruling-class unity may be that principle.

This brings us to the third point. The almost complete reversal in the pattern of support between the Proposition 18 and Proposition 5 campaigns suggests that effective coordination was achieved. In spite of the similarity of the two proposals, the highway lobby strongly opposed the first one, but gave essentially no money in opposition to the second. Likewise, while only two businesses (Rohr and Kaiser, both with token contributions) had given money in support of Proposition 18, during the later Proposition 5 campaign, businesses contributed more than $200,000 for Proposition 5. Of the 108 firms that had given money for or against either Proposition 18 or Proposition 5, only *three* companies were involved in both of the campaigns. That represents a turnover rate of 97%, further implying that some kind of coordination mechanism was operating among opponents and proponents.

Evidence supporting this interpretation comes from interviews. Executives told me that there were many discussions and debates within business organizations (such as Chambers of Commerce, and business social clubs) as to whether Proposition 5 should be supported. In the end, the business community was seemingly able to reach an accommodation of the disparate interests. One member of the Los Angeles Chamber spoke of the "great arguments" that took place within that organization over whether Proposition 5 should be supported. He pointed out that the pro-Proposition 5 forces eventually won:

> And when we won the fight, both of those guys [the presidents of an oil company and a railroad company] supported us . . .When the thing was over with and sixty guys had voted, and there was only—I don't know—five or six votes on their side, they weren't going to fight the trend.

This accommodation meant that business could take a unified position on Proposition 5, and corporations would not have to politically oppose other corporations. This gives us a particularly vivid example of the general finding in all of these five campaigns that business money never opposed business money, even though conflicts of interest would seem to demand opposition. Accommodative and cooperative tendencies were stronger.

Skeptics, however, could argue that these events merely reflected *conflict avoidance* on the part of powerful corporations. These firms did not want to go up against each other directly because it would be financially and politically costly. Indeed, one of the people I interviewed, a former senior executive of Bank of America, told me:

> Standard Oil and the other oil companies are extremely important customers and they have a lot of clout in many ways, and I think a lot of people are unhappy about being in opposition. You take a banker, and Standard Oil, Union Oil, Shell—you name it—Mobil, Atlantic Richfield are good customers and if they say, "We're opposed to this," It's awfully hard for the banker to say, "Well, we're in favor of it."

To the extent that this situation prevailed, then, one might believe that only the understandable desire to avoid confrontation was operating as an organizing principle, not positive cooperation and class unity. In other words, if mere conflict avoidance was *all* that was going on, we would expect to find no evidence of positive cooperation and coordination among supposedly competing firms: conflict avoidance is *passive* behavior, coordination is *active* behavior. Yet we do find evidence of active, effective coordination in these campaigns.

Presumably, banks compete with other banks and oil companies compete with other oil companies, according to both the standard competitive model of capitalism and the structuralist intraclass conflict model. These models would lead us to believe that effective political coordination among these competing firms is not likely to exist. However, it did exist in these campaigns.

If one compares the campaign contributions against Proposition 18 by oil companies with the amount of business done by each of the companies in California (i.e., gallons of gasoline sold each year), one finds a remarkable relationship. There is a very precise hierarchical ordering of the amount of money contributed. Gasoline sales account almost perfectly (i.e., 90% of the variance) for how much each firm gave, with those firms selling the most gasoline giving the most money. This suggests a very effective and closely controlled interfirm coordination mechanism, a kind of mechanism unexpected on the basis of pluralist and structuralist models.

An even stronger, and perhaps more interesting relationship, is found in the case of California banks. Here it is the total *assets* of the bank which perfectly predict (i.e., 98% of the variance) how much each bank contributes for Proposition 5. It is provocative to realize that banks define their *political* stakes on the sole basis of the amount of *capital* they control, with both the stakes and the capital being hierarchically ordered.

The evidence from these campaigns suggests that it is possible for the capitalist class, even in the face of real conflicts of individual and corporate interest, to overcome differences and to achieve effective political unity. Two points should be made here. At a minimum, this investigation demonstrates that "the profound division of the bourgeois class into antagonistic fractions" described by Poulantzas (1973), or "the fragmented, stubborn and short-sighted empirical interests of single capital units" described by Offe (1973) do not run nearly as deep as these statements imply. Second, even though divergent interests and conflicts do exist (as has been shown here) it may be possible for them to be largely *overcome* at the political level in the larger interests of ruling-class cohesion and effectiveness. This is perhaps not so surprising since even among hardened enemies ways are sometimes found to cooperate to further mutual interests. Certainly if the concept of *class* is to have any meaning at all, we must acknowledge the existence of important mutual interests among the members of that class, and a much more substantive and effective set of interests than is true of a random social group. Differences in economic and political interests among individual units do not necessarily result in political incapacity at more inclusive levels of organization, such as at the level of a social class. Indeed, if we return to the cases under analysis here, it can be seen that the ability of these "competing" banks and oil companies to get together and coordinate political strategy suggests that coordination might be even easier for firms that are not in direct market competition. If banks can coordinate with other banks and oil companies can coordinate with other oil companies, it is quite possible that oil companies can coordinate with banks, and that aerospace firms can work out strategies with electric utilities, when reasons exist for doing so. Indeed, the all-or-nothing pattern of political contributions discussed earlier shows that political strategy was effectively coordinated across a large number of diverse firms, but well within the boundaries of the capitalist class.

The evidence examined here seems too consistent to be accounted for by chance or simple conflict avoidance. Rather, it is likely that differences are ironed out and concrete strategies are generated, often in personal, face-to-face groups within the business community. When asked how potential differences among firms are handled, an executive stressed the role of intrabusiness communication.

> I'm sure the business community is not the only group of people who consult with each other. . . . It's a natural thing. So you kind of talk to the people you know and say, "What do you think about this?"

This "natural" process has much greater consequences for the business community than for other social groups since, as Schattschneider (1935: 287) reminds us:

> Businessmen collectively constitute the most class-conscious group in American society. As a class they are the most highly organized, more easily mobilized, have more facilities for communication, are more like-minded, and are more accustomed to stand together in defense of their privileges than any other group.

Under such circumstances, even the routine process of intraclass interaction and communication assumes enormous political significance. The dominance of the class begins with those who own the means of production *talking* to each other. It ends in class consciousness and class rule.

Domhoff (1974) has stressed the important role of social clubs in providing not only a forum for communication, but also in producing like-mindedness and cohesion among the business class. This reality was clearly echoed in the comments of a veteran oil executive, who told me:

> Well, up on Nob Hill there's the Pacific Union Club. It's the most exclusive club in San Francisco and it's just across from the Fairmont and the Mark Hopkins [hotels]. All right, the leaders of San Francisco business go up there for lunch and maybe they have a big round table with twelve guys around the table, guys alone, otherwise they come in sometimes and they bring in guests, and they know each other on a first name basis and they [breaks off]. . . . So they work together, partly on the basis of personal friendship, partly on the basis of devotion to the community, and I think they want to protect their own reputations as being cooperative.

THE STRUCTURALIST
PERSPECTIVE RECONSIDERED

This evidence casts doubt on those analyses that depict the capitalist class as riven with conflicts of interest and politically disorganized. The picture that emerges here is a capitalist *class-for-itself* as well as a capitalist class-in-itself. We should not underestimate the ability of capitalists to maintain social and political unity and to carry out effective class-based strategies, often without the necessity of relying on external agencies such as the state. They can do much within the confines of their class.

This does not necessarily mean, however, that capitalists can solve all of their internal conflicts or singlehandly ensure the smooth functioning of the accumulation process in the face of class conflict. Nor is this class invincible. In the cases studied here, the conflicts of interest had been worked out, but the side that put up the big campaign money did not always "win" the election (i.e., Proposition A of 1968 and Proposition A of 1974). Voter resistance to higher taxes for new transit systems could not be overcome in these cases. In addition, the corporate community had to rely to some extent on actions by the state. From the standpoint of the business class, the infrastructural element of transportation is a "public" good in that it is in the mutual interests of capital and it is not possible for individual capitalists to exclude other capitalists from using the new systems. Although business (particularly the Bay Area Council) was the moving force behind BART, it was necessary to get the proper legislation passed in Sacramento to create a public body (Bay Area Rapid Transit District) capable of planning the system, setting up the bond election, and managing the construction and operation of the new facility. Business controlled BART *through* public agencies of local and state government, but the state played a necessary organizing and legitimatizing role. The same was true in the two Proposition A campaigns which were formally initiated by the Southern California Rapid Transit District in close alliance with large centrally located corporations in Los Angeles. Here again the state played a subsidiary but necessary role.

In spite of the role of the state and the existence of conflicts internal and external to the capitalist class, the class was able to maintain effective political unity. I would argue that this finding is generally true for U.S. capitalism in the twentieth century. As this study shows, there is a great deal of political unity under the surface of what may appear to be class division. In this regard, we should not assume that such phenomena as corporate proxy fights and hostile mergers necessarily signify a fragmented capitalist class. The whole is more than the simple sum of its parts, and overarching common class interests tend to mute the effects of short-term struggles between individual economic units.

Nor should we take too seriously business complaints about government intervention in the market, such as those reported by Silk and Vogel (1976). Indeed, Vogel elsewhere points out that, although the state intervenes *less* in the U.S. economy than in any other capitalist country, American business leaders complain much more loudly about government restraints on the "free enterprise" system. He argues there is not much substance to these loud cries since "American corporate executives have been spoiled" by an ideology born of an earlier age in which corporate monopoly power developed long before significant intervention by the state became possible or necessary. Consequently, "Executives perceive the warfare-welfare state as an upstart" (Vogel, 1977: 69-78). Thus, business executives often sound as if they are being exterminated as a class when in fact only a few of their members are getting their knuckles rapped.

Although I maintain that this model of capitalist class cohesion fits the contemporary United States, one must generalize with care. Marxists have rightly emphasized historical contingencies rather than the search for general laws which are presumably true for all times and all places. It should be clear from the foregoing analysis that capitalists in the United States at least are *capable* of considerable effective organization. The question is: How far does that ability extend and over what kind of issues? To what degree does capitalist class cohesion vary by historical period and by specific circumstances external to the class (e.g., the strength of working-class opposition, the vitality of the accumulation process)? Do different capitalist societies exhibit different strengths of capitalist class organization?

Although he is not directly addressing the question of capitalist class cohesion, Stephens (1979) argues that working-class political organization, for example, makes a great deal of difference as to what policies are pursued by the state. He notes:

> The tremendous variation in (state) expenditure among capitalist societies cannot be accounted for by the varying functional needs of capital in various countries. Why does Swedish or Danish capital require that almost half of income be channeled through the state sector while Swiss and American capital only require one-quarter?

In the same way that working-class organization and state expenditures vary from one capitalist society to another, it is reasonable to expect that capitalist class cohesion may also vary. This is a proper subject for research.

Where there is substantial internal capitalist class disunity, the business of ruling would be made more difficult. The ability of capitalists to organize themselves as a class and to rule is a function of conditions both internal and external to that class. The structuralist perspective is useful in this regard because it draws attention to the economic, political, and social contradictions with which capitalists must contend, contradictions rendered more severe in times of economic crisis and subordinate class challenge. O'Connor (1973) and others, for example, have alerted us to the often contradictory requirements of maintaining both private accumulation and social legitimacy. This emphasis is well taken and is, in my view, the chief contribution by structuralists to the understanding of capitalist development and class relations. Here in the analysis of contradictions lies the special utility of structuralist (and similar) formulations. I would add, however, that *one* kind of contradiction—but certainly not the only kind—with which capitalists *may* be faced at certain times is internal capitalist class disunity. It definitely cannot be assumed as a constant. Historical and comparative analysis is called for here.

ONE REJECTION AND TWO PLEAS

This piece therefore should not be read as an argument against the structuralist perspective as a whole. Far from it, it should rather be seen as a rejection of the assumption of capitalist class disunity—and equally of the opposite assumption of unvarying cohesion. Such background assumptions need to be purged from our models and be made into problematics for research. In this regard, we have not progressed much beyond the old pluralist/elitist debate.

This piece should be read as a plea not only for research and the rejection of an untenable assumption, but for a theoretical synthesis as well. Instead of using models based on either unity or disunity, we need to construct new political models based on the most powerful explanatory features of existing instrumentalist and structuralist models.

It is of course beyond the scope of this chapter to undertake this task. In another place, I have attempted to sketch the beginnings of a similar kind of synthetic model, in this case as a response to the pluralist/elitist controversy in studies of community power (Whitt, 1979). As a result, that model is not directly applicable to the argument here. It is enough to note that what I have called the class-dialectical model would recognize the historical contingency of such factors as capitalist class cohesion, working-class opposition, and accumulation crises. Such a model may be able to serve as a suggestive paradigm for a future model that will bring together the best explanatory aspects of the models which are currently competing within power structure research and Marxist sociology.

At this point it can be argued that synthesis is a more rewarding strategy than continued proliferation of fine distinctions and theoretical models. Instead of academically contending, we should get busy assembling what we know into a synthetic model and doing empirical research to try to fill in the major gaps. This is a difficult intellectual task, but one that greatly needs doing.

NOTE

[1] The analysis by Block (1977) differs from most other structural critiques in an important way. He argues that although structuralists grant the state a degree of autonomy from ruling class influences, their models are also based on the assumption of ruling-class consciousness. Block rejects the idea of ruling-class consciousness entirely, presenting instead a model wherein there is a division of labor between those who profit from the market system (the capitalists) and those who protect that system by maintaining political and economic order (the managers of the state). Thus, capitalists do not have to be class conscious.

REFERENCES

BLOCK, F. (1977) "The ruling class does not rule: notes on the Marxist theory of the state." Socialist Revolution 7 (May/June): 6-28.

BRIDGES, A. (1974) "Nicox Poulantzas and the Marxist theory of the state." Politics and Society 4 (Winter): 174.

DeFREITAS, G. (1972) "BART: rapid transit and regional control." Pacific Research and World Empire Telegram (November/December).

DOMHOFF, G. W. (1974) The Bohemian Grove and Other Retreats. New York: Harper & Row.

ESPING-ANDERSON, G., R. FRIEDLAND, and E. WRIGHT (1976) "Modes of class struggle and the capitalist state." Kapitalistate 4-5: 186-220.

GOLD, D, C. LO, and E. WRIGHT (1975) "Recent developments in Marxist theories of the capitalist state." Monthly Review (October/November).

KELLEY, B. (1971) The Pavers and the Paved. New York: Donald W. Brown.

LEAVITT, H. (1970) Superhighway-Superhoax. Garden City, NY: Doubleday.

MOLLENKOPF, J. (1975) "Theories of the state and power structure research." Insurgent Sociologist 5 (Spring): 245-264.

O'CONNOR, J. (1973) The Fiscal Crisis of the State. New York: St. Martin's.

OFFE, C. (1973) "The abolition of market control and the problem of Legitimacy." Kapitalistate 1:111.

POULANTZAS, N. (1973) Political Power and Social Classes. London: New Left Books.

SCHATTSCHNEIDER, E.E. (1935) Politics, Pressures and the Tariff. New York: Prentice-Hall.

SCOTT, M. (1959) The San Francisco Bay Area: A Metropolis in Perspective. Berkeley: Univ. of California Press.

SILK, L. and D. VOGEL (1976) Ethics and Profits: The Crisis of Confidence in American Business. New York: Simon & Schuster.

SIMMONS, R. (1968) "The freeway establishment." Cry California 3: 31-38.

STEPHENS, J.D. (1979) The Transition from Capitalism to Socialism. London: Macmillan/British Sociological Association.

VOGEL, D. (1977) "Business distrust of government: an American paradox." Center Magazine 10 (November/December): 69-78.

WHITT, J.A. (1979) "Toward a class-dialectic model of political power: an empirical assessment of three competing models of power." American Sociological Review 44: 81-100.

——— (1975) "Means of movement: the politics of modern transportation systems." Ph.D. dissertation, University of California, Santa Barbara.

ZWERLING, S. (1974) Mass Transit and the Politics of Turmoil. New York: Praeger.

5

DECLINING CITIES AND CAPITALIST CLASS STRUCTURE

Richard E. Ratcliff

INTRODUCTION

This chapter addresses the coherence of the capitalist class in terms of its command of power in society and the extent to which dominant groups within the class pursue common programs of social and economic policies. The problem examined in this research, namely, the extent to which behavior by capitalists varies according to their positions within the structure of the class, has been included only marginally in other studies of the capitalist class. Put more generally, this study asks whether differences in the internal structure of the class lead to variations in policy that are of broad societal importance.

In contrast to most recent studies of the capitalist class in America, this research focuses on the class at the metropolitan rather than the national level. All banks and all bank directors in the St. Louis metropolitan area are examined in order to reveal the internal structure of the banking community. The direct concerns of the study are two: (1) the extent to which active involvement in civic policy by bankers is determined by their positional differences, and (2) the extent to which their positional differences and civic involvement influence the decisions made by banks concerning the flow of capital in the form of home mortgage loans within the metropolitan area.

THE INTERNAL STRUCTURE
OF THE CAPITALIST CLASS

A fundamental controversy has developed, especially among scholars working in the broad Marxist tradition, concerning the extent to which the capitalist class is dominated at its center by core groups that are both closely integrated structurally and generally united in the pursuit of common political and social policies. According to the more "structuralist" perspectives offered by Poulantzas (1973), Offe (1973), and others, there exists little coherent integration within the capitalist class and even less ability for capitalists to act in concert in the pursuit of common class-based policies. They argue that the class is dependent on the "capitalist state" to provide the coordination and most especially the discipline to develop and implement political, economic, and social policies that maintain and strengthen the interests of the class.

This perspective has been challenged by a number of recent studies that indicate the dominance of structurally integrated groups at the center of the capitalist class. Studies of capitalists in Chile have shown that kinship linkages reinforced by the common ownership of property and by interlocking directors create an internally differentiated class that is nevertheless dominated by coherent "segments" and interest groups (Zeitlin and Ratcliff, 1975; Zeitlin, Ewen and Ratcliff, 1974; Zeitlin, Neuman, and Ratcliff, 1976). This same research used the concept of an "inner group" to describe the network of core capitalists most integrated in terms of both property-owning family interconnections and the command of interlocking positions of administrative control over capitalist enterprises (Zeitlin, Ratcliff, and Ewen, 1974). Useem has pursued the inner-group concept in research on the American capitalist class, contrasting the inner-group thesis with alternate models of "business unity," which portray the class as structurally unified throughout, and of "business fragmentation," which emphasizes the atomizing effects of competition and other market forces (Useem, 1978a; 1978b). He argues that his research supports the existence of a dominant inner group whose members are far more likely to be found in positions of power over social policy. Mintz and Schwartz suggest that a coherent hierarchical structure is imposed on the capitalist class through the dominant role of banks and other financial institutions in controlling access to capital (Mintz and Schwartz, 1977). Domhoff has argued for a "class-hegemony paradigm" that portrays capitalist class domination as being maintained and reproduced through the extensive interconnections among class-based social clubs and policy-formation organizations (Domhoff, 1975, 1979; Bonacich and Domhoff, 1977).

The controversies over the structural unity and policy coherence of dominant capitalist groups defy easy resolution. Nevertheless, in the present chapter I will attempt to explore several issues of relevance to these questions. In our earlier research on St. Louis it has been shown that two distinct dimensions of the capitalist class structure could be identified which both separately and in combination help determine the centrality of capitalists within the class (Ratcliff, et al., 1979). The first of these dimensions is "economic power," defined as a capitalist's positions of administrative control and ownership in major capitalist enterprises. The second dimension is "upper-class prominence," defined in terms of connections to the exclusive social clubs and related organizations that are central to upper-class life. These dimensions are considered separately because they identify different bases of class centrality. The dimension of economic power concerns currently operating networks of control over major capitalist enterprises in the metropolitan area. The individuals who hold directorships in the largest corporations and the largest banks are clearly those who presently occupy the dominant positions in the economic structure. What is notable is that economic power thus defined identifies a functioning administrative structure, but does not necessarily indicate the continuity of individuals or groups of individuals within that structure. In contrast, upper-class prominence is defined by memberships in organizations that have been shown to have considerable continuity over time through the extensive and socially intimate bonds among intermarrying wealthy families and which thus embody the continuity of upper-class networks from generation to generation. (Domhoff, 1970; Baltzell, 1958).

The distinction between the two dimensions allows us to consider the significance of individual capitalists being more or less central within the class on either of the two dimensions. While the most central capitalists are those simultaneously occupying leading positions of power in major capitalist firms while also maintaining multiple memberships in exclusive social organizations, there are also notable inconsistent types. The most striking contrast is between those in command of economic power who are excluded from the most exclusive social networks and those who are core members of the exclusive clubs and organizations while remaining relatively uninvolved in leading capitalist enterprises. The contrasts between the full inner-group members and the two groups only partially tied to the central networks of power and prominence allow us to examine which factors seem most influential in mobilizing capitalists to become involved in public policy. In this chapter a detailed comparison is made of the relative importance of these two dimensions of class centrality in determining policy mobilization among capitalists.

This study is not directly concerned with the influence of the capitalist class on issues to be decided by government actions. In fact, the research begins with the premise that an exclusive concern with class-state linkages implies that capitalist class power is meaningful only in terms of its influence in state matters. Capitalist class power needs to be viewed in a much broader context, with groups within the capitalist class seen as attempting to pursue preferred "public policies" in a variety of different arenas. Nongovernmental civic organizations, which are central to this analysis, are important in this regard. This broader focus on questions of capitalist class hegemony in policy arenas outside of government also is significant for the controversy over the role of the state in organizing capitalists. It opens up the questions of whether the capitalist class is dominated by centrally interconnected groups that are able to pursue coherent policy choices that address classwide interests independently of any coordinating function provided by the state.

Our earlier study of St. Louis bank directors, a group which includes a broad range of business leaders, found that the command of civic policy positions was highly concentrated among those directors most central to the networks of economic power and social prominence (Ratcliff et al., 1979). The networks of both power and prominence were found to be significant determinants of the degree to which capitalists involved themselves as board members in leading civic policy organizations. The greatest concentrations of leading civic positions were held by bankers centrally located in both kinds of class networks, but those bankers who were tied to the center of one of the networks but not to both were considerably more likely to have important civic policy positions than were bankers with no such involvements. These findings suggest a pattern of centralized mobilization within the metropolitan capitalist class. Capitalists appear to be quite active in organizations that address issues relevant to capitalist class concerns, but that involvement is not evenly spread through the class. Instead, civic policy mobilization is concentrated in the rather small core groups of capitalists combining both power and prominence.

A central concern in the present study is to incorporate these two dimensions of class centrality in ways that allow us to see their effects on class mobilization in civic policy arenas. However, in this analysis an attempt will be made to incorporate both individual and group characteristics of class centrality. My aim is to consider not only the individual connnections that bankers have to the networks of economic power and upper-class prominence, but also to identify the capitalist class contexts in which the bankers are actually situated. The contexts of concern are still those defined by these two dimensions of capitalist class centrality but the measures of class contexts will not refer to each individual's personal class characteristics. Rather, the analysis will identify the aggregate class characteristics represented on the board of directors of the bank in which the individual holds a director position.

Two measures of the context of class centrality within which a banker is situated will be used, one relating to the dimension of economic power and the other to the dimension of upper-class prominence. With these measures I will determine whether bankers connected to the dominant networks of power and prominence are more likely than others not so connected to occupy positions in civic organizations regardless of whether they themselves have individual ties to the centers of power and prominence of the capitalist class. To the extent that the structural context as well as individual characteristics determine the level of civic involvement, we will be able to conclude that civic policy involvement is not just a function of individual characteristics but represents in part concentrated centers of power and prominence within the class which are particularly policy oriented.

After examining whether civic policy participation among bankers is not only determined by individual characteristics of economic power and upper-class prominence but also by their location in relation to central networks, I will then turn to a more fundamental question raised in this research regarding the internal structure of the capitalist class. I want to consider whether those banks characterized by the concentration of power, prominence, and civic policy participation are also associated with specific social policies. This issue is related to the question of capitalist class coherence that was raised at the outset. If the internal structure of the capitalist class were generally disorganized and if the dominance of individual motives among capitalists precluded common actions, we would expect to find neither the existence of tightly interconnected core groups nor a common pursuit of policy outcomes. Common policies at the core of the capitalist class would be particularly significant if these policies were distinct from those of the capitalist class in general.

In order to examine the linkages between the internal structure of the capitalist class and policy outcomes it is necessary to identify outcomes that are both significant and measureable. To this end, the analysis will focus on the lending practices of banks. At issue is whether the banks most centrally located within the structure of the capitalist class pursue lending policies consistent with what would seem to be their class interests, but that also have a fundamentally important impact on the larger metropolitan area. In a previous analysis it was found that the lending practices of the banks were related to their involvement in the central networks of economic power and upper class prominence (Ratcliff, 1979). The approach in this chapter will be to take the analysis one step further by determining how the lending practices of banks are influenced by the extent to which banks are centers of civic policy involvement. It will be argued that banks whose directors are most active in civic policy as well as being most closely tied to networks of power and prominence represent the centers of the most coherently organized dominant groups within the class and therefore the lending policies of these institutions should be most representative of the dominant groups in the class.

Before considering the data on these issues, it is necessary to explain the issues involved in the relationship between bank lending practices and civic policy mobilization. These relationships, which I discuss in the following section, are of particular importance in an older industrial city such as St. Louis.

CAPITALIST CLASS STRUCTURE AND THE DECLINE OF OLDER AMERICAN CITIES

In recent research on the American upper class, relatively little attention has been focused on the metropolitan level. Although local "economic dominants" and other capitalists were key concerns in the extended debate between "pluralist" and "elitist" conception of local power structures, interest in the internal structure of the capitalist class in metropolitan areas declined considerably as that controversy subsided. Instead, the class has been viewed either as a national group or else as a more abstracted entity. One notable exception to that trend is contained in Domhoff's recent reanalysis of "community power" in New Haven (Domhoff, 1978). In that study, Domhoff considers the linkages between local "economic and social notables" and the "national ruling class" and notes that analyses of community power have tended to go wrong in their general "failure to consider local power in relationship to the national ruling class and the needs of the national corporate economy" (Domhoff, 1978: 152).

The linkages between capitalists at the metropolitan level and the larger national economic system are particularly significant because current economic changes in the society have the potential to impose serious strains on local capitalists. These strains are particularly salient in older industrial cities that are caught in stages of "maturity" with relatively little economic growth if not actual decline. On one side, local capitalists in older industrial cities face challenges from two major shifts in the corporate economy. First, there is the continued growth through mergers and expansions of the largest several hundred private corporations. Such growth can threaten locally based corporations by rendering them uncompetitive. It can increase pressures to sell out to larger and usually externally headquartered firms. Or it can intensify the need for a local firm to build itself into a national firm. Second, there are the massive shifts in investments away from older industrial areas toward the "sunbelt" states and other higher-growth regions. Little analysis has been done of how these movements in investments affect the structure of local capitalists in older industrial areas. The shifts are normally seen as being led by capitalists who are seeking to realize new investment opportunities in the growing regions. Most of the studies have emphasized the resulting strains on the fiscal health of city governments and on the economic well-being of working-class groups. Relatively few researchers have considered how local capitalists have responded to this relocation of investments away from areas where they have built their own bases.

On another side local capitalists face formidable barriers against simply moving with these national economic trends. Despite the upper-class institutional structures that draw local capitalists into national networks, and despite the ability of some capitalist families to become truly national, the great bulk of capitalists base the largest share of their power and prominence on their local foundations. These foundations include not only the structure of the business enterprises from which their wealth directly flows and the commercial and distribution networks that sustain the businesses, but also the political linkages they benefit from and the other social relationships that facilitate the prosperity of their business. Moreover, their positions in the more general networks of power and prominence, which are important components of their class positions even when not directly tied to business dealings, also tend to spread out from local foundations. The overall effect of the locally based class networks is to make it difficult for the largest share of important local capitalists to be able to move their base completely, even if they were to desire to move with the dominant flows of capital out of the older industrial cities toward higher-growth areas.

It would appear that for important local capitalists the usual pattern is for a partial shifting of investments in the direction of higher-growth areas while still maintaining local bases. It should be noted that the "most important local capitalists" discussed here are tied to corporations of some national importance. About 25 corporations with headquarters in St. Louis rank either among the 1000 largest industrial corporations nationally or among the top 50 in their nonindustrial categories. Many other corporations among the 100 largest in St. Louis are of regional, if not national, importance in their particular industries. Though in recent years a fair number of large local corporations in St. Louis have been acquired by larger national corporations, very few have on their own moved their headquarters out of St. Louis. This pattern is similar to older industrial cities in general which have lost many corporate manufacturing jobs but, despite considerable publicity for the exceptions, relatively few corporate headquarters.

In contrast to popular media attention given to the attractiveness of warmer climates as a cause for the movements to the Sunbelt, it is notable that both business-oriented observers (Breckenfeld, 1977) and Marxist analysts (Gordon, 1977) have emphasized the desire of corporate leaders to get away from strong labor unions and the perceived difficulties with labor in general in older industrial areas by moving to largely nonunion and other "pro-business" settings in the Sunbelt. Local business spokesmen frequently state publicly that St. Louis's reputation as a strong union city both drives local manufacturing plants away and discourages the location of new plants. Moreover, most of the largest St. Louis corporations, such as Ralston Purina, Emerson Electric, International Shoe, Brown Shoe, Monsanto, and Pet, have in the last several decades transferred the great majority of their manufacturing jobs out of St. Louis, usually to smaller towns, Southern cities and other less unionized areas. The explicit antiunion character of such moves was emphasized in a recent *Business Week* analysis of the success of Emerson Electric. The chairman of the corporation was quoted as saying, "One of the key fundamentals that makes Emerson a low cost producer . . . is our labor policy." He also boasted that due to the company's aggressive antiunion policies, "since 1965 we've won 44 union elections and lost 2" (*Business Week,* 1976). The article notes that "to achieve that record [management] moved Emerson's plants out of St. Louis," and, according to the chairman, "deliberately situated them in rural areas."

The conflicting pressures to stay in the city, on the one hand, and to move their business operations to nonunion areas, on the other, place the metropolitan upper class in a particularly strained position. These strains are tied in important ways to the two empirical concerns of this chapter: the civic policy involvements of local capitalists and the lending decisions banks make regarding the capital they control. The linkages to lending policies are clear. Since investment capital is typically scarce, local corporations pursuing strategies of growth and relocation have a vested interest in the lending policies of the banks they help direct. In keeping with national economic trends and competitive pressures, the direction of such capital needs will typically be beyond the metropolitan area. Thus those capitalists tied to the largest corporations can be expected to be leaders in the process of "disinvestment" out of the St. Louis area. This process has been discussed more extensively elsewhere (Ratcliff, 1979).

The linkages to civic policy are somewhat more complex. The same capitalists who are involved in "disinvestment" also have been dominant in the formation and execution of local civic policy, and, due to the importance of their class positions, have a strong need to maintain that dominance. There is, of course, a significant connection between investment decisions and problems of civic policy in older industrial cities. The loss of manufacturing jobs, and the associated decline of central cities, which in most cases is where corporate headquarters are located, have been key determinants of the "urban crisis," and it is this "crisis" that is the focus of most important civic policy issues. In effect, locally based capitalists, forced to struggle to maintain their local hegemony unless they are willing to cast aside their local foundations, must seek to hold control of civic organizations working to overcome social and economic problems caused by corporate actions (Castells, 1976; Hill, 1978). Given the shortage of capital and, in any case, the unwillingness or inability of capitalists in a competitive system to invest corporate capital in the city, a key thrust of corporate policy can be the infusion of state funds into urban investments. However, any support for state capital investments intended to avoid the disruptive social and economic consequences of urban decline is paralleled by an active infrastructure of private civic policy organizations that seek to maintain social order. In addition to the basic questions of social order and the personal stake they have in their own home environments, the leading local capitalists need to support the "livability" of their headquarters city in order to facilitate the recruitment of the managerial and technical talent required by their corporations. This need in older industrial cities was emphasized by a corporate executive in Cleveland, who defended corporate support for cultural activities by saying "if we don't help to make the cities we work in good places to live in, it gets harder to attract . . . the best people" (*Wall Street Journal*, 1979). The role of local capitalists in these processes has been discussed elsewhere (Ratcliff et al., 1979).

Earlier research on this project has shown that civic policy involvements and mortgage lending practices run in a "contradictory" fashion. That is, bankers most central to networks of power and prominence in the capitalist class are *most* involved in civic policy in the metropolitan area, while the banks on which these centrally located capitalists sit are *least* involved in urban mortgage lending (Ratcliff et al., 1979; Ratcliff, 1979). These findings exemplify the tensions between local dominance and local withdrawal that are central to this analysis. Taking the absence of mortgage lending as one indication of the movement of capital away from local urban investments and toward corporate loans that are likely to be disproportionately exported from the metropolitan area (Ratcliff, 1979; Stone, 1978), the dominant groups in the capitalist class appear to be caught in the bind of trying to maintain local social stability while pursuing economic policies that undercut the viability of the urban area, especially for the low- and moderate-income neighborhood. These seemingly contradictory strategies are exemplified again in the actions of the chairman of Emerson Electric who was mentioned above in connection with moving company investments out of St. Louis. He is one of the most active "civic leaders" in St. Louis. Along with serving on local boards for United Way, the Boy Scouts, a top policy organization called Civic Progress, the Arts and Education Fund, and the St. Louis Symphony as well as being a trustee of Washington University, he gained considerable local publicity in 1977 when he led a private fund drive among corporate donors to collect $100,000 to preserve interschool athletic sports in the largely black high school system in St. Louis city.

The present analysis looks more carefully at the complex linkages between leading capitalists and the simultaneous processes of decline and stabilization in the St. Louis area. The empirical focus is on the precise points of greatest concentration in power, prominence, and civic policy mobilization in order to determine whether the internal stratification of the capitalist class is related to the processes of decline in the cities.

THE RESEARCH DATA

Data were gathered for all seventy-seven commercial banks operating in the two dominant urban counties in the St. Louis metropolitan area (St. Louis city and St. Louis County) as of 1975. Banks are ranked according to their total deposits. Missouri law restricts branch banking but does permit multibank holding companies. Any banks owned by multibank holding companies also are ranked separately by the total deposits of all banks in the particular holding company. In addition, data for all directors of these banks were developed concerning all corporate board positions held in large local corporations. Local corporations were ranked in size on the basis of sales information gathered from *Fortune* magazine, the *Dun and Bradstreet Million Dollar Directory,* and other business sources. The corporate data deal with board positions in the one hundred largest local nonbanking corporations. All memberships of bank directors in the five most exclusive local country clubs, men's clubs, and related organizations were determined. Board memberships were also determined in major local civic policy organizations in the areas of social welfare and social service, culture, and education, and the formulation and communication of business policy. The criteria used to select the social and civic organizations are discussed more fully elsewhere (Ratcliff et al., 1979).

The data on the mortgage lending practices are unique in studies of capitalist class structure in that they allow the analysis to consider in a systematic manner the aggregate consequences of a large number of economic decisions made by banks. These data only recently became available due to the reporting imposed on the banks under the Federal Home Mortgage Disclosure Act of 1975. This act requires banks to disclose the number and dollar value of all mortgage loans granted throughout the St. Louis Standard Metropolitan Statistical Area (SMSA). The data in this analysis are primarily for calendar year 1976 and concern the dollar amounts of mortgage loans granted in all individual census tracts in the St. Louis SMSA. The data for individual tracts have been aggregated on the basis of income and growth characteristics of the tracts. All mortgage loans considered here are on either new or existing residential (one to four unit) properties, with the great majority being for single family homes. Since the concern with urban disinvestment focuses on changes in older low- and moderate-income urban residential neighborhoods, the census tract areas from the St. Louis SMSA have been divided into groups according to, first, the median income level in the area, and second, the rate of population growth or decline since 1970. The greatest emphasis in this analysis is directed toward those census tract areas that were either stable or declining in population between 1970 and 1975 (no more than 5% growth) and had median family incomes in 1970 of less than $12,000. Areas meeting these criteria are referred to here as "stable, low and moderate income areas."

Two different measures of mortgage lending practices are examined in this analysis: (a) *the overall mortgage lending rate,* which is based on the volume of the bank's total mortgage lending activity in all geographic areas relative to the size of the bank measured in total deposits, and (b) *the mortgage lending rate in stable, low- and moderate-income areas,* which is based on the volume of the bank's mortgage lending in such areas relative to the size of the bank. The first measure equals the percentage that each bank's total dollars amount of mortgage lending in 1976 is of all mortgage lending by all banks divided by the percentage that its total deposits are of the total of all bank deposits in 1976. The second measure parallels the first except that it concerns only loans in stable, low- and moderate-income areas. These two measures are ratios which indicate the level of a bank's mortgage lending activity without being unduly influenced by the vast differences in the sizes of the banks (which range from $1.3 billion in assets to about $10 million in assets). It should be noted that these measures and the data parallel work done earlier on this project with data from 1975 collected for ZIP code areas rather than census tracts (Ratcliff, 1979). Thus, this chapter represents a replication, as well as an extension, with 1976 mortgage data of the research done for 1975 data.

DISCUSSION OF RESEARCH FINDINGS

The first set of tables, Tables 5.1, 5.2, and 5.3, relate to the issue of the determinants of civic policy involvement among bankers. The extent of such civic involvements is measured by the number of different civic policy areas, among three broadly defined areas, in which an individual banker holds at least one important board of director position. The three areas considered are, first, social welfare and social service, second, culture and education, and third, the formulation and communication of business policy. Two questions are considered in these tables. First, the data allow us to examine the importance of centrality to networks of economic power, as indicated by the size of the bank in which a person is a director and the number of directorships held in the largest local corporations, and centrality to networks of upper-class prominence, as indicated by ties to the most exclusive local social clubs and organizations, in determining the level of civic policy involvement. Second, the data will demonstrate the importance, in terms of mobilization of civic policy activists, of the capitalist class context of the boards of directors of the banks in which the individuals have their positions as that context is defined by other directors who form each board. As noted above, these measures of context describe more specifically the extent to which power and prominence are clustered within the capitalist class and more importantly allow for an analysis of the impact of that clustering on patterns of civic policy involvement among the capitalist class members.

As is revealed in Table 5.1, there are strong relationships between the level of civic policy involvements and the other measures of capitalist class centrality. The correlations range from a low of .460 for the number of corporate positions a person holds to a high of .549 for the extent to which

Table 5.1   Zero-Order Correlations Between Capitalist
Class Characteristics of Bankers and of Their
Institutional Contexts and the Range of Civic Policy
Positions Held by the Bankers

	2	3	4	5	6
(1) Number of Different Civic Policy Areas in Which Individual Holds Top Posts	.460	.467	.515	.549	.522
(2) Number of Board of Director Posts Individual Holds in Top 100 Local Corporations		.458	.388	.520	.455
(3) Deposit Size of Bank			.444	.791	.707
(4) Number of Top 5 Exclusive Social Clubs and Organizations in Which Individual is a Member				.482	.516
(5) Proportion of Other Directors of Individual's Bank with Director Posts in Top 100 Local Corporation					.790
(6) Proportion of Other Directors of Individual's Banks with Memberships in Top 5 Exclusive Social Clubs and Organizations	(N = 890)				

DESCRIPTION OF VARIABLES:
(1) The number (0 to 3) of different civic policy areas (social welfare and social service; culture and education; and the formulation and communication of business policy) in which the individual holds at least one important board of director post.
(2) The number of board of director posts held by the individual in the 100 largest nonbanking corporations headquartered in the St. Louis area.
(3) The total deposits (as of December 31, 1975) of the largest bank in which the individual holds a board of director post (Logarithmic transformation, base 10).
(4) The number of clubs and organizations in St. Louis which are ranked as being most exclusive in which the individual is a member.
(5) In the largest bank in which the individual holds a board of director post, the proportion *of all other directors* who hold board of director posts in one or more of the 100 largest local corporations.
(6) In the largest bank in which the individual holds a board of directors post, the proportion *of all other directors* who are members of one or more of the top five exclusive social clubs and organizations.

other directors that surround an individual hold top corporate board positions. Similarly, it should be noted that the variables of economic power and social prominence are strongly interrelated. While these interrelationships are expected, they do pose certain problems in determining the relative effects of the different factors.

The regression equation data in Table 5.2 deals with the impact of the corporate interlocks of individual bankers, the sizes of the banks for which they are directors, and the extent of their ties in the network of exclusive upper-class social organizations. It should be noted that these three variables produce a strong predictive model for civic policy involvement (R^2 = .377). By subtracting the incremental variance explained by different combina-

Table 5.2   Comparisons of the Explanatory Power of
Capitalist Class Connections in Determining the Holding
of a Range of Top Civic Policy Positions

Variables[a] Included in the Regression Equation	Standardized Regression Coefficients (Dependent Variable = The Number of Different Civic Policy Areas in Which Individual Has Top Posts)			
	Corporate Interlocks	Upper-Class Ties	Bank Size	R^2
A. All variables	.234	.329	.214	.377
B. Corporate interlocks and upper-class ties	.306	.396		.345
C. Corporate interlocks and bank size	.311		.325	.295
D. Upper-class ties and bank size		.383	.297	.336

Comparisons in Relative Changes in R^2

Equations Compared	Interpretation of the Comparison	Increment in R^2
1. A-D	Corporate interlocks net of upper-class ties and bank size	.041
2. A-C	Upper-class ties net of corporate interlocks and bank size	.082
3. A-B	Bank size net of corporate interlocks and upper-class ties	.032

a. Variables are described in Table 5.10.

tions of variables, it is possible to examine the relative importance of different factors. What is revealed is that each of these factors seems to have a
marked independent effect. It is notable that the strongest independent effect
is associated with the extent of upper-class organizational ties that an individual has. In other words, the closer a banker is connected to the centers of
upper-class prominence within the capitalist class, the broader the range of
civic involvements that such an individual will have. The impact of bank
size is only slightly less than the impact of corporate interlocks.

Thus, the positions of capitalists within the networks of power and prominence of the class strongly influence both their mobilization into directorship positions within major civic policy organizations and the likelihood that
they will hold positions in more than one civic policy area. This mobilization
certainly reflects their importance in terms of their corporate and banking
positions but also, in fact most strongly, reflects their linkages to those
private social organizations that more clearly characterize the existence of
truly class-based personal interconnections among the central groups of
capitalists.

The data in Table 5.3 represent a more complex presentation of the

Table 5.3   Comparisons of the Explanatory Power of
Capitalist Class Connection and One's Location in the
Context of Class Connections in Determining the
Holding of a Range of Top Civic Policy Positions

	Standardized Regression Coefficient (Dependent Variable = The Number of Different Civic Policy Areas in Which Individual Has Top Posts)					
Variables[a] Included in the Regression Equation	Top Corporate Interlocks	Upper-Class Ties	Bank Size	Context of Top Corporate Interlocks	Context of Upper-Class Ties	R^2
A. All variables	.180	.274	−.008	.237	.117	.412
B. Top corporate interlocks, upper-class ties and bank size	.234	.329	.214			.377
C. Corporate interlock context and upper-class tie context				.364	.234	.323
D. Corporate interlocks, upper-class ties, bank size and corporate interlock context	.183	.292	.015	.302		.407
E. Corporate interlocks, upper-class ties, bank size and upper-class tie context	.210	.281	.093		.216	.397
F. Top corporate interlocks and upper-class tie context	.306	.396				.345
G. Top corporate interlocks, upper-class ties, corporate interlock context and upper-class tie context	.180	.273		.233	.116	.412

Comparisons in Relative Changes in R^2

Equations Compared	Interpretation of the Comparison	Increment in R^2
1. G-C	Top corporate interlocks and upper-class ties net of corporate interlock context and upper-class tie context	.089
2. G-F	Corporate interlock context and upper-class ties context net of top corporate interlock and upper-class ties	.067
3. A-G	Bank size net of top corporate interlocks, upper-class ties, corporate interlock context and upper-class tie context	.000
4. A-B	Corporate interlock context and upper-class tie context net of top corporate interlocks, upper-class ties and bank size	.035
5. A-C	Top corporate interlocks, upper-class ties and bank size net of corporate interlock context and upper-class tie context	.089
6. A-D	Upper-class tie context net of top corporate interlocks, upper-class ties, bank size and corporate interlock context	.005
7. A-E	Corporate interlock context net of top corporate interlocks, upper-class ties, bank size and upper-class tie context	.015

a. Variables are described in Table 5.10.

research findings in that the effects of five different independent variables are examined. In addition to the three measures of top corporate interlocks, upper-class ties, and bank size, this table also includes the two measures of the context of corporate and class ties within which individuals are situated in terms of the bank boards to which they belong. These data reveal that the five measures explain 41% (R^2 = .412) of the variance in the measure of civic policy involvements. Thus, the addition of the two measures of capitalist class context does add to our ability to understand the determinants of the civic policy activities of bank directors. While these two measures of class context are not as powerful as the other three measures in their independent effects, the findings do support the notion that class context, as well as individual class interconnections, influence the mobilization of civic policy activists. One notable finding revealed by this table is that bank size, which had appeared to have a somewhat substantial influence, is revealed to have no independent influence once the effects of the class context measures are added. It is possible that the important factor influencing civic policy involvement is not the size of the bank, but the class contexts which have been established among the boards of directors of the banks. While these contexts are most likely to be established in the biggest banks, it would appear that there are both some more marginal large banks and some well-connected smaller banks. It is notable that the consistent finding of these tables is that actual interconnections with the centers of power and prominence within the class are most influential in determining civic policy involvements. If an individual bank director is connected to large corporations and connected to the most exclusive local social organizations, then that bank director is also likely to occupy important positions in leading civic policy organizations, and moreover, is likely to have such positions in a broader range of civic policy areas. Furthermore, even if the individual is not so interconnected himself, it is important whether or not he is surrounded by individuals who have such interconnections. In such contexts the individual banker, even though not well connected himself, is likely to be drawn into directorship posts in civic policy areas.

We now turn our attention to the mortgage lending behavior of the banks in the St. Louis metropolitan area. This analysis replicates an earlier study completed as part of this project (Ratcliff, 1979). In that analysis the concern was only with the dimensions of power and prominence as these influenced housing lending in the St. Louis metropolitan area in 1975. In this analysis we use data for 1976 and look not only at the measures of power and prominence, but also explore the question of whether the most active and most involved groups within the capitalist class are also associated with specific policies in the area of mortgage lending. The data presented in Tables 5.4, 5.5, and 5.6 allow us to examine this issue. The two different measures of bank lending behavior have already been described. The first measure, of the overall lending rate of a bank relative to its total deposit size, serves as an indicator of the extent to which the bank is involved in mortgage lending in the metropolitan area. The second measure, which is specifically focused on mortgage lending in stable and declining areas that are predominantly low and moderate income, relates to the question of the volume of a bank's lending, relative to other banks in those urban neighborhoods that have been most affected by urban disinvestment. The two measures of capitalist class interconnections included here are tied to the dimensions of economic power and upper-class prominence. First, banks have been distinguished according to the proportion of directors who have board positions in one or more corporations that rank among the one hundred largest in the St. Louis area. Second, the extent to which a bank's directors belong to one or more of the five most exclusive local upper-class clubs and organizations is considered. Two measures of the size of a bank are also incorporated in the analysis. The first of these measures equals the total deposits of the particular bank, and the second measure equals the total deposits included in the holding company, if any, with which a bank is affiliated. In the analyses presented here, these two measures of size have been transformed using a logarithmic function in order to produce a more normal distribution. Finally, in order to address the issue of the clustering of power within the class, these data include a measure of the proportion of members of each bank's board of directors who have board positions in at least one civic policy area.

The correlations among these variables are presented in Table 5.4. It is notable that the measure of a bank's ties to civic policy organizations yields stronger correlations with each of the measures of mortgage lending than do any other of the measures. Banks with more extensive ties to local civic organizations are relatively less involved in home mortgage lending. In general, a bank's greater centrality is associated with a withdrawal of capital from metropolitan housing investments.

The data in Table 5.5 allow for an assessment of the impact of these variables on the overall mortgage lending rate of the bank in 1976. The five variables included here yield a model that predicts 18% (R^2 = .179) of the variance in the mortgage lending rate. Certainly this model is not overwhelmingly powerful in predictive terms but it does reveal a definite pattern in the lending behavior of banks. It is notable that the measure of civic policy posts tied to the bank increases the power of the model considerably. The measure of civic policy posts contributes an increment of .057 to the total

Table 5.4   Zero-Order Correlations Between Bank
Mortgage Lending Practices, Corporate and Upper-
Class Ties of Bank Directors, the Total Deposits of
Banks and the Holding of Civic Policy Posts by the
Bank Directors

	2	3	4	5	6	7
(1) Overall mortgage lending rate of bank	.610	−.322	−.233	−.285	.028	−.375
(2) Mortgage lending rate of bank in stable, low- and moderate-income areas		−.345	−.129	−.310	−.040	−.351
(3) Proportion of bank's directors who interlock with top 100 local corporations			.729	.750	.227	.688
(4) Proportion of bank's directors who belong to top local upper-class organizations				.575	.267	.747
(5) Total deposits of the bank					.304	.559
(6) Total deposits of the bank holding company						.201
(7) Proportion of bank's directors who hold a top civic policy board post (N = 76)						

explained variance (R^2) that is found when only the four other variables are
included. Furthermore, the independent effect of the civic policy post measure is greater than that of either of the measures of upper-class ties or
corporate interlocks. This finding certainly does not mean that these other
factors are not important or that it is actually the civic policy connections
that are "causing" the lending pattern. Rather, it seems most reasonable to
take the civic policy measure primarily as an indication of the influence of
the clustering of power, prominence, and civic involvement which occurs
within the class. It is this clustering at the center of the class that is shown
here to be associated with important policy outputs. In effect, the conclusion
to be drawn from this table is that the banks most closely tied to the clusters
have, as demonstrated in their withdrawal of capital from home mortgage
lending, been most active in the general processes of urban disinvestment
within the metropolitan area. It also should be noted that these patterns are
only weakly affected by the size of the bank. Once again we find that bank
characteristics by themselves are not particularly influential. What is significant are the interconnections that the bank has with the networks of power
and prominence that exist within the metropolitan capitalist class.

The importance of the concentration of interconnections at the center of
the capitalist class for understanding policy outputs from the class are even
more clearly revealed in Table 5.6. Here the data concern the rate of mort-

Table 5.5 Comparisons of the Explanatory Power of Capitalist Class Connections, Total Deposit Size and Concentrations in Civic Policy Positions in Determining the Overall Lending Rates of Banks

Variables[a] Included in the Regression Equation	Standardized Regression Coefficients (Dependent Variable = the Overall Mortgage Lending Rate of the Bank in 1976)					
	Corporate Interlocks	Upper-Class Ties	Bank Deposits	Holding Company Deposits	Civic Policy Posts	R^2
A. All variables	-.139	.181	-.111	.120	-.377	.179
B. Corporate interlocks, upper-class ties, bank deposits and holding company deposits	-.236	-.016	-.137	.127		.122
C. Corporate interlocks and upper-class ties	-.325	.004				.103
D. Corporate interlocks, upper-class ties, and civic policy posts	-.205	.206			-.388	.163
E. Bank deposits and holding company deposits			-.323	.126		.095
F. Corporate interlocks, bank deposits, holding company deposits and civic policy posts	-.066		-.112	.136	-.294	.167
G. Upper-class ties, bank deposits, holding company deposits and civic policy posts		.136	-.175	.126	-.403	.173

Comparisons in Relative Changes in R^2

Equations Compared	Interpretation of the Comparison	Increment in R^2
1. B-C	Bank deposits and holding company deposits net of corporate interlocks and upper-class ties	.019
2. B-E	Corporate interlocks and upper-class ties net of bank deposits and holding company deposits	.027
3. A-D	Bank deposits and holding company deposits net of corporate interlocks, upper-class ties and civic policy posts	.016
4. A-E	Corporate interlocks, upper-class ties and civic policy post net of bank deposits and holding company deposits	.084
5. A-B	Civic policy posts net of corporate interlocks, upper-class ties, bank deposits and holding company deposits	.057
6. A-F	Upper-class ties net of corporate interlocks, bank deposits, holding company deposits and civic policy posts	.012
7. A-G	Corporate interlocks net of upper-class ties, bank deposits, holding company deposits and civic policy posts	.006

a. Variables are described in Table 5.1.

133

Table 5.6 Comparisons of the Explanatory Power of Capitalist Class Connections, Total Deposit Size and Concentrations in Civic Policy Positions in Determining the Mortgage Lending Rates of Banks in Stable, Low and Moderate Income Areas

Variables[a] Included in the Regression Equation	Standardized Regression Coefficients (Dependent Variable = the Mortgage Lending Rate of the Bank in 1976 in Stable, Low and Moderate Income Areas)					
	Corporate Interlocks	Upper-Class Ties	Bank Deposits	Holding Company Deposits	Civic Policy Posts	R^2
A. All variables	−.325	.492	−.113	.024	−.437	.236
B. Corporate interlocks, upper-class ties, bank deposits and holding company deposits	−.438	.264	−.143	.032		.160
C. Corporate interlocks and upper-class ties	−.537	.263				.152
D. Corporate interlocks, upper-class ties and civic policy posts	−.400	.495			−.445	.230
E. Bank deposits and holding company deposits			−.328	.060		.099
F. Corporate interlocks, bank deposits, holding company deposits and civic policy posts	−.128		−.117	.067	−.211	.152
G. Upper-class ties, bank deposits, holding company deposits and civic policy posts		.385	−.264	.037	−.498	.205

Comparisons in Relative Changes in R^2

Equations Compared	Interpretation of the Comparison	Increment in R^2
1. B-C	Bank deposits and holding company deposits net of corporate interlocks and upper-class ties	.008
2. B-E	Corporate interlocks and upper-class ties net of bank deposits and holding company deposits	.061
3. A-D	Bank deposits and holding company deposits net of corporate interlocks, upper-class ties and civic policy posts	.006
4. A-E	Corporate interlocks, upper-class ties and civic policy post net of bank deposits and holding company deposits	.137
5. A-B	Civic policy posts net of corporate interlocks, upper-class ties, bank deposits and holding company deposits	.076
6. A-F	Upper-class ties net of corporate interlocks, bank deposits, holding company deposits and civic policy posts	.084
7. A-G	Corporate interlocks net of upper-class ties, bank deposits, holding company deposits and civic policy posts	.031

a. Variables are described in Table 5.1.

gage lending in those communities in the metropolitan area inhabited largely by low- and moderate-income families and which have been stable or declining in population. These areas comprise over 40% of the population of the metropolitan area. While virtually all census tracts with a significant black population are included, the majority of the people living in the tracts included are white.

The empirical issue addressed in Table 5.6 is whether the banks whose boards are characterized by multiple ties to networks of economic power and upper-class prominence and whose members are highly mobilized in civic policy areas have been leaders not just in the withdrawal of capital from investments in housing in general but especially have led in the disinvestment of capital from older low- and moderate-income urban neighborhoods. The data indicate that such a pattern does exist. All five variables taken together explain 24% ($R^2=.236$) of the variance in the mortgage lending rates. Particularly strong relationships in the expected direction are associated with the measures of the corporate interconnections and the civic policy activities of board members. The size of the banks is not found to influence mortgage lending patterns independent of the effects of the measures of capitalist class interconnections. However, it is notable that the measure of ties to upper-class social organizations, while having a sizable impact on the explanatory power of the models presented, is related in an opposite direction to what was expected. This pattern, in a weaker form, was also apparent in Table 5.5. No clear explanation for this inconsistent pattern is apparent though there are some indications elsewhere in the data that several banks that are closely tied to upper-class social networks but relatively marginal to the networks of corporate power have been relatively active in lending to "gentrification" neighborhoods in St. Louis city where upper-middle-income families have been restoring old mansions. Such areas are typically located in low- or moderate-income census tracts and cannot be distinguished given the available data. If this explanation is valid, it would suggest that while the concentration of corporate linkages and civic policy mobilization is associated with the withdrawal of capital from mortgage lending in general and from lending in older urban neighborhoods in particular, the combination of upper-class linkages with a marginality from corporate and civic policy networks is associated with selective upper-income-housing lending in older parts of the city. It is notable that both the dominant pattern and this partial exception demonstrate that there is a central importance attached to the tendency for capitalist class networks to shape the flow of capital in metropolitan areas.

CONCLUSION

This research has shown that the portion of the capitalist class in St. Louis represented by bank directors is not correctly viewed as either a fragmented or a homogeneous structure of businessmen. Instead there exists a hierarchical system of stratification which separates and makes distinct a core network of capitalists closely bound together by multiple economic and social ties. We began the analysis by examining how two dimensions of class centrality, economic power and social prominence, identify the centralized patterns of integration within the class. We have looked at these patterns both as they are embodied in the linkages connecting individual bankers and as they form concentrated clusters of power and prominence on a limited set of bank boards. A major argument in this chapter has been that such clusters are a critical aspect of capitalist class structure that is missed when we study only the effects of individual characteristics. This research has shown that the civic policy mobilization of bankers is determined in part by the extent to which they are surrounded by class contexts with multiple ties to the centers of power and prominence.

By considering this concentration of civic policy mobilization as yet another dimension of capitalist class centrality, we have found that different economic policies are pursued by different kinds of capitalists. In particular, the core groups within the metropolitan upper class are shown to be clinging to positions of dominance in important metropolitan civic policy organizations at the same time as their economic policies in regard to mortgage lending indicate an ongoing disinvestment of capital from the metropolitan area. Given the magnitude of the investment shift out of older industrial regions such as St. Louis this pattern would appear to be fundamentally unstable and raises the question of whether such a metropolitan capitalist class will be able to maintain its grasp on local power as the investment trends continue.

REFERENCES

BALTZELL, E.D. (1958) Philadelphia Gentlemen: The Making of a National Upper Class. New York: Free Press.

BONIACICH, P. and G.W. DOMHOFF (1977) "Overlapping memberships among clubs and policy groups of the American ruling class: A methodological and empirical contribution to the class-hegemony paradigm of the power structure." Presented at the annual meeting of the American Sociological Association, Chicago, September.

BRECKENFELD, G. (1977) "Business loves the sunbelt (and vice versa)." Fortune 6: 132-146.

Business Week (1976) "Emerson Electric's rise as a low cost producer." November 1: 47.

CASTELLS, M. (1976) "The wild city." Kapitalistate 4-5 (Summer): 2-30.

DOMHOFF, G.W. (1979) The Powers that Be: Processes of Ruling Class Domination in America. New York: Vintage.

———— (1978) Who Really Rules? New Brunswick, NJ: Transaction.

———— (1975) "Social clubs, policy-planning groups, and corporations: a network study of ruling-class cohesiveness," in New Directions in Power Structure Research. Special issue of the Insurgent Sociologist 5 (Spring).

———— (1970) The Higher Circles: The Governing Class in America. New York: Vintage.

GORDON, D. (1978 "Capitalist development and the history of American cities," in William K. Tabb and Larry Sawers (eds.) Marxism and the Metropolis. New York: Oxford Univ. Press.

———— (1977) "Class struggle and the stages of American urban development," in David C. Perry and Alfred J. Watkins (eds.) The Rise of the Sunbelt Cities. Beverly Hills: Sage Publications.

HILL, R.C. (1978) "Fiscal collapse and political struggle in decaying central cities in the United States," in William K. Tabb and Larry Sawers (eds.) Marxism and the Metropolis. New York: Oxford Univ. Press.

McGUIRE, J. (1975) "City struggles with labor image," in Toward 2000: St. Louis's Horizons. St. Louis: St. Louis Post Dispatch.

MINTZ, B. and M. SCHWARTZ (1977) "The structure of power in American business." Presented at the annual meeting of the American Political Science Association, September.

MOLOTCH, H. (1976) "The city as a growth machine: toward a political economy of place." American Journal of Sociology 82: 2.

OFFE, C. (1973) "The abolition of market control and the problem of legitimacy." Working Papers on the Kapitalistate 1: 109-116.

ORREN, K. (1974) Corporate Power and Social Change: The Politics of the Life Insurance Industry. Baltimore: John Hopkins Univ. Press.

POULANTZAS, N. (1973) Political Power and Social Classes. London: New Left Books.

RATCLIFF, R. (1979) "Banks and the command of capital flows," in Maurice Zeitlin (ed.) Classes, Class Conflict and the State. Cambridge, MA: Winthrop.

RATCLIFF, R., M.B. GALLAGHER, and K.S. RATCLIFF (1979) "The civic involvement of bankers: An analysis of the influence of economic power and social prominence in the command of civic policy positions." Social Problems 26: 208-313.

STONE, M.E. (1978) "Housing, mortgage lending, and the contradictions of capitalism," in William K. Tabb and Larry Sawers (eds.) Marxism and the Metropolis. New York: Oxford Univ. Press.

USEEM, M. (1979) "Studying the corporation and the corporate elite." American Sociologist 14 (May): 97-107.

———— (1978a). "Inner group of the American capitalist class." Social Problems 25 (February): 225-40.

———— (1978b) "The social organization of the American business elite and participation of corporation directors in the governance of American institutions." Prepared for the European Group on Organizational Studies' Conference on Business Policies, Business Elites and Business Schools, Paris, November.

Wall Street Journal (1979) "Return to boosterism: more firms seek to improve their cities instead of giving up and moving away." July 11, 1979.

ZEITLIN, M., L. EWEN, and R. RATCLIFF (1974) "'New princes' for old? the large corporation and the capitalist class in Chile." American Journal of Sociology 80 (July): 87-123.

ZEITLIN, M., W.L. NEUMAN, and R. RATCLIFF (1976) "Class segments: agrarian property and political leadership in the capitalist class of Chile." American Sociological Review 41: 1006-1029.

ZEITLIN, M. and R. RATCLIFF (1975) "Research methods for the analysis of the internal structure of dominant classes: the case of landlords and capitalists in Chile." Latin American Research Review 10(3): 5-61.

————— and L. EWEN (1974) "The 'inner group': interlocking directorates and the internal differentiation of the capitalist class of Chile." Unpublished.

6

THE DEVELOPMENT OF AUSTERITY: FISCAL CRISIS OF NEW YORK CITY

Eric Lichten

INTRODUCTION

The most significant development characterizing the functioning of the capitalist state today is the arrival of an officially declared era of scarcity with an accompanying state policy of austerity. This era of scarcity with austerity has developed as a consequence of the severe crisis to both the capitalist mode of production and the capitalist state as evidenced by the oil crisis, recession, inflation, stagnation, lags in productivity, banking crises, the weakened dollar, and the international monetary crisis, as well as urban fiscal crisis. Working people, in both private and public sectors, as well as the poor have borne the burden of austerity as government expenditures for social welfare functions have generally been reduced while wages fall behind a continuing and severe inflationary spiral. The capitalist system is in crisis and the Keynesian mechanisms developed to mediate such crises continue to be inadequate to the task.

This chapter will discuss one such manifestation of this crisis. Here, we will be concerned with the fiscal crisis of New York City in its first and most

AUTHOR'S NOTE: The author would like to thank Michael E. Brown, William DiFazio, Dawn Esposito, Patricia Graham, John M. Goering, Meryl Sufian, and George Snekeder for their advice, support, and encouragement of his work.

important stage: that period between late 1974 and early 1976 when the organizational mechanisms to mediate such a crisis, and institute austerity, were developed. The fiscal crisis of New York City first became a prominent national issue when the city faced possible bankruptcy due to the closing of the municipal bond markets to its short-term notes and long-term bonds. Yet, the crisis mediation process began prior to, and continued after, this withdrawal of credit to the city in early 1975 and included the following: (1) the establishment of the *Financial Community Liaison Group* through which New York's major banks exerted influence during the early days of the fiscal crisis, (2) the creation of the *Municipal Assistance Corporation* by the New York State Legislature authorized to provide the city with temporary financing while restructuring its accumulated burden of short-term debt into long-term debt, (3) the institutionalization of an *Emergency Financial Control Board* authorized by the New York State Legislature to assume responsibility for controlling city expenditures and "assisting" the city in instituting a plan to balance its budget, and lastly (4) the alteration of strategy by the municipal labor unions to influence the developing policy of austerity.

By examining the actions of the above crises mechanisms we shall uncover the methods through which austerity, in the case of New York City, was instituted as public policy. Equally important, these methods will reveal the class structure of power in one of capital's most important cities. The location of this crisis in the public sector; the participation and conflict between organizations representing sectors of different classes; and the "solutions" arrived at to mediate the fiscal crisis, all point to the power, or lack thereof, of conflicting class interests as well as revealing the structure, functions, and contradictions of a municipal government in crisis. In a very real sense the study of New York City's fiscal crisis reveals the class nature of the capitalist state.

In the text that follows I will attempt to uncover the class structure of power revealed by New York City's austerity policy. I will begin by briefly discussing the current analyses of the fiscal crisis to highlight the ideology of austerity and the paucity of research in this area. Then, I will discuss the material basis of this crisis to locate it within the class struggle that moves capitalist society. I will follow with a discussion of the history of the fiscal crisis in order to outline the process through which it developed. Lastly, the actions of the aforementioned crisis organizations will be analyzed in order to demonstrate the class bias and function of austerity.

CURRENT ANALYSES OF FISCAL CRISIS

The literature analyzing the fiscal crisis of New York City is, at present, inadequate in empirical substance and theoretical significance. In part, this may be attributed to the lack of completed and published empirical research; after all, the crisis is both recent and ongoing history. Nevertheless, it may also be the result of the methodological difficulty in studying the concrete machinations of the powerful *as they act*.

For the most part, the literature has been confined to analyzing and theorizing about the causes of the fiscal crisis. According to these analyses, the causes are seen as a consequence of either one, or a combination, of the following: (1) Powerful Unions—In this theory the municipal labor unions created the social conditions for the development of the fiscal crisis by forcing destructive and fiscally unsound wage and benefit settlements from past city administrations in return for labor peace. Edward Banfield provides an example of this:

> I don't see what's to stop the unions from shaking the city down for whatever money it can accumulate. The laws have prohibited striking all along. . . . If the people of New York will tolerate strikes by public employees, against the law, and not tolerate politicians who crack down on strikes, then I can't see that it will be possible to get New York to live within its budget. It would require a fundamental change by the unions [Shanker, 1977:8].

Indeed, an empirical elaboration of this thesis is provided by the Temporary Commission on City Finances (TCCF), a government-appointed research commission whose function has been to study the city's budget and analyze its expenditures and revenues. According to TCCF, labor costs constituted the largest single item of expenditure in the city's budget in the years immediately preceding the fiscal crisis. In fact, in fiscal year 1975, according to the TCCF, labor costs accounted for almost one-half of total budgetary expenditures (Eighth Interim Report, TCCF, 1976: 22).

The "powerful union" theory is a popular one and can be seen daily in news articles on the fiscal crisis. Indeed, this interpretation is so popular that it is now taken for granted as fact, and therefore has elicited countering studies commissioned by the Municipal Labor Coalition (Program Planners, Inc., 1976, 1977). It must be noted, however, that this analysis differs fundamentally from a Marxist interpretation of the power of the organized and mobilized sectors of the working class. In this regard, we shall discuss one Marxist interpretation, provided by Donna Demac and Philip Mattera (1977), in the latter part of this section.

(2) Powerful Banks—This analysis lays the "blame" for the crisis at the doorsteps of the city's major banks. In this interpretation the bankers withheld their support for city securities in order to arbitrarily raise the interest rates and to transform the structure of city government. An example of this theory is provided by Jack Newfield and Paul Du Brul (1977) who write that

> it was the bankers that did the hoodwinking [about the security of New York City debt obligations]—lying to the thousands of hapless investors, to the press, and even to the City Hall sharpies who were left holding the bag after a fullfledged market panic had commenced. The true story [is that] New York didn't jump: it was pushed [into fiscal crisis].

The problem here is that the banks are construed separately from the structure of the credit market, and more significantly, from the crises within the banking establishment and within the capitalist economy as a whole. Removed from the structure of capitalist society, the bankers seem to be totally independent actors. This analysis "personalize[s] and, in so doing, seriously obscure[s] the larger social processes at work" (Tabb, 1978: 241).

(3) Management Crisis—A third explanation focuses on the lack of rationalization of city management functions. In this analysis, the politically motivated organizational structure of city agencies allows for corruption, inefficiency, waste, and low productivity by the city's employees, In this, a management perspective, the fiscal crisis is viewed as the result of a lack of managerial control. This allows for "gimmickry" in reporting city expenditures and revenues. The Congressional Budget Office (1977), in its report on the fiscal crisis, pointed out that

> one cannot ignore the city's questionable accounting procedures and loose fiscal management in relation to the current fiscal crisis. These procedures masked the fact that New York officials were failing to make the difficult choices that were required if the city's expense budget was to be truly balanced as required by law. The fault does not rest with the city alone. Many of the "gimmicks" which allowed the budget to appear balanced were tolerated or even suggested by state officials and were certainly not secrets to the banking community. These gimmicks produced small deficits which were allowed to accumulate and grow, producing a problem of large and unmanageable proportions.

This analysis suggests a rationality crisis in the methods of administering the processes of government. Furthermore, this suggests that a contradiction exists within the state system itself:

> In the administrative system, contradictions are expressed in irrational decisions and in the social consequences of administrative failure, that is, in

disorganization of areas of life. Bankruptcy and unemployment mark unambiguously recognizable thresholds of risk for the non-fulfillment of functions [Habermas, 1973: 63].

Accordingly, actions to "rationalize" management, or administration, become necessary for the state to fulfill its operational, and perhaps contradictory, functions of providing a basis for the accumulation process and its legitimation. Crisis then, becomes a context within which "rationality" may be instituted at the expense of the city's workers.

(4) Welfare State—This explanation suggests that the fiscal crisis was caused by the expansion of expenditures for the clients of the welfare state. In this view, fiscal crisis results from responses made to urban poverty either by a city government humanely responsive to the needs of the poor (Newfield and Du Brul, 1977) or one that was forced, by pressures applied by the mobilization of poor people, to take their needs into account (Piven and Cloward, 1971, 1975, 1977). Regardless of the theorist's emphasis, here the welfare state is itself called into question as a viable, functioning mechanism to meet social needs.

There remain two analyses that deserve further attention. In one, provided by Demac and Mattera (1977), the development of the fiscal crisis is placed as the result of the intensifying organization and mobilization of the working class and the poor. This increasing militance, evidenced in poor people's movements, rank-and-file wildcat strikes, and low rates of productivity, constitutes a struggle for a social wage; that is, a wage separated from the production of exchange-value. The fiscal crisis and the development of austerity constitute capital's counteroffensive designed to reestablish the relationship between wages and productivity—a connection constituting the basis of expanded accumulation:

> Something had to be done, and before long, capital's counter-offensive was launched. At its center were the imposition of a climate of austerity, the creation of scarcity, and the attempt to reimpose the discipline of work [Demac and Mattera, 1977: 120].

This approach therefore attempts to establish class struggle as the basis of the fiscal crisis, and austerity as the solution to the fiscal crisis.

James O'Connor (1973) sees the fiscal crisis of the state as generalized to local and national levels and as operant in governmental units regardless of appearances of fiscal health. According to O'Connor, the fiscal crisis results from an "overload" of fiscal demands made upon the state in its attempt to fulfill the twin, but contradictory, demands of fueling capital accumulation while legitimizing the capitalist system. These demands develop as the costs of production, in particular the social costs, become an impediment to the accumulation of capital. Capital thereby requires, in a structural context, that these costs of production be "socialized," while profits remain privately appropriated. At the same time, however, the state must legitimate both the economic system, which it supports with funds, and itself. This requires the state to obscure its class function as it attempts to balance these contradictory needs—which translate to conflicting budgetary pressures. O'Connor (1973: 9) argues:

> Although the state has socialized more and more capital costs, the social surplus (including profits) continues to be appropriated privately. The socialization of costs and the private appropriation of profits creates a fiscal crisis, or "structural gap," between state expenditures and state revenues. The result is a tendency for state expenditures to increase more rapidly than the means of financing them.

O'Connor argues that once the structural determinants of the fiscal crisis have been established, the depth of the crisis is mediated by the actions of "special interests." These interests represent O'Connor's (1973: 9) recognition of the mobilization of class conflict:

> We argue that the fiscal crisis is exacerbated by the private appropriation of state power for particularistic ends. A host of "special interests"— corporations, industries, regional and other business interests—make claims on the budget for various kinds of social investment. [In addition] organized labor and workers generally make various claims for different kinds of social consumption, and the unemployed and poor . . . stake their claim for expanded social expenses. Few if any claims are coordinated by the market. Most are processed by the political system and are won or lost as a result of political struggle.

The necessary socialization of the costs of production, along with the demands by the various sectors of the capitalist, working, and poor classes, create the conditions for the fiscal crisis, as well as the politicization of class struggle. The intervention of the state in the political economy of capitalism creates the conditions altering the discipline imposed by the market and by the connection between profits, wages, and productivity (Offe, 1972, 1973).

The work by both Demac and Mattera, on the one hand, and O'Connor, on the other, attempts to ground the fiscal crisis within a class struggle over the appropriation of the social surplus. Since they view this crisis as stemming from the class process of the society as a whole they are able to integrate the preceding analyses into their own. The organization and mobilization by the banks, the unions and poor people, as well as the city's administrative inefficiency, make sense once they are located within such a structural context. The fiscal crisis, then, becomes part of the historical development of capitalist society; and the austere structure of fiscal crisis is understandable within the state's functions.

Despite the strength of these analyses, however, there still exists a lack of concrete research. These analyses, like those mentioned before, fail to study the crisis process itself. We are not shown how the crisis develops and how it is mediated to produce austerity. We must realize that austerity is not instituted by the powerful in one bold, grand move; especially if we analyze crisis as the result of a process of class struggle. These analyses lack the very information and data which we need to demonstrate that there is a ruling class; that austerity is introduced and developed at the behest of a class. In the following section I will theorize that the fiscal crisis was the consequence of class struggle within a rapidly declining economic base. Then, we will be able to understand austerity as capital's reaction to the strength of certain factions of the working class.

THE MATERIAL BASIS OF THE CRISIS: CLASS STRUGGLE IN THE PUBLIC SECTOR

During the latter part of 1974 the most powerful factions of the banking and financial sectors of New York City's corporate establishment became concerned with the already huge and growing debts accumulated by the city to cover past and present budget deficits. By this time these debts totaled more than $10 billion, half of which were issued in short-term notes and due to mature within a few months. Indeed, debt service for 1974 alone exceeded $1.25 billion and represented nearly 20% of city operating funds (revenues minus categorical grants and transfers from capital funds) and 12% of total city revenue. Furthermore, the budget deficit for fiscal year 1974 was a huge $1.977 billion portending increased borrowing by the city in fiscal year 1975. An October 1974 report by Bankers Trust warned that the city would have to roll-over 1.2 billion dollars in debt before the year's end. This represented nearly 25% of the total short-term debt and would further burden the city's budget for fiscal 1975, necessitating budgetary maneuvers to secure adequate funds. This in turn could only serve to decrease the marketability of the city's debt offerings. To Bankers Trust and the rest of the financial community this indicated that the city's finances were in deep trouble and might cause it to cease being an attractive investment. The spectre of New York City being unable to borrow operating funds from the municipal credit markets became realistically possible for the first time in

the post-World War II era. Only in 1933 had the city faced similar circumstances, only to be bailed out by the city's banks who ran the city for the next
four years.

This very huge debt was the result of the city borrowing funds to cover the
growing gap between rapidly increasing operating expenses and inadequate
revenues from sales and real-estate taxes. The practice of borrowing to
supplement shortages of revenues began in 1971, though the city's short-
term debt began to steadily rise as early as the 1965-1966 fiscal year. A look
at the following table 6.1 (Newfield and Du Brul, 1977: 163) shows that the
short-term debt multiplied nearly five times during the years between 1965
and 1974.

Table 6.1   New York City Short-Term Debt

Fiscal Year	Debt in Billions of Dollars
1965-1966	1.6
1966-1967	2.0
1967-1968	2.4
1968-1969	3.2
1969-1970	4.4
1970-1971	6.5
1971-1972	5.2
1972-1973	4.0
1973-1974	7.3

Furthermore, since 1971 most of the short-term debt was incurred solely to
cover existing debt service; in other words, the city was borrowing to pay the
maturing debt of the very recent past. The city had begun to borrow from
creditors to pay its creditors.

This growing gap between expenses and revenues, now commonly understood as fiscal crisis, was the result of severe economic crises, on the one
hand, and the organized strength of the city's workers and the demands of the
city's poor for an adequate standard of living, on the other. To make this
claim is to suggest that the fiscal crisis is the result of class struggle and that it
has a material base in the actions of both the capitalist and working classes.
The financial community, suffering from heavy losses in real estate specula-
tion as well as "shaky" investments in the Third World, recognized that the
fiscal crisis presented a rare opportunity to repress the growth and strength
of the city's work force through the institutionalization of austerity. At the
same time, the fiscal crisis posed a real and serious threat to the stability of
the banking system and the solution to this crisis would be framed to save
those with large investments in city paper, including and especially New
York's major banks.

We have already stated that this fiscal crisis develops out of a crisis in the economic base of the city. This crisis has been discussed elsewhere (Mermelstein and Alcaly, 1977; Tabb, 1978). Here we will be content to summarize the data demonstrating the underlying causes of fiscal collapse. Then we will be able to better understand the threat and opportunity that the fiscal crisis presented to a ruling class desperate to reimpose its discipline over an organized and militant public work force.

THE COLLAPSE OF THE CITY'S ECONOMY

From 1950 to the present New York City has seen its manufacturing base eroded by both economic recession and the movement of manufacturing out of the central city. Between 1950 and 1975, for instance, the city lost nearly 50% of its manufacturing employment, including 13,426 firms and 324,000 jobs between 1960 and 1974 (Ninth Interim Report, 1976: 4). Between 1969 and 1976 alone, as the city began to increase its debt, more than 500,000 jobs were lost, nearly one-half of these in factory employment, leaving more workers dependent upon public assistance for support. Indeed, according to the Ninth Interim Report of the Temporary Commission on City Finances:

> 1970-1975 period . . . the local economy experienced a severe contraction, losing 468,900 (12.5 percent) of its jobs. . . . Between 1970 and 1975 every industrial sector declined, including services and finance, insurance, and real estate, and some declined precipitously: contract construction, 29.3 percent; transportation and public utilities, 17 percent; wholesale and retail trade, 13.6 percent; and manufacturing, 31.1 percent. The losses in the services and finance, insurance, and real estate sectors were smaller than elsewhere—1.9 percent and 8.1 percent, respectively—but contrasted sharply with the rapid growth each sector experienced in the 1950s and 1960s [1976: 4-5].

Nor were the city's largest corporations immune from contributing to the city's economic decline. In 1965, for instance, the city was the headquarters for 128 of the top Fortune 500 corporations, but by 1975 the figure had dropped to 62 with 38 of these corporations relocating to the less costly suburbs or regions of the country (Goering and Lichten, forthcoming). The city was losing employment and revenue from both its manufacturing and corporate headquarter sectors. In the process the economic base of the city's economy was transformed.

With this overall significant decline in the city's economy came an increased unemployment rate, a transformation to a service oriented economy, and a revenue base which could not maintain pace with expanding city expenses. The city found itself providing support and services to the unemployed and, for a lucky few, jobs to cushion the downturn in the local economy. As the city's unemployment rate climbed from 4.8% in 1970 to 10.6% in 1975 and "wage and salary employment dropped 13%, from 3,797,700 in 1969 to 3,287,800 in 1975 . . . municipal employment rose by 30,000" (*Fiscal* Observer, 1978: 1). These were indeed years in which municipal employment grew in leaps and bounds as the city increased its full-time employment by 43% between 1960 and 1970. This provided an organizing base for the city's municipal unions as they increased their membership by 300%, thereby increasing their potential influence within the city's power structure. At the same time, the city could not possibly employ all those left jobless with the resulting increase in the size of the welfare rolls. In the decade between 1960 and 1970 the proportion of the city's population receiving public assistance increased from 324,200, or 4% of the population in 1960, to 1,094,700 or 14% in 1970 (Piven and Cloward, 1971, 1975).

As the city's welfare rolls increased, poor people mobilized to agitate for better housing, higher welfare rates, better medical treatment, day-care centers, job training, and direct participation in the city's public education system. The wageless poor were demanding a social wage; an adequate level of income to support a materially decent standard of living even without direct productivity to serve capital or the capitalist state. And while some of the funding to support these services came from New York State and federal grants, often requiring matching city funds, the city itself contributed a growing proportion of its own revenues. Table 6.2 (Eighth Interim Report, 1976: 52) demonstrates this growing dependence upon city, state, and federal revenues to support the social wage and to pick up the pieces left by capital's crisis and mobility. As the data demonstrate, expenditures for welfare assistance increased during the 1961-1976 period. This was due to both

Table 6.2 Expenditure by City Function (percentages)

Function	Total Expenditures		Percentage Increase or (Decrease)
	Fiscal Year 1961	Fiscal Year 1976	
Welfare	12.3	22.6	10.3
Hospitals	8.2	9.7	1.5
Higher Education	1.9	4.5	2.6
Subtotal	22.4	36.8	14.4
Police	9.5	6.4	(3.1)
Fire	4.9	2.8	(2.1)
Sanitation	5.4	2.7	(2.7)
Education	25.6	18.4	(7.2)
Subtotal	45.5	30.3	(15.1)

Continued on page 149

Function	Total Tax Levy Expenditures Fiscal Year 1961		Fiscal Year 1976		Percentage Increase or (Decrease)	
Welfare	5.6		11.6		6.0	
Hospitals	8.8		5.4		(3.4)	
Higher Education	1.2		2.1		0.9	
Subtotal		15.6		19.1		3.5
Police	12.0		11.1		(0.9)	
Fire	5.9		4.7		(1.2)	
Sanitation	6.2		3.8		(2.4)	
Education	21.0		14.9		(6.1)	
Subtotal		45.1		34.5		(10.6)

SOURCE: Adapted from tables provided by The Temporary Commission On City Finances.

an infusion of federal and state monies and an increase in the proportion of expenditures allocated from the city's collected tax revenues. And while this in itself does not adequately demonstrate a burden on the city's revenues, it nevertheless indicates a shift in the expenditure patterns as the city's economy moved into a serious decline. Indeed, if we turn to table 6.3 (Eighth Interim Report, 1976: 1), we can see this more clearly. While welfare expenditures constituted 12.3% of city revenues in fiscal year 1961, by fiscal year 1971 welfare expenditures had increased to 22.5% of total city resources. Compare this to the proportion of revenues allocated for police, fire, and sanitation services, all of which decreased over this time. Nevertheless, a word of caution is advisable here. Much of this revenue was allocated from grants and programs mandated and funded by both the federal government and New York State. For example, the Temporary Commission on City Finances (1976: 1) noted that

> State and Federal aid contributed significantly to the growth and reorientation of City expenditures during the 1961-1976 fiscal period. State and Federal aid increased from $565.2 million, or 23 percent of the fiscal year 1961 budget, to $5.7 billion, or 47 percent of the fiscal year 1976 budget.

The Commission then cautions us that

> Welfare and Hospital costs, which include Medicaid, are nearly $4.3 billion and represent the major functional expenditure problems faced by the City. Although 75 percent of welfare and medicaid benefits are paid for by State and federal aid, combined welfare and hospital expenditures exceed combined police, fire, sanitation, and education expenditures.

Nevertheless, according to the Temporary Commission's own data, the proportion of city taxes expended for welfare functions increased only 6.5% between fiscal years 1961 and 1971. And while much of the pressure to increase these funds came from the poor themselves, along with their allies

Table 6.3   Percentages of Resource Shares Allocated
to Major Functions of the City of New York: Fiscal Years
1961, 1966, 1971, and 1976

Function	FY 1961	FY 1966	FY 1971	FY 1976
Police				
Expenditures	9.5	9.1	7.3	6.4
Tax levy	12.0	11.5	12.9	11.1
Employment	12.8	12.5	12.3	12.0
Fire:				
Expenditures	4.9	4.5	3.4	2.8
Tax levy	5.9	5.9	5.8	4.7
Employment	6.2	5.6	5.4	4.8
Sanitation:				
Expenditures	5.4	4.4	3.4	2.7
Tax levy	6.2	5.7	5.2	3.8
Employment	6.8	5.8	5.4	4.7
Education:				
Expenditures	25.6	24.7	20.6	18.4
Tax levy	20.9	20.7	18.9	14.9
Employment	Education data were not comparable through- out this period			
Welfare:				
Expenditures	12.3	14.1	22.5	22.6
Tax levy	5.6	7.5	12.1	11.6
Employment	4.3	6.2	8.9	9.2
Higher Education:				
Expenditures	1.9	2.3	4.0	4.5
Tax levy	1.2	1.3	3.0	2.1
Employment	2.1	3.2	5.4	7.1
Hospitals:				
Expenditures	8.2	8.6	9.4	9.7
Tax levy	8.8	9.5	6.4	5.4
Employment	19.2	15.0	14.1	15.2
Total percentage of expenditure	67.8	67.7	70.6	67.1
Total percentage of tax levy	60.6	61.9	64.3	53.6
Total percentage of employment	51.4	48.3	51.5	50.3

in the welfare rights movement, much of this money went to support a growing maze of city agencies servicing the poor, and not necessarily to the poor themselves.

Despite this, we might still argue that the growth and redirection of the city's budget reflected the urban insurgency characteristic of the 1960s. The process of allocating city resources reflected the militance of the city's impoverished and working-class population. There was rebellion in the city and a redirected budget was the price to be paid for some semblance of order.

A major beneficiary of this militant era were the city's labor unions. Throughout America's major cities, beginning with the mid-1950s, a new wave of labor organizing resulted in the unionization of more workers than in any period with the exception of the Great Depression of the 1930s (Bok and Dunlop, 1970; Aronowitz, 1973; DiTomaso, 1978). In fact, the workers most likely to be harshly affected by the current austerity, that is, municipal and public employees, were the most successfuly organized and experienced the most rapid expansion of unionization during this preausterity expansionary period. Public employees at all governmental levels, federal, state, and city, were organized to such a great extent that their numbers actually doubled between 1960 and 1968 alone. By 1968 union strength among public employees had grown to over two million members (Bok and Dunlop, 1970: 313). For example, membership in The American Federation of State, County, and Municipal Employees (AFSCME) swelled from 150,000 in 1950 to 400,000 in 1972. In New York City alone, District Council 37 of AFSCME grew to include more than 100,000 workers (O'Connor, 1973: 237). To further highlight the extent of the organizing effort among public sector workers we must recognize that this was a period in which the proportion of American workers belonging to unions actually decreased. Furthermore,

> By 1974 government employees at all levels accounted for 13.5% of all unionized employees, up from 10.7% in 1968. During the same years, the proportion of the unionized labor force in this country declined, from 23.0% in 1968 to 21.7% in 1974; this in itself is a dramatic decrease from the high point in union organization of 35.5% of the labor force in 1945. Therefore, the influence of public employees among unionized workers is even greater than would appear at first glance, and they are one of the few areas of the labor force where unionization is increasing [DiTomaso, 1978: 192].

In cities across the nation public sector workers were organizing, lobbying, and, most importantly, striking, regardless of legal barriers forbidding the strike by many public workers. Hence the significance of the public employee unions cannot be underestimated, having effectively shut down cities in the recent past, for however brief a time. In New York City, for instance, 25% of all union members are in the public sector. By 1969 these public unions had grown to such an extent as to have organized the public workers in 80% of cities with populations greater than 10,000; this from a low figure of 33% in 1938. This very rapid organizing experience caused analysts to declare that "the 1960s have already earned a place in labor relations history as the decade of the public employee" (Bok and Dunlop, 1970; 313).

Along with this organizing experience public workers became among the most militant workers, often confronting the governmental unit with jurisdiction with demands for higher wages, better health and retirement benefits, shorter hours with better working conditions, and an increase in the size of the public workforce. Across the nation the strike by public workers became commonplace whether it be legal or not, with or without the sanction of the union hierarchy or the support of the public. Indeed, in most cases these strikes were illegal and were met with forceful resistance from governments intent on keeping expenditures as low as possible. In any case, strikes by public workers involved more workers for longer periods of time, as public employee unionization picked up increasing numbers of members. "In 1953, there were only thirty strikes against state and local governments; in 1966 and 1967, there were 152 and 181 strikes, respectively (O'Connor, 1973: 238). Furthermore, 310,000 state and local government employees conducted 490 strikes in the year ending October 1975 according to the Census Bureau. This was a 72% increase over the number of strikes in fiscal 1974, as governments began to crack down on public workers (*Seven Days,* 1977). At the very least, these workers had demonstrated their resolve to increase their wage and benefit packages. The more progressive unions, on the other hand, formed alliances with clients to unite in a common effort against capital's government. Social workers in New York City were an example of the effort to unite workers and clients in a common struggle. Regardless of union strategy, public workers had indicated their potential power in the administration of city services.

Furthermore, money which might be expended toward making business more profitable was now being allocated for increased wages and benefits to city workers. Local business often found itself with increased taxes while fewer local funds were allocated to meet its production requirements and investment needs. The result was a "consistent, though varying, level of pressure from business to keep expenses in the public sector low in order to free investment monies for the private sector, or at least to channel public monies through contracts with private enterprise" (DiTomaso, 1978: 191). As city expenses increased, local business began to apply pressure for a decrease in the costs of labor; in other words, decreased wage and benefit packages to the city's workers. The Citizen's Budget Commission, a private nonprofit research advisory organization whose trustees are prominent members of New York's corporate sector, warned as early as 1969 about the possibility of fiscal crisis as expenses increased and revenues decreased. These warnings began even as the city's debt increased, yet they went unheeded. This was not because they were unfounded; rather, it was due to the politicization of the class struggle. Worker's demands could be ignored only at the expense of "public order" and essential city services. For the first time on such a large scale, public employees were showing their potential power.

It was within this context of the politicization of class struggle that public sector workers organized, mobilized and pressured the state sector for increases in the value of their labor power. Profit criteria are absent in the public sector and the value of a worker's labor power ceases to be measured by either the profitability of the business or the productivity of the labor power. As a result, wage and benefit packages seem to lose the inhibition and limitations of the marketplace. Wages are set solely by the strength of the contending classes, or rather by the conflict between public workers and the government. More importantly, public workers recognize this and expected higher wages as their right, often establishing a wage and benefit parity with the highest-paid workers in the corporate sector. The mystification and ideology of wage levels being tied to productivity and profitability become transparently political and lose their influence over increasingly militant public workers. Consequently, workers demanded and often won unprecedented settlements, thereby forcing government to redirect some revenues from capital's need to the workers themselves. This threatened both the administrative function of the capitalist state—to provide the social stability necessary to maintain the legitimacy of capitalism—and its economic function of encouraging and assisting the accumulation of capital. Indeed, the cost of performing the legitimation function and maintaining the "loyalty" of the working class threatened the accumulation function as potentially "productive" and profitable expenditures were drawn away from the private sector. This redirection of state funds away from capital posed a threat to the partnership between government and industry. Seen in this light, the fiscal crisis, the loss of manufacturing and corporate jobs, and the eventual withdrawal of credit and financing from the city all result from capital's response to this heightened and politicized mobilization of public sector workers, along with the "clients" of the welfare state. Capital needed to reassert its control over government policy so that its needs, and not the needs of workers and poor people, would be met. Control over the budgetary mechanisms of New York City became the strongest and most direct method to reimpose control.

FINANCE CAPITAL, BANKS AND FISCAL CRISIS

So it was that in late 1974, with the city's debts piling up, the financial community began to show its "concern" over the city's fiscal stability. In separate, independent internal memos, analysts at the Chase Manhattan Bank, Citibank, Bankers Trust, and Morgan Guaranty Trust all expressed reservations over the marketability of future city bonds and notes. Indeed, even the Clearinghouse Association, representing New York's major clearinghouse banks which had underwritten and marketed city securities in the past, had been alerted to the potential danger of the city offering debt not covered within its constitutional limits, and the possible cool reception of investors to such an offering. For example, the Securities and Exchange Commission reported that a December 1974 letter from Richard L. Tauber, a Vice President of Morgan, "advised" a substantial investor that the city was indeed in a financial crisis:

> The letter stated that although the author believed that the rating agencies [rating city securities] would give the city the benefit of the doubt, a downgrading was very possible if the financial deterioration of the city continued; this would narrow the market for City securities. The letter recommended that the client reduce his holdings of City securities by not renewing maturing obligations and by tax loss trading [SEC, 1977, Ch. 1: 3].

Yet, at that very moment, the *Wall Street Journal* (December 4, 1974) carried a report that substantiated great demand for the last offering of city securities. Individual investors were quite excited about purchasing part of the December 2, 1974, offering of $400 million in Revenue Anticipation Notes (RANs) and $200 million in Tax Anticipation Notes (TANs). In part this was due to the high interest rates: 9.4% on the TANs and 9.5% for the RANs. The demand was also partly caused by the "low" $10,000 denominations. We can surmise from this that smaller investors were being attracted to these city notes even as bankers were warning their major clients to divest of city securities.

Still, the banks continued to circulate internal memoranda warning of trouble ahead. One such memorandum from Amos T. Beason, a Vice President, Municipal Credit and Finance, Morgan Guaranty Trust, to Frank Smeal, Executive Vice President of Morgan Guaranty Trust, suggested that part of the problem was that

> city officials did not appear to comprehend the seriousness of the situation. It was asserted that, in the recent past, the City's problems were solved by more borrowings, budget gimmicks and increased Federal and State aid receivables. The reported attitude among dealers and investors was that the New York City financial institutions and the State and Federal governments would not permit the demise of the City to occur. However, investors were said to need *concrete signs* [my emphasis] that the City's problems were being addressed by City officials and the financial institutions [SEC, 1977, Ch. 1: 40].

Indeed, the memorandum continued to suggest that the bank

> apply some financial discipline to the City's operation . . . [and then recommended the following course of action]

(1) a substantial moratorium on capital expenditures
(2) a substantial cut in the City payroll
(3) the development of "honest three-year plans" on revenues and expenses
(4) a review of the City tax structure
(5) an analysis of the City's overall debt structure . . . by officials of the City, State and City's business community . . . [with] the results of the study [including] suggested remedial legislation [SEC, 1977, Ch. 1: 40-41].

The memorandum went on to suggest that the banks should agree to fund the city by lending substantial capital in short-term loans if the city undertook a rigorous program of fiscal recovery. Indeed, the banks had already decided that austerity was necessary—even prior to the refusal of investors to buy city securities.

All the while, the Mayor and the Comptroller of the city could not agree on the size of the budget deficits, nor the methods to close the budget gap. The public bickering, along with the actions of the clearinghouse banks, pushed interest rates higher. Indeed, on October 16, 1974, the city issued $478.58 million in long-term bonds at an average interest rate of 7.3318%. A November issue of $500 million RANs and $115 million TANs were marketed at an average rate of 8.3359% by a syndicate led by Morgan Guaranty. But by December 2 the interest rates had climbed to 9.5% for the RANs and 9.4% for TANs. This indicated a marketing problem; it also indicated that the banks' perception that the city was becoming unmarketable might have affected the marketing process itself.

Even so, the squabbling between Mayor Beame and Comptroller Goldin certainly could not assure investors of the city's financial stability. As the city moved to greater and greater debts, the actions of the city's elected officials only served to verify the deep trouble that lay ahead. According to Jac Friedgut, Vice President for Municipal Securities at Citibank:

The major impact of the dispute was felt after a bidding syndicate had already purchased a new bond issue from the city but before the bonds were resold by the underwriters to the public. Prices on the bonds fell sharply as investors felt the need for a higher interest rate to compensate them for greater uncertainty, and the underwriters were forced to sell bonds into the market at very substantial losses. Meannwhile, the Technical Debt Advisory Committee [of bankers] had warned the comptroller that the city's heavy schedule of short-term debt offerings were likely to meet market resistance, resulting in higher interest rates [1977: 3].

So it was that interest rates continued to climb. With this, the city's debt service increased, necessitating further borrowing. The data in Table 6.4 (SEC 1977, Ch. 3: 19) demonstrate the increased costs of borrowing.

Table 6.4   Debt-Service Expenses

Fiscal Year ending June 30	Debt Service	Expense Budget	Percentage of Budget Devoted to Debt Service
1970	705,753	6,722,824	10.5
1971	781,819	7,744,761	10.1
1972	847,433	8,659,194	9.8
1973	1,099,101	9,560,928	11.5
1974	1,175,973	10,287,546	11.5
1975	1,826,965	11,895,019	14.0

As the data indicate, by fiscal year 1975 the city was allocating 14% of its budget to pay off its accumulated debt.

In November 1974 the city began cutting its expenses. Its solution then was to be the same as throughout the next three years: expenses would be cut by layoffs, attrition, and austerity. November saw 1,500 layoffs of civil servants and provisional workers followed by 3,725 the next month. The December layoffs, however, included uniformed workers and teachers. In addition, up to 2,700 workers faced forced retirement. The financial community continued to press for more layoffs and stricter control of expenditures in a series of meetings with the city. The financiers were willing to cooperate with "saving" the city, but the price for this cooperation was the forthcoming austerity program.

In January 1975 the city continued to lay off its workers, with 4,050 police officers, firefighters, teachers, and other city workers "axed" for an alleged saving of $15 million. Union concessions and funds, however, were able to save many of these jobs, at least for a short while.

January 1975 was also important, for the financial community began to formalize its influence over city policy. On January 9 the Financial Community Liaison Group (FCLG) was formed. Its membership included the major officers of the city's largest financial institutions and was chaired by Ellmore Patterson, chairman of Morgan Guaranty Trust. Other prominent members included David Rockefeller, Chairman of the Board at Chase Manhattan Bank; William I. Spencer, President of Citibank; Alfred Brittain III, Chairman of the Board at Banker's Trust; Donald C. Platten, Chairman of the Board at Chemical Bank; John F. McGillicuddy, President of Manufacturers Hanover; as well as Donald T. Regan, the Chairman of the Board of Merrill, Lynch; and William Salomon, Managing Partner of Salomon Brothers. Heading the staff of the FCLG was David Grossman, Senior Vice President of Chase and former budget advisor to Mayor Lindsay, aided by staff members from other major banks and brokerage firms. The function of the FCLG was to establish a formal mechanism through which the financial community and the city could work cooperatively to reopen the municipal credit markets to the city. Essentially, this committee established the power of finance capital over the city's fiscal affairs. At this point, that power was exerted through a mechanism, the FCLG, which had no legal authority to mandate the city's actions and policies. Yet the FCLG was able to exert a powerful influence over both the municipal credit markets and the city. Still, this power was informal and depended upon an atmosphere of "cooperation" and "responsibility." In this regard,

> the underwriters and the City were brought together in a series of meetings at which the fundamental concerns about the clash between the City's budget gap and its constant need for new debt were aired in great detail. Among the principal problems discussed were the inability of the City to continue on the path of ever-increasing budget gaps and short-term note issuances, the use of budget gimmicks to disguise the true state of the City's deficit, and the need for immediate City action to remedy the situation. A recurrent theme during these meetings was a recognition of the scope of the problems, the need for immediate action, the consequences of the failure to take such action, and the difficulty, given political realities, of taking effective action [SEC, 1977, Ch. 4: 16].

At the meetings between the FCLG and the city, the FCLG stressed that effective and significant expenditure-cutting actions must be taken if investors were to be impressed and, indeed, reassured that the city was not a risky investment. On February 11, 1975, the staff of the FCLG decided that its major activities should concentrate on analyzing the "City's budget problems . . . [and developing] a long range plan for the City's financial management" (SEC, Ch. 4: 59). The staff would concern itself with the methods through which the city financed itself. Indeed, the FCLG, in order to reassure investors, would assert that "reforms" be made both in these financing methods, and in the city's budgetary processes.

Yet, the financial community had long been involved in advising the city on its debt offerings, their integrity, and on market accessibility. Indeed, William Scott, former Third Deputy Comptroller of the City of New York, stated during an interview with me on December 14, 1978 that the city's mayors, and especially Mayor Beame, were

> led by a group of technical advisors mostly arising, all of them arising, from the banks and financial community who for many, many years had no obligation to what the city did so long as the bonds were saleable. They never asked for full disclosure [of the city's problems]; they never forced issues; they never had real prospectives. They had a bond counsel who conveniently came up with reasons why the city should be able to sell its bonds and the types of bonds they were selling. There was political pressures to do certain things with city

money—to roll them over, to roll over notes in the anticipation that the interest rates were going down, which was a bad guess. If you're able to roll them over, you're able to sell them later at a lower interest rate. There were poor decisions made based upon poor information, but based upon the only information that was available. You always had to look with some suspicion on the advice you received because in a city this size who do you go to for financial advice about bonds, whether they're saleable and what rates they should be paid, except to the people who are going to buy and sell them.

Still, the financial community pressed for more influence over the city's financial affairs, and, in so doing, assisted the climate of investor insecurity pushing the city to fiscal collapse. In order to gain more control over the process the financiers would find it necessary to exert control over both city financing arrangements and city expenditures. Hence, they would find it necessary to control the budgetary processes of the city. This, in turn, would require formalized, legal authority.

An influential staff member of the FCLG was Jac Friedgut, the afore-mentioned Vice President for Municipal Securities at Citibank. In a Febru-ary 25, 1975, meeting of the FCLG, Friedgut circulated a memorandum in which he suggested that the city must institute a complete and rigid program of reducing city expenditures. Included in this memorandum (SEC, 1977, 1: 104) were suggestions that the city institute a

(1) review [of] . . . all City programs and . . . cutback in low priority items;
(2) freeze on jobs;
(3) joint effort [with] the business community to (secure) federal and State funds;
(4) increase [city worker's] productivity;
(5) [reduce] debt and an immediate termination of the issuance of debt for operating expenses.

These recommendations, if followed by the city, would require huge budget-ary cutbacks. These cutbacks would be necessitated by the reduction of operating funds due to the absence of funds acquired through the credit markets. In effect, Friedgut was suggesting that the city operate only on its revenues, without substantial credit. New York City had not accomplished this in a decade and such a program would seriously erode the quality of essential services.

February and March 1975 were very difficult for the city as its securities increasingly became more difficult to market. One such debt offering of Revenue Anticipation Notes (RANs) on March 13 was marketed only after bankers had secured a guarantee that certain New York State per-capita aid would be designated to retire the notes when they matured in three months.

This offering of RANs underscored the trouble that the city was having in marketing its securities. Before it would market these notes, the financial community *demanded* that the revenues to repay them be secure and identified. Only in the event of bankruptcy could there be a question about repayment. In an interview with me in January 1979, Jac Friedgut of Citibank and the FCLG emphasized the significance of the events that transpired during the negotiations and marketing of these notes: "What happened was we were offering investors, and Citibank ran that particular note-sale, a very short coupon (three months), a good rate, and much better security, and an identifiable source of repayment, than had ever been offered before . . . [Yet] they stayed away in droves. So the skelter came together in my mind on that Friday, the 14th [of March], was (a) that the city was in really big trouble and (b) whether or not they [the city] knew the reasons for investor's sense that the city was indeed in trouble." Only one-half of those notes were successfully marketed; the underwriting syndicate was left holding the remaining notes.

In a previous memorandum circulated on March 5, 1975 (SEC, 1977, Ch. 1: 134), Friedgut recommended that the city *"bite the bullet"* (emphasis mine) and institute a strict austerity policy under which the city would live within its means. In order to do this, he recommended reducing expenditures with a freeze on all labor costs, including wages and benefits, and an across-the-board reduction in city services. Still, Friedgut maintained that his recommendations were not to be conveyed to the Mayor to pressure him; rather, they would be communicated only if the Mayor asked for advice and specific recommendations. His "bite-the-bullet" memorandum was intended for William Spencer, President of Citibank, who was to meet with the Mayor. It can be surmised that Spencer communicated these recommendations to the Mayor. Friedgut maintained that "if the city recognized any of the depths of its troubles and the depth of investor suspicion of the city, and therefore did something very dramatic to show that they intended to get control of their finances," then investors might be willing to invest in city securities. Otherwise, the erosion of investor confidence would continue, as already evidenced by the unsuccessful March 13 sale of Revenue Anticipation Notes.

On March 17 Mayor Beame met with David Rockefeller, Ellmore Patterson, and William Spencer in a meeting whose function was to be kept from the public. The bankers wanted to convey the urgent and serious nature of the crisis, with the erosion of investor confidence, to the Mayor. Yet, they feared that

knowledge of the participants, purpose and the message of this meeting could trigger a real panic in the market for New York City securities and have a serious impact on markets, worldwide, because of the extensive ownership of the billions of dollars of New York City securities and especially because of the concentration of that ownership among the large New York City banks [SEC, 977, Ch. 1: 187].

At this meeting, the bankers told the Mayor that the traditional market sources of funds were no longer open to New York City. Nor could these banks, the Mayor was told, with one-quarter to one-fifth of their capital invested in city securities, afford to hold additional securities. Essentially, Mayor Beame was told that the city could no longer borrow from the municipal credit markets or the clearinghouse banks: the city's lifeline of funds to cover its operating expenses and to retire maturing debt had been closed. Before it would reopen, the bankers told the Mayor that the "confidence of the banks and the underwriters must be restored" (SEC, Ch. 1: 189).

The bankers were operating with information supplied to them by Jac Friedgut (Citibank) and Frank Smeal (Morgan Guaranty Trust). Friedgut confirmed, during our interview, that Beame was told that "the city was running out of gas and had to do something very dramatic" (interview with Jac Friedgut, January 4, 1979).

On Tuesday, March 18, Mr. Friedgut met with the New York City congressional delegation in Washington. Ed Koch, then a Congressman and now the Mayor of New York City, was the secretary of the delegation and had arranged the meeting. Friedgut described that meeting to me in these terms:

> I had been told that everything would be off-the-record and wouldn't be given to the press, and I spoke very frankly and candidly . . . I felt that sooner or later . . . that Washington had to be dragged in . . . and before they got Washington in . . . they should realize not only what is Washington's role, but what is New York City's role . . . I told them that the dimension of what has to be done on an annual basis is $500 to $800 million worth of budget balancing dollars; that this would involve biting the bullet on the city front and also having to go to Washington and getting some additional aid . . . As part of my presentation I said . . . that unless the city takes very drastic steps, the city's paper would be unsaleable at any price. Now we were talking about the . . . increase in the interest rates and how Beame had been very critical that the interest rates were so high. And I said it won't even be a question of price; it will be a question of availability. And that unless something dramatic is done, city paper would be unsaleable at any price.

These statements were leaked to the public and soon the city's securities were unmarketable at any price. Further exacerbating the erosion of confidence in city securities was the unloading of city securities by the major New York banks. At the same time that they were underwriting city securities and meeting with the city administration "to keep the market open," these banks were divesting themselves of their own holdings of city securities. Newfield and DuBrul (1977: 37) reported that "the big New York City banks, as well as major banks across the nation, quietly dumped approximately $2.3 billion in New York City securities on the market between the summer of 1974 and March, 975." The banks were involved in the dual role of underwriting and divesting of city securities. All the while they "advised" the city of possible measures to secure investor confidence in the stability of the city's finances. Yet, their actions could only lead to a glut in the municipal securities market which was already burdened by the enormous amount of city debt. They continued, however, to recommend that the city reduce expenditures for municipal workers and decrease the quality of services for the residents of New York City.

In April 1975 the city could not borrow to meet its expenses and found itself dependent upon New York State to provide the funds to escape bankruptcy. The price to be paid for this aid was a crisis budget and the eventual layoffs and/or attrition of approximately 67,000 jobs. The city's debt was now at $11 billion with $4.5 billion in short-term securities due to mature. For the first time, but not the last, the city was faced with the real possibility of bankruptcy.

There were not very many people in support of a city bankruptcy. The city government, its unions, and the banks all wanted to devise a miracle plan to prevent such an occurrence. The banks could not afford bankruptcy for they still held a large amount of city securities. The unions feared the consequences of bankruptcy just as much as any other party. For one thing, they were not sure of the sanctity of their contracts in such an event. They feared that a federal judge might abrogate the contracts and unilaterally force layoffs, lower wages, and increased productivity. Furthermore, a bankruptcy might lead to the destruction of union pensions. This led the unions into a no-strike position, as well as the commitment, made later on in the course of the crisis, to keep the city afloat with union pension money. The unions felt obliged to embark on a conservative course which would only lead to austerity on the one hand, and a reduction of the potential power of the city's labor movement on the other.

From the beginning of the fiscal crisis the city's unions felt it necessary to adopt a "pragmatic" approach. This pragmatism, or realism, accepted that the fiscal crisis was real and severe. Therefore, cutbacks in city expenditures were necessary, even at the expense of the city's workers. As one union leader stated in an interview with me, the unions were willing to make what they deemed to be necessary sacrifices "because those sacrifices had to be made. There was no getting away from it." And while there were discussions of more militant alternatives, such as strikes, sick-outs and slow-downs, the union leaders inevitably returned to a strategy guided by notions of pragmatism and responsibility, thereby extending their cooperation and their pension funds to the city.

The unions were trapped by their own ideology *and* by the layers of control that were being imposed upon them. Their own trade union philosophy, reformist though often militant, disallowed the development of concrete alternatives to austerity. They feared a general strike and its consequences more than they feared the layoffs and reduced wages and benefits that an austere budget would bring. A general strike might produce bankruptcy, leading to judicial intervention. This might cause the unions to lose the little control that they had over the situation, or so they felt. As union official Al Viani stated to me in the same interview cited above:

> What our approach essentially was from the very beginning was that we don't want unilateralism. We recognize the severity of the problem. Whatever is done, we want it done as a result of negotiations with the union. We don't want anything imposed upon us. We would cooperate because that was the only way that we could get some measure of control as to what was really going to happen. Had we taken a very hard line, bankruptcy would have given control to somebody else. There might have been legislation that took control away from us. So tactically we said we could take a hard line and maybe look good with the troops initially, in the short run; in the long run, if we don't have a say with what happens then we will really be out of the picture and they'll really just run right over us.

It was this fear that was guiding union strategy.

Still, union strategies were being channeled by superimposed layers of control over which they felt they had little control. A general strike seemed impractical to them, in part because they did not know who they were striking against. They felt a strike against the city would not directly force finance capital to reconsider its lack of support and reinvest in the city's securities. Furthermore, as the crisis continued to develop, a union strike would not only have to confront the city, but also New York State and the federal government.

In a very real sense, then, the unions were powerless to present an alternative to austerity because (1) they accepted austerity as a necessary evil, and (2) capital had already begun to organize government to enforce austerity (as will be explained in the next section). The unions, quite frankly, were unprepared to oppose the altered economic political conditions that austerity presented.

FISCAL CRISIS AND THE CORPORATE SECTOR

With the city facing near-bankruptcy, its only alternative was to seek financial assistance from both New York State and the federal government. The city recognized that it could not rely on the city's major banks for substantial assistance; that had been made clear by the banks' actions during the preceding months. Further exacerbating the problem, President Ford announced that the city would not be "bailed-out" with federal funds.

Bankruptcy did not seem to be a viable option to the city or its corporate sector. To avoid such a fate, some of New York's most powerful corporate executives began to devise a "rescue" plan. Richard Shinn, President of Metropolitan Life Insurance Company; Felix Rohatyn, a partner in the investment banking firm Lazard Freres and a director of ITT and six other major corporations; and Frank Smeal of Morgan Guaranty Trust purportedly arranged the structure and functions of the Municipal Assistance Corporation (MAC) on May 26, 1975. MAC formalized the power of the financial and corporate class over the city's long-range fiscal planning. Governor Carey's appointments to the nine-member MAC board included eight members with banking and brokerage connections. They were Felix Rohatyn; Simon Rifkind, a corporate lawyer and director of the Sterling National Bank; Robert Weaver, director of the Bowery Savings Bank and the Metropolitan Life Insurance Company; Thomas Flynn, a director of the Household Finance Corporation as well as trustee of the American Savings Bank; William Ellinghaus, President of the New York Telephone Company, director of Bankers Trust and a trustee of the Dime Savings Bank; John Coleman of Adler, Coleman and Company, a brokerage firm; Francis Barry, president of Campbell and Gardiner, a brokerage firm; and George Gould, chairman of Donaldson, Lufkin, Jenerette Securities. The only appointee without these connections was Donna Shalala, a professor at Columbia University and an expert on state financing. Yet, she, by her own admission in an interview with me, was not within the circle of decision-makers:

> During that period it was Felix Rohatyn and only Felix Rohatyn . . . It was a very small group of people [making-decisions]. MAC was usually represented by one person or by two at the most. Ellinghaus, when he was chairman, with Rohatyn. You didn't put all the MAC people into a room, with all the Mayor's people and all the Governor's people. So in a sense, while I knew

what was going on, and I certainly felt consulted, I didn't feel that I was a
central person in the negotiations [to refinance the city and institute an austerity plan].

It has already been shown that New York's major banks were deeply
implicated in the events which led up to the crisis. We saw that through the
FCLG finance capital was exerting its influence over city. Yet, with MAC,
the financial community began to exert more control, in a formalized,
legally authorized state board. One union leader described the power of the
banks at this point to me this way: "The banks were doing business all the
time. They [had been getting] 9½ interest . . . and they were cracking the
whip." The newest "whip" was to be the Municipal Assistance Corporation.

The staffing of MAC quite obviously demonstrated the power that the
financial and corporate factions of the capitalist class were able to exert at
this point. In a very real sense, their view of the crisis became the prevailing
ideology. The interests of the city were presented as parallel to capital's
interests. At the same time, those interests necessitated reductions in the
city's workforce, as well as reduced wages for those workers who remained.
Austerity was to be introduced even as MAC was to renegotiate the city's
short-term debt into long-term, state-guaranteed MAC bonds. In the process the city was to be saved from bankruptcy.

Donna Shalala revealed in our interview the Governor's concerns and the
financial community's power when she described how staffing decisions
were made:

> It was seen as a financing problem, and the Governor's first inclination was to
> find people who were politically acceptable but knew the substance [of the
> problem] . . . Remember, the problem was credibility with the financial com-
> munity and therefore he was urged to make a series of appointments that
> would be looked at by the financial community, as well as by the unions and
> other people, as respectable people; people who, even though they had some
> connections with the banking community didn't have a particular axe to grind
> or weren't antiunion particularly.

Regardless, the unions did not exert veto power over appointees. More
importantly, they were not consulted about the legislation creating MAC
until *after* it had been drafted. Ed Handman, public relations director of
District Council 37 of the American Federation of State, County and Municipal Employees, New York City's largest public employee union, described
the union's influence over the legislation to me as follows:

> The same thing was happening all the time: when a crisis came they had to run
> to the unions . . . so that we could solve the problem. And then anytime
> something new was happening they would do it themselves without asking the

unions [for assistance] . . . So the legislation [creating MAC]—they drafted that themselves. And one morning we were having a Municipal Labor Coalition meeting and we suddenly learned that they got the legislation ready to go and they hadn't even shown it to us. So we had a press conference and everybody was here waiting for it and the word got to the governor that we were angry—so they held it up. And we went . . . over the legislation. But basically it was the same and an example of a unilateral document. We made some minor changes at the moment. We were in a frustrating position. They would draft something without us [Ed Handman, interview, December 6, 1978].

The unions were constantly working with plans submitted by the banks. The MAC legislation was one such instance in which members of the corporate sector drafted legislation without prior consultation with the city's labor unions. Furthermore, the function of MAC itself served the interests of the financial community; it was intended to establish the security of investments in the city. MAC was authorized to market $3 billion of Municipal Assistance Corporation bonds. These bonds would be issued by MAC as an agency of New York State. It would have the credit backing of the state and not the city. The bonds would be retired upon maturity by a fund set aside and protected by law. The fund would consist of state taxes imposed on retail sales within the city, as well as a stock transfer tax. It was a financing instrument, controlled by finance and corporate capital.

On June 30, 1975, under pressure from both the state and federal governments, as well as the continuing pressure from the financial community, Mayor Beame unilaterally ordered a wage freeze applicable to the city's labor force. The unions, in a meeting at the Americana Hotel one month later, capitulated to these demands and signed an agreement deferring a portion of their wages. The bankers' demands for a reduction in labor costs were being met. Still, there was no rush by investors to show confidence in a city moving through the initial stages of austerity.

On July 10 MAC began marketing its first series of long-term bonds. It was a $1 billion issue, with a high interest rate of 9.25%, tax free. Nevertheless, only $550 million of this was successfully marketed to the public, despite an "A" rating from the municipal bond rating agencies. The underwriting banks and brokerage houses were forced to absorb the remaining $450 million.

It was clear that investors were demanding more austerity before they would express their confidence in the city. The prominent banking and corporate appointees to MAC were not enough to inspire confidence in MAC; it had been too closely identified with New York City. Despite the security of separate funds and the status of a New York State agency, investors refused to commit their capital to MAC bonds.

On July 17 a group of bankers led by David Rockefeller, Chairman of Chase, Frank Smeal, Executive Vice President of Morgan Guaranty Trust, and Walter Wriston, Chairman of Citibank, met with the MAC board to propose the direction that the city must take. At this meeting the bankers asserted that the MAC board must take more control over the city's finances and budget. Furthermore, they suggested an end to free tuition at the City University of New York, a raise in the transit fare, a wage freeze, further reductions in the size of the city's labor force, and deeper service cutbacks. In addition, the bankers questioned the ability of the mayor to take the "dramatic" steps necessary and urged a fiscal program be implemented and monitored by an outside agency or control board. They were suggesting that it was necessary for a nonelected control board to administer the city. According to Newfield and Du Brul (1977: 184-188), Mayor Beame was then advised by MAC that further and much more drastic austerity measures were necessary.

By August it was apparent that MAC was not able to perform its function. The investment community was "on strike," denying the city funding even through a state agency such as MAC. The corporate sector, and especially the city's banks, were pressing for a stronger, more powerful control board. In September, the Emergency Financial Control Board (EFCB) was created. This board had the power to

> (i) review, control and supervise the financial management of the city, (ii) . . . approve . . . a plan that will provide the basis for a return of the city to sound financial condition, (iii) control . . . the disbursement of city funds, under which debt service requirements will be met as a first priority, (iv) review and audit city operations . . . to assure that sound management practices are observed or restored [New York State Financial Act, 1975: 2].

It was, in all respects, a formal and legally authorized austerity board, Most importantly, its function was mandated by law and it was able to institute austerity regardless of any potential resistance from the city's unions, workers, or residents. It had been isolated from potential popular movements against austerity.

Serving on the EFCB were Governor Carey, Mayor Beame, State Comptroller Levitt, City Comptroller Goldin, and three members of the corporate sector: Felix Rohatyn, William Ellinghaus, both members of MAC, and David Margolis of Colt Industries.

The most powerful member of the EFCB was Felix Rohatyn. By this time Felix Rohatyn had become the major decision-maker in plans to introduce austerity. He devised and approved financing plans; he smoothed over any rough spots with both the banks and the unions. "He had the power of his prestige [originating from the corporate sector]; tremendous power because of his prestige and visibility in this situation. He was simply trusted by a large number of people that were involved in the process and therefore I think he had enormous power during this period. And he in fact shaped the financial settlements" (Donna Shalala, interview). Indeed, this wizard of the corporate world was setting the fiscal policy of the city, though within the constraints set by the deteriorating position of New York City in the credit markets. Still, with all his prestige and power he could not successfully market MAC bonds without the establishment of the EFCB.

The function of the EFCB was to institute tight control over the city and its policies, and to force austerity in the form of control over expenditures and finances. To this end, the EFCB asserted its authority over *all* major contracts that the city entered into—including and especially the city's contracts with its labor unions. Consequently, the board began to force, within the context of a new three-year plan, layoffs, attrition, and a general reduction in city services. This action, it was thought, would reassure investors that the city would reform its profligate ways. Jac Friedgut explained the control board's function to me this way: "the only way that people will buy MAC bonds will be if you make it very clear that the state is not only borrowing on behalf of the city, but that it's also clamping down on the city and getting the city back into line." And that meant getting the city's labor unions back into line.

The city still had difficulty marketing its obligations and paying for its reduced services. In November 1975 President Ford reacted to the city's austerity program and approved a $2.3 billion seasonal loan program. Still, the city needed a continuous flow of capital invested in either MAC or city notes and bonds. The banks refused to bankroll the city while it was in its precarious and "risky" fiscal condition. A source of funds would have to be found and soon.

This source ended up being the city's labor unions. Pension funds would be diverted from other investments into city and MAC bonds and notes. William Scott, former third Deputy Comptroller of the city, told me that the plan to use the pension funds was devised by

> Steven Clifford, who was a deputy to the City Comptroller. He worked out what is today the financing system. And he showed it to the Comptroller . . . [who later showed it to] Felix Rohatyn and George Gould. And the plan was presented to them that morning. And it showed how each month's capital needs were going to be met, the expense budget, all the rest was laid out and it required that each month so much money was to be coming from the pension

funds . . . It was all worked out entirely without the unions. The unions didn't enter into [the planning process].

Subsequently, the unions were informed of the plan and acquiesced. One labor leader, however, refused to commit pension money to the city. Albert Shanker, President of the United Federation of Teachers, did not have the authority to commit these funds; that was up to the union members who had been elected trustees by their fellow union members. And they had refused. The trustees then came under intense pressure as the city moved closer to default. The Mayor, Governor, Felix Rohatyn, and George Gould all attempted to pressure the trustees into the commitment. They were brought to the Governor's office and were guaranteed that they would not be personally liable for any penalties that might arise from their investing in risky securities. Rohatyn and Gould personally visited during the meeting and tried to convince the trustees that the investment was indeed prudent. Finally, after relentless pressure, the trustees committed the teachers' pension funds.

The significance of these investments should not be underestimated. By investing their pensions, the city's unions committed their members' futures to the fiscal stability of the city. Furthermore, the investment tied the unions to the three-year austerity plan, thereby taking away from union strategy any action which might force the city into resisting austerity. A general strike or huge wage increases might endanger union investments. The unions had been pushed into being both the city's creditors and its workers' representatives, a position which could only compromise its potential militance. So it was that the unions found themselves funding an austerity program which was hurting their membership.

Within this strategy, Felix Rohatyn and his colleagues had integrated a potentially antagonistic union coalition into the structure of austerity. Yet, it was done in such a way that the unions would not be able to exert the power that investors often do. The unions' potential power had already been constrained by the EFCB and its legally authorized and mandated program of controlling, while reducing, the city's finances and expenditures. In such a way, the unions' opposition to austerity was pacified. Ed Handman summarized the lack of union power to me in this way:

> Union power is highly exaggerated. The union's power is on certain levels; it exists. The union has a certain subjective power. There's a power when you have influence on politicians . . . There's a power when you have influence on politicians . . . There's power that comes from people who think that if they do something to hurt you you're going to pull the whole city out on strike . . . On the other hand, we don't really have power . . . Our power in this case came from the threat of bankruptcy and the threat of chaos."

But this threat had been resolved and the method through which it was resolved reduced the potential of the unions as a counterforce to austerity.

CONCLUSION

In our analysis of the fiscal crisis we have been able to reveal the methods through which New York City's government was transformed by capital to mediate a severe economic and political crisis. The methods involved finance capital's withholding financing from the city, the development and staffing of both a New York State control board (the Emergency Financial Control Board) and a state financing corporation (the Municipal Assistance Corporation), as well as establishing the social constraints to inhibit labor resistance as austerity was instituted. It is clear that those who developed and initiated this structure of austerity were powerful members of the capitalist class and represented various factions of finance and corporate capital operant in New York. These influential members of the capitalist class developed the instruments through which austerity was adopted, instituted, and enforced.

During crises periods power structures become visible. New methods to mediate crises must be developed to replace or reform the old. This often involves transforming the mechanisms of government. So it was in this case that New York City's government, ineffectual in its response to capital's needs and demands, was superseded and thereby transformed by governing bodies developed at capital's behest.

In this case austerity was introduced with very little resistance. Workers lost their jobs; poor people saw the already low quality of their health care decline with the closing of medical facilities; students at the City University payed increased tuition for larger-sized classes, or they dropped out for lack of tuition funds; day-care centers were closed, thereby forcing many of the city's working poor to quit their jobs and return to welfare dependency; and the infrastructure of the city—its roads, bridges, and tunnels—continued to erode. All of this was justified by the ideologies of scarcity and equal sacrifice to the community.

Yet, New York's working class and poor were forced to sacrifice disproportionately; its capitalist class actually benefited from austerity. There was a redirection of tax benefits and city and state funds to improve business conditions and lower the costs of doing business in New York, as well as generously high interest rates from Municipal Assistance Corporation bonds. Furthermore, capital's shaky investments in city securities were saved from possible bankruptcy proceedings in which investors might have lost some of their investment. Certainly, there was not an equality of sacrifice. Indeed, the extent of sacrifice was determined by the class basis and function of austerity. Austerity was instituted by capital, for capital. It was introduced at the expense of the city's workers, poor people, and its working- and middle-class residents; without their approval or control.

Austerity was further justified by an ideology of scarcity. In this case, New Yorkers were told there was a scarcity of investment money coming to the city. Yet, this scarcity was the result of deliberate decisions by investors and financiers, and especially New York's major banks, to withhold funds until their needs were met by a redirection of government priorities. There was no absolute scarcity of investment money; rather, it was redirected to more profitable ventures. The banks had lost a great deal of money in real estate ventures that could be written off against other profits on tax reports, and no longer needed the tax-free securities that the city offered. Finance and corporate capital were warning that they would not allow government the option of meeting the needs of its working class.

This case study tells us much about the functioning of government and the actual structure of power in a capitalist society in crisis. The continuing political-economic crisis has caused the capitalist class to devise new strategies of control and mediation. Keynesian policy has been reformulated so that capital may be served by budgets based on austerity. The formerly expanding budgets of the welfare state have been slashed and redirected to bolster a mode of production in perpetual crisis.

In the process, austerity has become the basis of a new class politics. It has become the ideological and political formula for the reassertion of power by the capitalist class, as well as for the restructuring of the capitalist state. Through austerity the class function of the capitalist state becomes more recognizable as the rationality of capital is asserted over the human needs of the working class and the poor.

REFERENCES

ARONOWITZ, S. (1973) False Promises. New York: McGraw-Hill.

Bankers Trust Internal Report (1974) in Securities and Exchange Commission Staff Report on Transactions in Securities of the City of New York. Committee on Banking, Finance, and Urban Affairs. Washington, DC.

BOK, D.C. and J.T. DUNLOP (1970 Labor and the American Community. New York: Simon & Schuster.

Congressional Budget Office (1977) "New York City's fiscal problem," in David Mermelstein and Roger Alcaly (eds.) The Fiscal Crisis of American Cities. New York: Vintage.

DEMAC, D. and P. MATTERA (1977) "Developing and underdeveloping New York." Zero-work: Political Materials 2: 113-139.

DI TOMASO, N. (1978) "Public employee unions and the urban fiscal crisis." Insurgent Sociologist 8: 2-3.

Eighth Interim Report to the Mayor by the Temporary Commission on City Finances (1976) "An historical and comparative analysis of expenditures in the City of New York: expenditure by object."

Fiscal Observer (1978) Vol. 2, Nos. 12 and 13, June 15.

FRIEDGUT, J. (1977) "Perspectives on New York City's fiscal crisis: the role of the banks." City Almanac 12, 1 (June).

GOERING, J. and E. LICHTEN (forthcoming) in Scott McNall (ed.) Political Economy: A Critique of American Society. New York: Holt, Rinehart and Winston.

HABERMAS, J. (1973) Legitimation Crisis. Boston: Beacon.

MERMELSTEIN, D. and R. ALCALY (977) The Fiscal Crisis of American Cities. New York: Vintage.

New York State Financial Emergency Act for the City of New York (1975). September 9.

NEWFIELD, J. and P. DU BRUL (977) The Abuse of Power: The Permanent Government and the Fall of New York. New York: Viking.

Ninth Interim Report of the Temporary Commission on New York Finances (1976) "The effects of taxation on manufacturing in New York City." December.

O'CONNOR, J. (1973) The Fiscal Crisis of the State. New York: St. Martin's.

OFFE, C. (1973) "The abolition of market control and the problem of legitimacy." Kapitalistate 1 and 2.

——— (1972) "Advanced capitalism and the welfare state." Politics and Society 2, 4.

PIVEN, F. F. and R. A. CLOWARD (1977) "The urban crisis as an arena for class mobilization." Radical America 11, 1: 3-8.

——— (1975) The Politics of Turmoil: Poverty, Race and the Urban Crisis. New York: Vintage.

——— (1971) Regulating the Poor: The functions of Public Welfare. New York: Vintage.

Program Planners, Inc. (1977) "New York City municipal labor coalition presentation to Honorable William Proxmire." December.

——— (1976) "An analysis of employee compensation levels." June.

Securities and Exchange Commission (1977) Report on Transactions in Securities of the City of New York. Committee on Banking, Finance, and Urban Affairs. Washington, DC: U.S. Government Printing Office.

Seven Days (1977) April 11.

SHANKER, I. (1977) "Urban experts advise, castigate, and console the city on its problems," in David Mermelstein and Roger Alcaly (eds.) The Fiscal Crisis of American Cities. New York: Vingage.

TABB, W. K. (1978) "The New York City fiscal crisis," in William K. Tabb and Larry Sawers (eds.) Marxism and the Metropolis. New York: Oxford Univ. Press.

WYNDHAM, R. (1975) "Going broke the New York way." Fortune (August): 44-24.

7

THINK TANKS AND CAPITALIST POLICY

Irvine Alpert and Ann Markusen

INTRODUCTION

In this chapter, we undertake an analysis of two public policy institutions: Brookings and Resources for the Future. It is our view that these organizations perform a brokerage function between private capital and the state. We characterize their operations as a production process in which the product is policy, ideology, and plans (PIP). Historically, we show that corporate leaders established these institutions as somewhat "independent" agencies in response to the changing nature of capitalism and the state. We examine in detail the internal operation of the production process: market research, product testing, organization or production including labor inputs and technology, marketing and sales effort, price and income of the PIP product. Our analysis underscores the central role of a professional-managerial class. We hypothesize that the motivation and consciousness of this group facilitates the smooth operation of RFF and Brookings, and endows their

AUTHORS' NOTE: We would like to thank the Washington, DC Kapitalistate Collective, especially Heidi Hartmann, and Dan Feshbach; and Roger Montgomery, Bill Domhoff, Deborah Lubeck, Paul Lubeck, Bob Alford, Dudley Burton, Allan Zabel, and Anatole Anton for their critical support. We are particularly grateful to many individuals at both Resources for the Future and the Brookings Institution for their time and conversation. We thank Brookings, which provided office space to Markusen, and the University of California, which supplied financial aid to Alpert.

product with a certain degree of independence. However, the contradiction between internalized recognition of political "reality" and the claim to independence occasionally produces conflict.

The explicit characterization of PIP production as a material and ideological process contributes to the debate between structuralist and instrumentalist views of the state. The instrumentalist view focuses on how capitalist class and corporate interests influence the inputs into state policy formation; the structuralist view focuses on how policy output supports capitalist institutions (Esping-Anderson et al., 1976). Our work bridges this gap by examining one segment of the policy production process, in which the material base of professionals is central. Professionals operating with an entrepreneurial consciousness transform private sector and state requirements into apparently independent policy plans and justification. This process is a part of the entire machinery for propagating what Gramsci calls the ideological hegemony of capitalism (Hirsch, 1975: 79): "The philosophy of the ruling class passes through a whole tissue of complex vulgarization to emerge as common sense." We also contend that these particular institutions play a role in unifying a system-supporting position on various issues before the state that transcends particularistic private sector or bureaucratic interests.

Our method is that of participant observation. We were fortunate to experience both major postures—the unknown and the known observer. Markusen joined Brookings as an Economic Policy Fellow before deciding to analyze the function of the professionals within it. Her interest arose directly from conflicts experienced over her own policy work and is as much a self-analysis as a view of other professionals. Alpert introduced himself as a researcher, explicitly interested in the history and operation of RFF.

Our positions in and exposure to both agencies satisfy the criteria laid out by Lofland (1971) as features of good participant observation: physical and social intimacy with the observed, truthfulness, significant descriptive results, and direct quotation. However, since we hold a class-conflict view of American social reality, we expect that our analysis might be challenged by some members of the institutions under scrutiny. This is a standard problem in the analysis of organizational patterns, as Lofland (1971) also notes. The comprehensive portrait drawn by the researcher is not like the one held by members of the institution and may be seen as unflattering to its public image. This is particularly apt in the case of Brookings and RFF, whose public image is in large part what they sell.

THE "INDEPENDENT" PRODUCTION OF POLICY, IDEOLOGY, AND PLANS

For our purposes, we define a particular set of institutions in the capitalist economy as "independent producers of planning and ideology." These include policy analysis groups like Brookings and RFF, as well as universities and the press. While the lines cannot be drawn absolutely, we distinguish these elements because they claim an independence from private capital and state manipulation and because their product is information, plans, and justifications, rather than commodities or other services. In defining this "independent" sector, we exclude for-profit consulting firms such as Arthur D. Little, Mitre Corporation, and Booz-Allen from the present analysis, even though they sell their ideological product to both corporate and state sectors. While on rare occasions "for-profit" and "independent" institutions collaborate, their images and functions are quite separate. We also exclude ideology production carried out directly by the state and corporate sectors for their own internal use—e.g., corporate R & D and government agency research reports—because they are directly under the control of those sectors. We argue that those organizations frequently use the ideology and policy plans that are produced by the "independent" producers.

By plans we mean those ideas and suggestions that encompass the entire array of policy formulation, change in governmental structure and behavior, and definition of researchable problems. Planning is a deliberate attempt to manipulate the future of society, especially through state intervention. Planning is preoccupied with economic questions, including social displacement through economic forces and reproduction of the labor force. Capitalism requires planning because of the instability and periodic crises produced by the sum of private decisions regarding production activity, decisions based on profit motives. It is our hypothesis that the emergence of "independent" groups like Brookings doing planning at the national level is a uniquely American phenomenon. In Europe, capitalist nations have generally lodged planning functions directly within the state sector. Cohen (1977) documents the evolution of French planning. The governments of Scandinavia and the Netherlands are well known for their extensive economic planning. In the United States state planning has been retarded by the ferocity of anti-big government sentiment and the successful constitutional attacks on the most explicit centralized planning agencies of the New Deal. When state economic planning was once again proposed in the early 1970s, as a response to the breakdown of Keynesian methods of indirect manipulation of the economy, it met similar resistance (Cohen, 1977: xii-xvi). The new call was issued by people (e.g., Herbert Stein) long associated with "independent" planning institutions, supporting our view that planning has simply been detoured into this associated sector.

By ideology we mean both forms distinguished by Mannheim (1952: 49-62). At the paradigmatic level (Mannheim's total conception), ideology takes shape with the evolution of capitalist economic and political institutions and becomes embedded in the analytical methods used in the planning process. Thus notions like individual preference, the productivity of capital, the public interest, and the market are ideological constructs which imbue the work of planning institutions. Such concepts are generally produced and polished in academia, and incorporated by professionals through graduate school training. They are not grounds for argument or reformulation within the planning process. However, extensions and applications of the general ideology are produced in these institutions, which are ideally situated to sense private sector needs (through forums described below) and to respond with a new twist consistent with state structure and process. Thus a large part of the product of these institutions is purely ideological: justifications for existing conditions (e.g., high unemployment is due to more women and children entering the labor market) and justifications for certain policy approaches (e.g., incentives for pollution control are more efficient than government controls). These ideological formulations are subject to a good deal of internal debate and hammering out, corresponding to Mannheim's definition of the particular conception of ideology.

We contrast the "independent" production of ideology with the production of commodities for profit in the private sector and for use in the state sectors. We are not suggesting that this sector, which is in fact quite small in terms of employment or percentage of GNP, is a coequal of the state and corporate sectors, but that it is different and plays a unique role between the other two. It is a growing sector, which needs further analysis.

The aura of institutional independence which we believe is the chief distinguishing characteristic of this sector is secured through various arrangements. First, the income to such institutions (i.e., the exchange value of their ideological product) is not paid directly from the corporate coffers nor from the state treasury. It is received through a series of mediating institutions, which act as the immediate buyers of the ideology: NSF and similar government-funded granting agencies, the Ford Foundation and similar private foundations, or endowments with Board of Trustees oversight. This diffuse financial support is not the result of government or business withholding of funds. On the contrary, internal codes of conduct in each institution prohibit them from accepting extensive and readily available support from those sectors. For instance, Brookings has long had an internal rule which prevents government-sponsored research from its annual budget:

> To safeguard the Institution's independence, revenue from government grants and contracts has not been allowed to exceed 15% of total operating revenue in recent years [Brookings, 1976: 31].

Secondly, the independent image of these ideological producers is promulgated by the high degree of professional participation in the management and production process of the institution. As we will suggest below, the class position of professionals requires that they adamantly assert their independence, regardless of their objective role. This ideology of the ideology producers, as we have called it, enables the institutions named above to appear as independent, objective servants of the public interest.

THE HISTORICAL ROOTS

It is our hypothesis that such "independent" ideological producers were consciously set up by certain members of the capitalist class, with state complicity.

In 1927 the Brookings Institution was formed by combining three young PIP-type organizations: the Robert Brookings Graduate School of Economics and Government, the Institute of Government Research, and the Institute of Economics. The fledgling organization was funded by the Carnegie, Rockefeller, and George Eastman foundations, as well as the Brookings' family wealth. Then, as now, the trustees were drawn from elites in business, education, and law. As Domhoff documents through network analysis in his book, *The Higher Circles* (1970), Brookings and other "think tanks" were set up by members of the ruling class or their agents in order to deal with issues affecting the relations between the private sector and the burgeoning state sector.

By the post-World War I period, large and powerful monopoly corporations had become dominant economic institutions. At the same time the state sector was growing rapidly as economic bigness and distortions threatened stability. In 1921, the federal budget process was established, confirming that the state sector had become a permanent and significant actor in the economy. A major function of Brookings was to analyze the annual budgetary process, attempting to ensure that the corporate sector's needs were met. Brookings members have a long history of participating in corporate and state sector activities in many forms ranging from informal advising to top-level posts.

In 1951 President Truman appointed CBS chairman William Paley to head a President's Materials Policy Commission (PMPC). The purpose of the committee was to examine the rate and use of natural resources and determine their adequacy for corporate growth. Although its findings were deemed important by the business and popular press, Paley felt that there was a need for a full-time, nongovernment research group to carry on the work begun by the commission. The Ford Foundation was also convinced that there was an urgent need for such an organization. As early as 1949, Ford staff members were suggesting that the "resource problem" needed attention. By 1951 Ford was actively searching for an organization or institute which would focus upon resource allocation and use rate from a social science policy perspective.

In 1952 Paley established Resources for the Future to continue the work undertaken by the PMPC. Within a few weeks of its creation, the new organization became the instrument for a natural resources program that had been developed under the aegis of the Ford Foundation by a group of which Mr. Paley was a member. Subsequently, Paley and Chester Davis, a Ford representative, were able to assemble a board of directors and organize an initial program.

The major problems facing the original staff and directors of RFF concerned resource sufficiency for the growing international competition between capitalist and socialist spheres. In an era when growth was of paramount importance, many corporate and state sector leaders realized the need for a planned environment where all factors of production, including resources, could be accounted for in purely economic terms. The Paley Commission laid the groundwork, but it was the responsibility of the original RFF staff to legitimate what was to become an entirely new way of dealing with natural resources (Wolanin, 1975: 148).

The establishment of separate policy research groups provided a solution to problems of legitimacy that plagued previous in-house efforts. As multinational corporations came to dominate the economic order, new means of legitimating the order were required. Neither industry nor government research and education efforts could rid themselves of public suspicion—of profit-making motives in the first case and of big-brother megalomania or pandering to vested interests in the second. Since it is clear that producers of ideology do not directly produce surplus value, but are funded out of profits made elsewhere (and thus must support exploitation) the link tends to become obscured, rendering the ideology more powerful.

THE PRODUCTION PROCESS

The production of ideology and policy plans can be conceptualized as analogous to the production of commodities for exchange. The point of this exercise is to distinguish, from a Marxist point of view, the difference between ideological production and commodity production under capitalism. This distinction is critical because the nature of the ideological production process obscures the hegemonic role of capital in the state. We use the same categories used in an economic or Marxist approach. This comparison is outlined in Table 7.1. Briefly, institutions like Brookings and RFF organize inputs and employ various technologies to produce an output: policy, ideology, or plan. The output is exchanged for receipts which are in turn used to pay off the costs of factor inputs. Using specific examples from both Brookings and RFF, we describe this process as follows.

The product of a nonprofit public policy organization is ideology and suggestions for policy. It is not policy as such. Public policy is decided upon by the actors in the state sector, in response to class conflict, bureaucratic interest, interest group demand, and the need for managing the entire complex socioeconomic system under modern capitalism. We distinguish several needs in the state and private sectors which these products address. First, in some cases previous state actions or policies have failed to solve a problem. Confusion over which course to pursue may result from bureaucratic inability or unwillingness to see the whole. In such cases, think tanks may be in an ideal position to survey both private and public sector "needs" and arrive at some suggestion which may temporarily resolve the impasse. For instance, RFF pioneered the economistic method of viewing the country's resources in terms of exchange rather than use value. As Hans Landsberg (1964: 4), an RFF fellow, says, "Physical barriers are more a philosophical concept than a practical barrier. In recent years, especially since the pioneering report of the President's material policy commission [RFF's predecessor in the early 1950s], scarcity has been thought of in terms of cost rather than physically running out." This policy emphasis undermined the conservation movement's critique of economic growth. It values resources in terms of their growth performance, not their intrinsic value.

Conflicts between bureaucratic vested interests and system requirements constitute another source of demand for think tank products. Bureaus for regulation of particular industries or for legitimation may develop historically into vested interest groups within the state which have a stake in maintenance of expensive programs long after their need. A new administration or congressional coalition may require a more rational policy approach

Table 7.1 Capitalist Commodity Production and Ideology Production

	Inputs	Production Technology	Motivation	Market Research and Product Test	Output	Price	Income
Commodity production	Land Labor Capital	Motor power cybernetics, etc.	Profit Wages Rent	R and D, PR, Advertising Sales Op	Commodities and Services	Determined by demand and by cost of production plus normal rate of return	Sales Receipts
Ideology production	Labor: Professionals Nonprofessionals Materials: library Machines: computers	Social science paradigms Technical language and mathematics Computers and data	Income Status Name	Seminars, lectures Interlocks, Conferences, Informal conversants Manuscript circulation Round table Trade journals	PIP: policy plans; books testimony conference rationalizations Name: for institution for professionals	Determined by the degree of independence that the agency can muster and, by usefulness of the particular item	Grants Endowment Book sales Consulting fees

to attack such bureaus. An example is the formulation by RFF and Brookings jointly of the incentives approach to pollution control. In *Pollution, Prices and Public Policy* (1975), Allan Kneese and Charles Schultze argue that we should rely upon market-like tax signals to producers rather than employ regulatory standards under threat of fines or closure. Carter's administration is pursuing such incentive schemes. This policy suggestion/ ideology aims to defeat, discipline, or prevent from expanding entrenched bureaucracies like EPA and OSHA, which impose expensive requirements on the private sector and require large amounts of public funds to administer.

Another instance is the policy analysis that serves only to justify, or legitimate, state actions or the status quo. For instance, the book *Equity and Efficiency: The Big Trade-Off* (1975), by Arthur Okun, provides a conceptual framework for viewing all state actions as movements toward either equality or efficiency. Relying on a vulnerable set of assumptions from welfare theory, the argument assumes that we cannot have both, and it is used time after time by policy-makers arguing for capital subsidies and against welfare programs. This book is also used extensively in introductory economic courses.

We do not intend to suggest here that each policy suggestion or ideological formulation is immediately transformed into state policy. But such products do shape the nature of the public debate, in the press and universities as well as in government circles. Theodore Ynetrna, in a response to critics, · said of Committee for Economic Development output:

> We are often asked how we know that trying to adhere to these standards pays off. This is a legitimate question. However it is sometimes asked in a way that seems to call for an illegitimate answer. We are expected to show that what we recommended in January is done in June. There are some cases like this, but they are not usually significant. Almost always if what we recommended in January is done in June, there is a strong possibility that it would have been done anyway. The more significant test is whether there has been a *gradual shift* in the *climate of public opinion* in which public policy is made, as a result of national discussion and debate in which CED has actively participated [Schriftgiesser, 1967: 48].

This statement underscores the conscious production of ideology by such groups.

PIP is produced as a product for exchange and will find purchasers if it is useful in rationalizing or legitimizing the system. The product in the case of these particular institutions, however, is not simply PIP, but an accompanying aura of quality because it is the product of "independent" institutions. Thus the by-product of the production process is the good name, both of the institution, and of the individuals whose names are associated with it. This by-product is inseparable from the product itself, since a particular justification (e.g., current high unemployment is due to large numbers of youth and women entering the labor force) is more prestigious if it issues forth from Brookings than if it is promulgated by the *Wall Street Journal* or the National Association of Manufacturers. From the producer's point of view, this by-product can simultaneously be accumulated as "goodwill" for the institution and as "human capital" for the individuals involved, two notions from conventional economics that are not inappropriate.

Therefore, the product of these agencies appears to vary widely in its political tone. Some policy ideas or books will advance liberal solutions, concentrating on expanding the legitimation functions of the state, such as welfare. For instance, Henry Aaron's book *Shelter and Subsidies: Who Benefits from Federal Housing Policies* (1972), documents the subsidization of upper- and middle-income groups at the expense of lower-income groups. Other pieces may concentrate on subsidies to capital; *Capital Needs in the Seventies* (1975), by Barry Bosworth et al., explores the best ways of promoting capital accumulation through government policy. Sometimes, these institutions even publish studies that run contrary to their established position on a particular issue. For instance, RFF published a study on the liquid metal fast breeder reactor which attacked the economic and ecological viability of this technology, despite RFF's general support for the breeder reactor. In other instances, however, studies have been suppressed. These incidents are not very common, for reasons explored below: the screening of hirees and the motivations of professionals.

The product of PIP institutions is packaged in books, testimony, advice, and conferences. For example, Resources for the Future has published numerous books and reports which had sold more than half a million copies by 1976 and are widely used in colleges and universities. Brookings's conferences for leaders in the private sector involved 1,700 executives in one-week seminars from 1970 to 1976. Brookings also sold 1,029,817 books from 1972 to 1976 (Brookings, 1976: 16-18).

Perhaps even more importantly, the embodied skills engendered during a stay at the institution can be sold or loaned to other sectors for long periods of time, an exchange of human capital which enriches both the institution and the recipient agency or corporation. For instance, one Brookings staffer spent several months at NBC managing the political content of David Frost's interviews with Nixon, another wrote the Republican party platform in 1976, one became head of the Council of Economic Advisors, and another an Assistant Secretary of Health, Education, and Welfare.

The product of these institutions is not simply justifications and rationale for individual policies or economic realities, but an overall attitude that pluralism is in fact the appropriate paradigm for analyzing the American socioeconomic process. Thus a major result of their work is to divert attention from conflictual situations and replace the consciousness of conflict with a vision of cooperation, compromise, and solution.

MARKET RESEARCH, PRODUCT TESTING, MARKETING, AND SALES

The PIP process includes market research and product testing that must precede and shape the decisions about what product to produce, and the marketing and sales efforts that accompany the exchange process. The same activities, in this case, perform both market research and marketing functions. In this stage, signals emerge that identify the major problems/policies which capital and state need to address/legitimize. The needs are sometimes easy to spot in conflict or social chaos (e.g., current immigration policy being reviewed by Brookings). Other needs are less apparent (e.g., sophisticated empirical techniques or environmental measurements worked on at RFF). In the case of Brookings and RFF, this process occurs in an elaborate set of activities which bring representatives of capital, the state, and staffers of these institutions together in both formal and informal settings where mainly *verbal* exchanges hammer out the prevailing attitudes. At Brookings, these are organized under the rubric of "The Advanced Study Program":

> Since the program's inception in 1959, we have conducted some 1,300 educational programs in which more than 61,000 leaders in public and private life have examined public policy questions in an atmosphere that stimulates a free' exchange of views with visiting specialists. Since 1970 the program has drawn an average of 3,800 participants a year from the senior executive levels in government, business, labor unions, civic groups, and the professions. In addition to regularly scheduled programs, special seminars have been held for members of Congress, religious leaders, editors, lawyers, physicians, foundation officials, psychologists, psychiatrists, educators, and other professionals [Brookings, 1976: 18].

The bulk of these forums are aimed at "senior government officials" and "leaders in the private sector."

These events provide a service to participants. They are important forums for unifying the capitalist class perspective on state policy and transmitting that to state policy-makers. The institution uses the events to expose its staff members to the business communities' and bureaucrats' perception of current conflicts and to their reactions to various proposed solutions. Such roundtable discussions, seminars, informal lunches, conferences, and lectures consume a large part of staff members' time. In addition to these in-house activities, individual members of the staffs of both organizations research their market and market their research in a variety of forums outside of the institution. They consult, attend seminars, testify at hearings, give speeches, lecture at universities, advise government agencies, and serve on international advisory commissions. Staff members also read the trade journals, business magazines, and competitors' publications in order to discern the salient positions and the nuances of acceptable ideology. They read, write for, and edit trade and professional journals. A not uncommon example is Sam Schurr, Codirector and Senior Staff Fellow of the Energy and Materials Division of RFF, whose annual activities are listed as follows in the Annual Report:

> Sam H. Schurr Member, Synthesis Panel of the National Academy of Sciences Committee on Nuclear and Alternative Energy Systems; member, the International Institute for Applied Systems Analysis Subcommittee on Energy Systems of the National Academy; completed assignment with the Federal Power Commission Technical Advisory Committee on the Impact of Inadequate Electric Power Supply; member, editorial board of *Energy Policy;* member, editorial advisory board of *Energy Systems and Policy;* associate editor of *Energy–The International Journal;* at the invitation of the Department of State, lectured on "Energy and Economic Growth" in Munich, Germany, to an invited audience from the Max Planck Institute for Future Development and the University of Munich Institute of International Economics, and in Cologne, Germany, at the Energy Economics Institute of the University of Cologne; met with leaders of the Italian energy industry in Rome; consulted with members of the Swedish Secretariat for Future Studies Group on Energy and Society in Stockholm; participated in the International Symposium on New Problems of Advanced Societies at the Hamburg Economic Research Institute; gave paper (with Joel Darmstadter), (another RFF staff member), "Some Observations on Energy and Economic Growth," to the Seminar on Perspectives on Energy and Growth at the Aspen Institute for Humanistic Studies in Colorado [1976: 89-90].

In addition to the methods described above, the institutions also use circulation of drafts and manuscripts, pilot articles in trade journals, and informal conversations to test their product. Particularly important in product testing are the internal conversations that staff members have with each other, documented in a later section of this chapter. Occasional changes have been made in manuscripts that are displeasing to clients. The process of rendering individual work palatable to clients is quite sensitive, since it transgresses the institutional ideology of independence. In the rare case where it is necessary, an individual's work is censured by management, which arbitrates between the client and the producer. The infrequency of censorship reflects the success of the hiring and promotion system in weeding out recalcitrant or insurgent analysis.

Marketing activities are increasing in this current period of financial change. Recently, when RFF hired University of California Ex-Chancellor Charles Hitch they also employed a new "Information Officer and Assistant to the President," Kent Price (Hitch's former associate from UC), whose explicit job is to market the output of RFF. This consists of arranging meetings, publicizing books, scheduling news conferences, and other public relations work. Price is also searching for alternative sources of institutional finance.

Market research and product testing are dramatically one-sided. There is literally never any systematic consultation with recipients of social policy or the anonymous collective constantly referred to as "the public interest." An examination of the highlights of staff activities for fiscal 1976 at RFF reveals that only a handful of events were advertised and open to the general public. One notable exception was the 1975 RFF/League of Women Voters Workshop Series for examination of community issues in land use.

PRODUCT PRICE AND INSTITUTIONAL INCOME

The public policy institution raises its money in different ways, most of which are indirectly connected to varying degrees with the state and capitalist sectors. We noted above that the most obvious sources of funding may undermine the independent image of such institutions, so that indirect money is an important medium. Brookings, for instance, receives very little of its income directly from corporate donations or state contracts. Corporate donations are currently not much in excess of $100,000 (less than 2%) and the institutional restriction on government funds keeps this source low. Its major funding comes from large block grants from the Ford Foundation and from a relatively ample endowment. Honoraria and book sales add to these basic sources.

The determination of product price is a thorny issue. The relationship between value and price has always been problematic in both neoclassical and Marxist analyses. We believe that PIP work is in fact ultimately financed out of surplus from the private sector but is productive in the overall sense of supporting capitalist institutions. We contend that the better the job the institution does at creating forceful arguments and PIPs, particularly for the compelling problems at hand, the more support it will receive and the more prestigious its name. Thus, the macroeconomic policy-making at Brookings has long enjoyed substantial support because it has produced successful ideology about the aggregate functioning of the economy (not the best forecasting models but the best policy perspectives). A specific instance is the argument formulated by Charles Schutze, prior to becoming head of the Council of Economic Advisors, that government spending has not really gone up, but in fact gone down a little because, when corrected for inflation, *real* output has not increased as much as in other sectors. This argument relies on a clever use of an assumption that productivity in the government sector is zero, so that all increases in spending are purely inflation.

Furthermore, the price paid Brookings will be influenced by the current state of competition in the PIP industry. While an oligopoly of professionals undoubtedly exists, where economists and related specialists control their own numbers, certify themselves, and determine what is good research, there is substantial competition among ideological agencies which acts as a subtle disciplinary force on the production possibilities of each. Professionals ultimately see their primary allegiance to their profession, not to their institution, so that they will migrate to a university, to a private consulting firm, or to a competitor if they deem its fortunes and prestige to be on the rise. Thus institutions like Brookings must perform cosmetic surgery periodically as the politics of the state change and the nature of conflict in the economy changes. Currently, competition from the American Enterprise Institute is pressing Brookings toward a more conservative position. In an era like the 1960s, when conflict was sharply etched and extensive protest organizations thrived, Brookings could afford to be more liberal, since the state and corporate sectors needed stronger legitimizing ideology (Bay Area Kapitalistate, 1977).

When the demand for PIP products falls, particular institutions may rethink their direction or aggressively market their existing product to new clients. For instance, with the threat of Ford Foundation withdrawal of general funding for Brookings and RFF, recent administrative initiatives within each institution aim to win greater financial support from both state agencies and private firms. To better facilitate this process, trustees of both institutions have recently hired managers who are well known for their businesslike and business-oriented posture. In 1974, RFF hired Charles Hitch, who was formerly associated with the Department of Defense, the

Rand Corporation, and once served as chancellor of the University of California. He has served on CED, CFR, and numerous business associations. In 1977, Brookings hired Bruce MacLaury, formerly head of the Minneapolis Federal Reserve Bank. He is well known for organizing a business forum in the Midwest for joint discussion and input into public policy.

The "price" paid for PIP is thus determined by the usefulness of the particular item to the client, by the degree of independence that the institution can claim (thus the aura of prestige attached to its policy analysis), by the degree of competition prevailing within the ideological sector, and by conditions in the economy as a whole.

PRODUCTION FUNCTION: INPUTS AND TECHNOLOGY

In order to produce PIP output, the institution hires labor and/or harnesses up current staff members to work on specific projects. The process is highly labor intensive; 71% of Brookings's 1976 expenditures consisted of payroll costs. Within the process, work is hierarchically divided among management, senior fellows, associates (equivalent to young faculty), dissertation and graduate student research assistants, and the clerical and service staff. Other inputs include library books and periodicals, and machines like photocopiers and computers. It is the work of the upper-level professionals that gives the PIP output its particular character, the apparently individualistic quality of research and production, discussed in the next section.

The professionals themselves come equipped with a technology for ideology production that includes paradigms from the social sciences, access to data, knowledge of computer techniques, and an accumulated set of professional connections. These are the technology of the ideological production process. The technology changes rather rapidly, in part because concrete conditions tend to expose the particular weaknesses of yesterday's policy formulations. The paradigmatic basis, however, is tenacious.

The organization of the production process is carefully watched by the management. Think tanks must be on the frontiers on social, economic, and political issues. A good argument cannot be made in successive years if it is not useful to prevailing powers. Management will reorganize the process from above if external conditions require a change in tone, emphasis, or personnel.

PROFESSIONAL MOTIVATION AND CONSCIOUSNESS: PIP PACKAGING

In its research, Brookings functions as an independent analyst and critic, committed to publishing its findings for the information of the public [Brookings *Bulletin*, 1976: 32].

Our view of the role of professionals in the PIP production process differs from those advanced by other attempts to analyze information production and the material base of professionals. The study by social scientists of information production (e.g., Machlup, 1962) presupposes that resources are allocated to produce *better* information that enhances the market mechanism under capitalism. There is no analysis of the possibility that resources might be used to create misinformation, confusion, or ideology in a world of class struggle.

Recently, the distinctness of professionals has become a major issue. Moving beyond the 1960s analysis of the "new working class," such authors as the Ehrenreichs (1977) and Bledstein (1977) argue that professionals have a consciousness and unique position of privilege that warrants labeling them a separate class. The Ehrenreichs argue from a Marxist position; Bledstein produces an historical-cultural critique. Another attempt to locate the class position of professionals is Poulantzas's (1974) distinction between manual labor and mental labor, where the occupational quality of professional work divides but does not sever two arms of the working class. In this section, we look closely at Brookings and RFF professionals in order to reveal their material base in specific work situations. We hope this will contribute to an understanding of one segment of the professional-managerial class.

The motivation of professionals and managers of these institutions is twofold. We assume that the board of trustees of such institutions hire managers (e.g., McLaury and Hitch) who will advance the effort to produce an ideology which supports the basic structure of capitalist institutions. They in turn hire the staff. Professional staffers are motivated by the income and status that accrue to them because of their connection with a prestigious institution. They are also accumulating human capital (both name and skills) which can be exchanged at a later time for a position or higher income at a university, in government, or at another institution. The concrete manifestation of this human capital is the individual's vita, which displays the actual products (books, articles, reviews, and speeches) and the connections of the individual. The Good Name of the institution is the aggregate of such individual products and names.

These two aspects of professional motivation distinguish the ideological production process, at least in these institutions, from the experience of most workers in the capitalist economy. Most workers under capitalism produce products whose sale is not connected with their names. For professional ideology producers, their name is a necessary characteristic of the product. Furthermore, their future economic security (unless they want to return to nonprofessional jobs) depends not only on their skills, but on their record of accumulated products.

An examination of the seventy senior research fellows at Brookings in 1976 reveals that the average length of association was less than seven years. Generally, fellows aspire to positions within business or the university and view a stay at Brookings as a stepping stone. There is no tenure at Brookings. Following a successful performance in another sphere, a professional may be asked to return to Brookings for another round. This process brings back to Brookings a wealth of information and expertise from these other domains. A notable example was the influx of Brookings senior fellows and associates into the Carter Administration: Charles Shultze to head the Council of Economic Advisors, Henry Aaron to head HEW's Planning and Evaluation division, Barry Bosworth to direct the President's Council on Wage and Price Stability, and Edward Fried to become U.S. Executive Director of the World Bank. Although the average length of stay for RFF senior staff members is somewhat longer than at Brookings, the turnover in junior staff is quite rapid. Senior members do take leaves to work in the government, universities, and private organizations. But because of the specialized nature of RFF work in the past, senior members have tended to stay for far longer periods.

These facets of work life for professionals in such institutions result in a highly individualized production process, which requires a fair degree of decision-making (although not independence, as we show below), and a tremendous degree of pressure to perform correctly, so that each project is momentous. The fact that professionals working in the same place generally constitute each other's major social base deepens the pressure. A social-psychological study, akin to those endlessly administered to workers, might be valuable evidence of the impact of these pressures on personal life.

The higher-level professional is a hired worker, who sells labor time to the institution with the expectation that he/she will produce an individualized product which pioneers a "new" PIP device (or variations on an old and accepted one) for its clients. Generally, the hiree will be someone who is already familiar and comfortable with Brookings or RFF style, trained by older professionals in the conventional paradigms. This process is strengthened by the numerous formal and informal networks existing be-

tween the universities and both organizations. We explore these interrelationships below.

The PIP workers, in order to determine what will be a saleable product to
Brookings and its clients, survey Brookings's past products and listen carefully to the conversations of fellow, especially senior, workers and the
visiting government and business leaders. Eventually, they may try out their
incipient arguments at the weekly Brookings staff lunches. Here they field
criticisms, discover analogous arguments from others' ongoing work, and
make working alliances with fellow staff members. The weekly Brookings
staff lunches are an institution in themselves. Every Friday, thirty to forty
senior and associate staffers sit around a huge oak table and eat a catered
meal, while Joseph Peckman, Chief of Economic Studies, moderates a
lively discussion on three or more current public policy debates. For instance, a typical session might begin with Peckman asking a foreign policy
expert about the most recent status of arms control negotiations, proceed to a
directed question on rationalizing military pensions, and end with a discussion of welfare "chiseling." This environment fosters the testing of professional product, through tough questions about a PIP's political viability,
ideological rationale, and correct use of social science paradigms. Although
serious policy issues are debated in this forum, participation is limited to
Brookings fellows and their guests; members of the press are visibly absent.
Junior staff fellows are not allowed to eat at the table, but may sit around the
perimeter and listen to the forging of PIP.

Brookings and RFF share the same building; more precisely, RFF, Aspen
Institute of the Humanities, and the Institute for Social Science Research all
rent space from Brookings. Consequently, these groups frequent the same
cafeteria in the building. Here, informal conversations take place among the
staff members of the various organizations as well as among staff members
of the same tier within the organization. Tables are hierarchically populated,
so they are visibly segregated into black women (secretaries), white women
(librarians and secretaries), and older white men (senior fellows), while
black men and women run the kitchen. There are also a number of special
dining rooms for small to medium-sized luncheons and dinners. There are
some exceptions to the general hierarchical pattern. Direct observation
showed us that the most racially and sexually integrated group is the
youngest layer of professionals—graduate students and associates.

In sharp contrast to this elaborate set of hiring practices, signals, and
discussions which shapes their notions of acceptable PIP development,
professional staff members project a strong image of objectivity and individual control of the production process. Such claims to independent analysis

are a vital part of the product, as we have noted above. Several institutional features support this independent image. First of all, staff members are generally paid salaries rather than by piecework; therefore they are given appointments based on their general skills and past performance rather than for a specific piece of work. Second, the internal grooming process teaches upcoming professionals this self-image of independence as they experience the old-timers around the dining table. Prescribed personal style emphasizes being bold, even arrogant. Third, Brookings reserves the right to publish work that they do on contract with any group; this means that they claim they do not do any secret research. However, in the past they have occasionally decided not to publish the results of sensitive studies. Another device supporting the aura of objectivity is the artificial limitation of the realm of possible solutions to a relatively narrow range. Government or business planning is acceptable; socialist planning is not. At a Brookings lunch, a discussion of the neutron bomb once began with the statement that since we decided ten years ago that we want tactical nuclear weapons, the only question is which is the best killer. A similar RFF response to one of the coauthor's queries about nationalization as an energy-production alternative suggested that it was beyond the range of reasonable alternatives.

The self-image of Brookings and its staffers is an outstanding example of the Marxist notion of false consciousness, a distorted view of the reality of one's own objective position. Brookings and RFF professionals act as if they were entrepreneurs, selling an individual product on an open market. They act as if the best-crafted product will win the highest price and prestige. The requirements of their own hiring and tenure, and the process forming their pragmatic view of PIP possibilities, usually are not explicitly understood. Of course, it is of no use to the institution or the individual to comprehend the internalized constraints that each member acts within. In fact, they are obscured by frequent debate (which also helps fine-tune the ideology) and by mutual reassurance that they are scientists, seeking the objectively best answer. Staffers concur that since the world is complex, only experts are capable of comprehending it. "The basic facts that bear on the main issue must be distilled from a great body of technical material, analyzed objectively and made available to the people" (Resources for the Future, 1954: 6). Professionals are the self-selected distillers.

This professional self-image is not born at Brookings as such, but is embedded in the entire higher education process. The majority of staffers at both Brookings and RFF are either economists or political scientists with advanced degrees. Each of these disciplines has a prevailing paradigm which asserts its objectivity: pluralism in political science, neoclassical and

Keynesian economics. (Interestingly, only one sociologist is employed at RFF and his task is to study RFF internally!) Many of the staff members of both organizations were trained at the elite universities (e.g., MIT, Harvard, Yale, Columbia, Princeton, Johns Hopkins, Chicago, Berkeley, Stanford, Cal Tech).

Promising graduate students are financially rewarded by both institutions via fellowships and grants to work on some aspect of PIP. In fiscal 1974-1975 Brookings reported seventeen fellows doing predoctoral studies with its support. Brookings also supports an Economic Policy Fellow Program (on Ford Foundation money) which for a number of years has brought ten to fifteen young academic economists (junior faculty) to Washington to work in various government agencies (Markusen's sponsor). RFF recently terminated a fellowship program which aided "qualified" graduate students to finish their doctoral dissertations. RFF is considering replacing this educational liaison program with resident fellows, policy fellows, and guest scholars, much like Brookings.

Staff fellows also migrate to the universities for visiting appointments and frequent lectures and seminars. Brookings staffers take such leaves more frequently than do RFF staffers. In the former case, some academics cycle through as guest fellows several times in their working lives. Other links with universities arise from normal professional contact: conventions, professional associations, editorial work, and public forums.

The strength of Brookings and RFF PIP work as contributions to the social science literature in general is documented by our analysis of the *Social Science Citation Index*. A comparative statistical summary of 1976 data shows us that RFF senior staff members are quoted on the average twelve times per year and Brookings senior staff members are quoted an average of twenty-five times a year by other social scientists. The average rate for all social scientists is less than four citations per year. It has been shown by Chubin (1973) and Cole and Cole (1972) that frequency of citation in the index is a valid measure of impact within science and social science disciplines.

This process is mirrored with PIP institutional relationships to the state and private sectors. Formally, this occurs when Brookings or RFF staff members accept jobs or advisory positions within government administration. Informally, it occurs in the various meetings mentioned earlier. Brookings also sponsors the Federal Executive Fellowship Program, designed for "senior federal officials" who wish to do research on leave from their offices in the bureaucracy. Brookings hosts programs for government officials: Conferences on Public Policy, Conferences for Science Executives on policy issues on science and technology, and Conferences on Business and Contemporary Society. In similar conferences with top business leaders, staff members exchange information and perspectives.

All of these forums and interrelationships engender the development of the PIP producer as a researcher grounded in a particular profession and paradigm, with a well-honed sense of the politically pragmatic and saleable policy analysis.

CONFLICT WITHIN THE PIP PRODUCTION PROCESS

Despite the discipline that we have documented, conflict within the process develops from time to time. This is because of the internal contradictions between a process that is quite rigidly demanding of orthodoxy but which requires an aura of independence. Professionals within the institution internalize constraints on analytical possibilies, but the claim to independence is essential to both the individual and the institution. It is the rationale for and guarantor of the highly paid and status-laden position that each holds. In fact, one issue of frequent militancy on the part of professionals is the assertion of the objectivity of their work.

This militancy is the makings of the saleability of their product. The best ideologies are those which have committed adherents. In this case, the grooming of individuals to be producers of PIP succeeds so well because it stakes their entire material and psychic survival on their performance. Unlike school teachers, who also produce ideology, there is no security nor academic insulation for this particular group, who are paraded before camera, and ferried in and out of government, to speak directly to the public or to prompt political or business leaders on the best rationale for a particular policy decision. The clash between truly democratic and humanitarian sentiments and the realities of the political world can be quite traumatic for individual staff members of both organizations.

One manifestation of this militancy is the current concern among staff members over the new financial directions being forced on the institutions by the withdrawal of Ford funds and stiff competition from other institutions. Professionals within each institution shudder at the threat to their "objective" reputations. Our research indicated that RFF, in response to this potential reputational erosion, has set up screening committees to judge research requests. Research on timber practices, paid for by Weyerhaueser, for instance, will be permitted only if this committee guarantees RFF's position would not be compromised. If the financial independence of each institution wanes, it may be that the burden of proving independence will increasingly be shouldered by the professionals themselves. The recent popularity and growth of public policy schools (as opposed to public administration schools) may be one source of improved professional image and claims to objectivity. This new profession would complement extant relationships between the universities and these institutions, which will be documented below.

On a rare occasion a staff member may produce overly idealistic or truly oppositional analyses that make waves. In 1974 RFF published Thomas Cochran's (1974) critique of the fast breeder reactor. According to inside sources, an influential division head (who has close ties to the energy industry) led an internal opposition to the publication of this manuscript, which held it up for several months. Cochran, by no means a radical, had argued that the liquid metal fast breeder reactor has no environmental nor economic advantage over light water reactors already in operation. Cochran is no longer associated with RFF. Another infamous case at Brookings involved Morton Halperin, who opposed the war in Vietnam before it was fashionable in Brookings circles to do so. (The reader will remember that Halperin was to be a target for Nixon's dirty tricks hit list, visualized as firebombing Brookings).

Rejection of progressive analysis may originate outside the institution. For instance, Joseph Peckman, Director of Economic Studies at Brookings, reportedly lost out in the competition for Treasury tax czar because his idealistic proposals for overall tax reform, the product of many years of labor, were not acceptable to political leaders like Russell Long. Instead, Long was able to convince Carter to place his chief Senate staff aide in that position.

Progressive analysis is most often tolerated in the sphere of social equity issues. This is consistent with Piven, Alford and Friedland's (1977) hypothesis that issues concerning the distribution of income or social services are fought in forums relatively accessible to the various factions fighting over the crumbs, while the big decisions supporting private capital (tax credits, tariff policy, debt financing, energy technology, etc.) are hidden in bureaus and couched in analyses inaccessible to the general public. For instance, Henry Aaron's (1972) book accounted for the subsidies implicit in all of the federal housing programs, including FHA mortgage arrangements, and concluded that housing policy as a whole benefits the middle and upper classes. However, such analyses tend to be backward looking rather than focused on a current policy issue or debate. In general, there is noticeable lack of vehemence about malnutrition, poverty, or unemployment. Professionals are more apt to object strenuously if their analysis is accused of supporting an unequal or worsening income distribution, than register dismay at the phenomenon of inequity per se. For instance, the possibility that employing incentives for pollution control might lead to a worsened income distribution provokes defensive responses that income distribution ought to be handled in a separate sphere through welfare policy. Another line of defense against pressure to formulate progressive solutions to social equity problems is to invoke the notion that democracy and capitalism have done so well in the past that they have raised popular expectations beyond the possibility of satisfaction.

Thus, while these institutions generally operate efficiently in supporting capitalist hegemony, occasional contradictions do exist. Staff members with distinctly different political views or strong moral sensibilities ultimately change their views, are weeded out, or will gravitate to other working situations. For instance, Tom Cochran is now working for a public-interest environmental group. In our judgment, therefore, these institutions are populated mainly by seemingly detached, self-confident, frequently arrogant and politically malleable professionals. Each may have private conflicts about the nature of his or her work, but accepts the institutional constraints to perform within certain analytical and philosophical guidelines. It seems that the younger staff members within both institutions tend to experience the contradictions more acutely than do their older associates, who have found ways of justifying their involvement in this process. The latter seem to feel that "this is better than nothing."

This section has been difficult for us to write because we found some of the men and women in these institutions amiable and helpful to us in our respective research. A few have strong convictions about the value of their work and, in an abstract way, feel they are making the world a better place for people to live in. They perceive the power of Brookings and RFF, and hope to use it as a vehicle for social change. And, in fact, some of their suggestions might be progressive if they were implementable. This qualification represents our own conflicts about progressive sentiments versus political realities of these institutions as we see them. In the long run, we believe that it is impossible for individuals to hold a stance oppositional to the ideological bent of the institution as a whole. If nothing else, personal friendships and collegiality make this extremely difficult.

CONCLUSION

In this chapter we have provided a framework for analyzing the production process within policy, ideology, and planning institutions like Brookings and RFF. We have emphasized the central role of professional motivation and consciousness in the act of transforming requirements of the private and state sectors under capitalism into policy/plans/ideology: Our work supports previous analyses by Domhoff (1970, 1979) and other theorists who assert that state policy under capitalism is a subject of concern and organized action within the ranks of corporate leaders. Our documentation traces how institutions like Brookings and RFF, via their professional agents, collect input from the private and state sectors and process it into policy formulations and supporting ideology. This is not meant to suggest that there are not important structural mechanisms within the state itself that inhibit or do not require direct manipulation; in fact, there are. Nor do we wish to suggest that all suggestions are implemented; they are not. However, the issues that Brookings and RFF attack are precisely those that present an enigma to existing state structure and programs. Therefore, their work aims at producing improvements in the structure and operation of the state.

Our contribution lies in our analysis of these institutions as *producers* and in our emphasis on the use of professionals in sustaining the aura of "independence." In doing so, we have provided a bridge between the structuralist and intrumentalist views. We hope that our contribution will encourage people involved with political theory to move beyond what we consider to be a pseudo-debate. Moving beyond this debate will allow us to return to the main issue of our times: the transformation of the state, the economy, and the society into a truly human environment.

REFERENCES

AARON, H. (1972) Shelter and Subsidies: Who Benefits from Federal Housing Policies. Washington, DC: Brookings Institution.
Bay Area Kapitalistate Collective (1977) "A review of setting national priorities." Kapitalistate 6.
BLEDSTEIN, B. (1977) The Culture of Professionalism. New York: W.W. Norton.
BOSWORTH, B., J. DUESENBERRY, and A. CARRON (1975) Capital Needs in the Seventies. Washington, DC: Brookings Institution.
Brookings Institution (1976) Brookings Bulletin 13 (Fall-Winter).
CHUBIN, D. (1973) "On the use of the social science citation index in sociology." American Sociologist 8, 4: 187-191.
COCHRAN, T. (1974) The Liquid Metal Fast Breeder Reactor: An Environmental and Economic Critique. Baltimore: John Hopkins Univ. Press.

COHEN, S.C. (1977) Modern Capitalist Planning: The French Model. Berkeley: Univ. of California Press.

COLE, J. and S. COLE (1972) "The Ortega hypothesis." Science 178, 4059 (October 27): 368-375.

DOMHOFF, G.W. (1979) The Powers that Be. New York: Random House.

——— (1970) The Higher Circles. New York: Random House.

EHRENREICH, B. and J. EHRENREICH (1977) "The professional managerial class." Radical American 11, 3: 7-24.

ESPING-ANDERSON, G., R. FRIEDLAND and E.O. WRIGHT (1976) "Modes of class struggle and the capitalist state." Kapitalistate 4/5: 189.

HIRSCH, G. (1975) "Only you can prevent ideological hegemony." Insurgent Sociologist 5, 3: 64-82.

KNEESE, A. (1975) Pollution, Prices, and Public Policy. Washington, DC: Brookings Institution.

LANDSBERG, H. (1964) Natural Resources for U.S. Growth. Baltimore: Johns Hopkins Univ. Press.

LOFLAND, J. (1971) Analyzing Social Settings. Belmont, CA: Wadsworth.

MACHLUP, F. (1962) The Production and Distribution of Knowledge. Princeton, NJ: Princeton Univ. Press.

MANNHEIM, K. (1952) Ideology and Utopia. New York: Harcourt, Brace.

OKUN, A. (1975) Equity and Efficiency: The Big Trade-Off. Washington, DC: Brookings Institution.

PIVEN, F., R.R. ALFORD, and R. FRIEDLAND (1977) "Political conflict, urban structure, and the fiscal crisis." International Journal of Urban and Regional Research 1, 3.

POULANTZAS, N. (1974) "On social classes." New Left Review (March-April): 27-59.

RESOURCES FOR THE FUTURE (1976) Annual Report.

——— (1954) Annual Report.

SCHRIFTGIESSER, K. (1967) Business and Public Policy. Englewood Cliffs, NJ: Prentice-Hall.

WOLANIN, T.R. (1975) Presidential Advisory Commissions. Madison: Univ. of Wisconsin Press.

8

WHICH BUSINESS LEADERS HELP GOVERN?

Michael Useem

Though the web is not seamless, considerable social cohesion and political self-awareness draws together the members of the American capitalist class, as studies by Mills (1956), Baltzell (1964), and Domhoff (1970) have made abundantly clear. But it is also well known that the middle and working classes, despite substantial internal unities of their own, are nonetheless divided along occupational, work, racial, and gender lines, and that these divisions can decisively shape the content and character of their political expression (see, for instance, Hamilton, 1972; Silverman and Yanowitch, 1974). Divisions within the dominant class may have equally significant political consequences.

Previous inquiry suggests that potentially important lines of differentiation lie along at least three axes within the capitalist class. These lines, if significant, would divide the class into three cross-cutting sets of distinct strata: (1) financiers and industrialists; (2) those overseeing large corporations and those responsible for small business firms; and (3) those with multiple-firm connections and those affiliated with only a single corporation. Previous research indicates that all three lines of differentiation are important, but their relative importance has not been established. Nor has the possibly varying political role of the distinct strata been assessed. Draw-

AUTHOR'S NOTE: Financial support for this research has been provided by the U.S. National Science Foundation, and invaluable research assistance has been rendered by Gladys Delp, Carmenza Gallo, John Hoops, David Swartz, and Linda Trehnholm.

ing on new evidence, this chapter examines the relative importance of these lines of internal differentiation for one area of political activity—the direct participation of corporate officers and directors in the goverance of other institutions, including government agencies, business policy associations, and cultural organizations.

The term capitalist class, used interchangeably here with, simply, businesspeople refers to those who own or manage major business firms and their immediate kin. Management is taken to include the firm's top officers and members of the board of directors. Owners would primarily consist of those with substantial stockholdings, but exact definition will prove unnecessary since adequate ownership data are unavilable in any case. The capitalist class is internally differentiated when subsets of its members are located in positions with distinct interests. All businesspeople are united, of course, by a common set of dominant interests (foremost of which is continuation of business profits and prosperity), and internal differentiation refers only to secondary interest cleavages. Those sharing a set of secondary interests are conventionally labeled class strata, fractions, or segments (see Zeitlin et al., 1976), and these terms will be used interchangeably in this chapter.

The only area for which we have data on political activity is the direct involvement of businessleaders in the affairs of three types of institutions other than business firms themselves: local, state, and federal government agencies; regional, sectoral, and national business policy associations; and cultural institutions, including art organizations, research organizations, and colleges and universities. Participation in the governance of these "outside" institutions takes many forms, but we shall be primarily concerned with the businesspeoples' service on advisory committees and governing boards, and their temporary tenure as full-time administrators.

THREE MODELS OF INTERNAL DIFFERENTIATION OF THE BUSINESS ELITE

Numerous lines of internal differentiation of the business elite have been identified as potentially significant, including divisions between the established corporate wealthy and new entrepreneurs; Anglo-Saxon Protestants and other ethnic groups (e.g., Baltzell, 1964); Northeastern businessleaders and "Southern rim" businessleaders (e.g., Sale, 1975); and those who oversee military contract firms (comprising the "military-industrial complex") and other industrialists (e.g., Rosen, 1973; Russett and

Hanson, 1975). Three lines, however, have preoccupied analysts far more than any others, in part because the evidence suggests that these are the most pronounced internal cleavages, and in part because their political implications are more profound. These lines of internal differentiation of the capitalist class, and their implications for the participation of business executives in the governance of other institutions, can only be briefly set forth here.

FINANCIAL AND INDUSTRIAL SEGEMENTS

Financiers and industrialists, by virtue of the distinct and partially opposed economic circumstances they face, are likely, according to a *sectoral* model, to form distinct class segments. Though united by their primary commitment to the continued profitability of private enterprise, the two segments are viewed as divided by two divergent sets of secondary concerns. The first division stems from the fact that industrial firms are heavily reliant on banks and insurance companies for short- and long-term financing; in the 1965-1974 period, for instance, between 40 and 45% of the total funds used by nonfinancial businesses came from external sources, and approximately two-thirds of this was provided by financial institutions (Kotz, 1978: 6). As debtors, industrialists are united by their common concern for the availability of large amounts of capital at low interest rates; as creditors, bankers are equally well united by their common concern for the maintenance of high interest rates and low-risk corporate behavior that will not endanger loan repayment.

The second source of division between bankers and industrialists, according to this model, stems from their differing spans of concern. Industrialists are necessarily worried primarily about the prosperity of their own firm, while bankers must be concerned with the collective prosperity of a large number of firms to which credit has been extended. Practices of individual firms, such as "price wars" or illegal antilabor policies, can often be costly for business as a whole even though individually profitable. A further wedge, then, may be created between industrialists and bankers over the practices of individual companies.

Not only are industrialists and bankers often divided by these two contrary concerns, but, according to the arguments of some, the divergent interests result in an asymmetric relation between the two business sectors. The dependency of the industrial corporations on the financial institutions is said to be increasingly one of unequal exchange, with the latter's size and control over an essential resource placing them in a better position to dictate the terms of exchange than are the former. Furthermore, the banks' interconnections with a large number of other firms provides them with a resource base for imposing their terms on recalcitrant corporations, a power that industrials cannot impose in return by virtue of their relative isolation from other corporations (these arguments are developed in U.S. Congress, 1968; Fitch and Oppenheimer, 1970; Mariolis, 1975; and Kotz, 1978).

Both of the aforementioned factors led to the expectation that bankers should more often participate than industrialists in the governance of other institutions. The more powerful position of bankers should place them in a better position to promote one another for service with other institutions; and, at the same time, these institutions should be more likely to recruit bankers since they add greater prestige and are capable of mobilizing greater resources than are industrialists. Moreover, banker interconnections with a large number of client firms facing a diverse range of conditions also provide them with a more generalist view of the needs and outlook of all business, not just the narrow concerns of a single firm or type of industry, as is likely to be the orientation of many industrialists. In his study of the business elite which dominates the U.S. foreign policy bureaucracy, for instance, Kolko (1969: 199) suggests that it "was in the nature of their diverse functions as . . . financiers for many corporate industrial and investment firms . . . that these men preeminently represented the less parochial interests of all giant corporations." Thus, from the standpoint of both business and the outside institution, bankers should be preferred as advisers and governing board members since they are in a better position to represent the interests of business as a whole.

SMALL-FIRM AND LARGE-FIRM SEGMENTS

Managers and owners of large firms, according to the second, *size* model of internal differentiation, are likely to form a segment with secondary interests distinct from those who oversee small firms. The nation's largest firms, operating in monopolistic or at least oligopolistic conditions and relying primarily on the "primary" labor force, are far more able to accept prolabor legislation and costly state-induced social reforms than are smaller firms, whose precarious competitive existence dictates opposition to any labor or government actions restricting their profit margins. Large firms can generally pass higher labor and government-mandated costs to consumers through the imposition of price increases, whereas the competitive market faced by smaller firms makes this far less feasible, with higher costs thereby necessarily absorbed in lower profits. On a broad range of issues, then, ranging from attitudes toward negotiations with labor to federal legislation on minimum wage and environmental protection, these class segments have opposing interests (this thesis receives fullest elaboration in O'Connor, 1973, but similar arguments have been propounded by many writers including Marris, 1964; Monsen and Cannon, 1965; Baran and Sweezy, 1966; Galbraith, 1967; Weinstein, 1968; Poulantzas, 1975; and Miller, 1975).

The far greater resources commanded by those associated with large corporations than by those associated with small firms should make the former more able to insist on having their representatives sit on institutional governance bodies. And, seen from the other side again, leaders of large businesses should make more desirable appointees in any case, since they bring greater influence and visibility to the governing body than do smaller businesspeople. Thus, according to this model, the larger the corporation, the more likely management is to participate in the governance of other institutions.

SINGLE-FIRM AND MULTI-FIRM SEGMENTS

The third, *multi-firm* model of internal class differentiation suggests that an elite stratum has formed within the capitalist class, a segment characterized by the connections of its members with at least several major corporations. While most businessleaders are primarily identified with the interests of a single firm, a not insubstantial number have developed connections with several, and at times many, corporations. These connections take the form of large stockholdings, close ties of kinship, and simultaneous service as an officer of one firm and director of one or more other firms. As in the case of bankers, multi-firm businessleaders are in a position to be more aware of the aggregate interests of a broad sector of business than are their single-firm counterparts. Thus, the interests of the multi-firm segment are more coincident with the general interests of the capitalist class than is the case for other businesspeople (this thesis is argued in Mills, 1956: 121-122; Perrucci and Pilisuk, 1970; Zeitlin et al., 1974; Koenig et al., 1976; Useem, 1978a; and Ratcliff et al., 1979).

For reasons paralleling those advanced in connection with the other two models, higher institutional governance participation rates are expected for multi-firm businessleaders than for the single-firm businessleaders. Compared with the single-firm segment, multi-firm businesspeople have a greater resource base on which to promote one another for outside positions of governance; their broader range of influence makes them more attractive recruits from the standpoint of the outside institution; and the multi-firm connections place them in a better position to recognize and promote general business interests.

In sum, then, these three models of internal differentiation generate three distinct hypotheses concerning the rate of participation of business elites in the governing affairs of other institutions. Higher rates of participation should be observed among (1) bankers than industrialists, (2) large businesspeople than small businesspeople, and (3) multi-firm businesspeople than single-firm businesspeople. An implicit baseline of comparison for all three of these hypotheses is an additional hypothesis bases on a fourth model that holds that the capitalist class is without any significant internal division. By implication, most business executives are equally likely to participate in the governance of other institutions, and, it can therefore be hypothesized, participation rates should be unrelated to the lines of internal differentiation identified above.

THE CONSEQUENCES OF UNEQUAL CLASS SEGMENT PARTICIPATION

If businessleaders take into account their secondary business interests when they participate in the goverance of other institutions, as can be reasonably assumed, and if their voice in these circles has substantial, if not decisive, influence on the policies adopted, the relative magnitude of the impact of the three lines of differentiation on participation rates can have important implications for the policies and general orientations of the outside institutions. Overrepresentation of bankers would imply that the outside institutions tend to take actions at least marginally more favorable to the interests of finance; to the extent that bankers also concern themselves with the overall interests of capital, this would also imply that the institutions' policies are oriented toward the more general needs of business. The overrepresentation of large businesspeople, by contrast, would imply that government agencies and the other outside organizations are more often responsive to the concerns of big business than the needs of small business. And the overrepresentation of multi-firm business elites would imply that the more general interests of business receive greater weight in policy formulation than do more narrow interests of particular sectors or specific firms. Of course, direct study of the institutions' policies would still be needed to verify any of the implications suggested by the results here.

The presence or absence of the participation patterns predicted by each of the models also contains implications for the validity and general importance of the models themselves. Assuming the measurement procedures are valid, the presence of one of the predicted patterns would enhance the likelihood that the corresponding line of differentiation is of fundamental importance for not only political involvement but for other areas of individual and corporate behavior as well. Thus, if participation in the governance of other institutions is observed to be strongy shaped by one of the lines of division, this would heighten our confidence that this line differentiates other elements of class organization as well, such as the formation of subcultures, friendship networks, career strategies, and kinship and intermarriage patterns. Corporate behavior may be affected as well. If the multi-firm line of differentation is pronounced, for instance, corporations more centrally connected with the multi-firm network of businessleaders may take actions which differ from those that are more isolated (Ratcliff, 1979, reports such as consequence for the area of bank lending policies). Conversely, the absence of an anticipated pattern would suggest, though certainly by no means prove, that the hypothesized line of differentiation may be weaker than is generally assumed by proponents of the model. Thus, evidence on this limited domain of outside institution participation provides one additional datum on which to build a fuller picture of the internal social organization of the American capitalist class.

PREVIOUS RESEARCH

The overrepresentation of business executives on the governing bodies of outside institutions has been amply documented in numerous previous studies (for a sampling, see Hartnett, 1969; Freitag, 1975; Landau, 1977; DiMaggio and Useem, 1978). Few studies, however, have systematically assessed the degree of overrepresentation of the major class segments hypothesized here. Some studies have suggested that commercial and investment bankers appear in governing boards, advisory committees, and top government posts even more often than other business leaders, but no fix on the differential rates is offered (e.g., Kolko, 1969). Other studies of business elites in the "higher circles" of government suggest that most come from the largest corporations, but again specific rate differentials as a function of corporate size have not been made available (e.g., Dye and Pickering, 1974). One exception is an investigation of the local governance activities of bank directors in St. Louis by Ratcliff et al. (1979); they find that bank size is strongly correlated with bank director participation rates in the governance of local charitable organizations, cultural organizations, and a business policy association. Those affiliated with the five largest banks participate in the governance of these institutions at a rate more than six times the rate observed for directors affiliated with the sixteenth to seventy-eighth largest banks.

Still other studies suggest that multi-firm executives are more often sought for governing boards, advisory committees, and government posts than are others, but again scant specific rate evidence is available (e.g., Domhoff, 1970). One study of the directors of the largest 797 business firms in 1969 by Useem (1978b) did reveal that the multiple directors (those who sat on the boards of several of the corporations) were far more likely than single directors to be involved in the governance of a variety of outside institutions, including the federal government; participation rates were found to vary by a factor of two or even more. However, no effort was made to compare these differential rates with those associated with other class divisions.

Thus, there is suggestive evidence indicating unequal participation along the three hypothesized axes, and at least two studies report unequal rates for the corporate size and multi-firm axes of differentiation. No systematic evidence is yet available, however, on the relative significance of all three dimensions.

RESEARCH PROCEDURE

Data are drawn from a set of corporate directors and officers sampled as follows. An annual list is prepared by *Fortune* magazine of the one thousand largest U.S. industrial corporations and the fifty largest firms in each of six additional sectors. Two hundred and ten of these companies were selected for intensive examination according to their sector and size at the end of 1977 (*Fortune*, 1978)). In each sector the companies were rank ordered according to their size. The sampled firms include industrials ranked 1 to 60 and 451 to 500 according to their sales volume; commercial banks ranked 1 to 25 and 41 to 50 (ranked by assets); insurance companies ranked 1 to 15 and 41 to 50 (assets); diversified financial firms ranked 1 to 10 and 41 to 50 (assets); retail firms ranked 1 to 5 (sales); transportation companies ranked 1 to 5 (operating revenue); and utilities ranked 1 to 5 (assets).

The identities of the six top officers (typically the chairperson of the board, president, and several senior and executive presidents) were obtained from a standard source, Dun and Bradstreet's 1977-1978 edition of the *Million Dollar Directory*. In cases where all of the top six officers were also on the board of directors, two nondirector officers were also sampled. In addition, the identities of all nonofficer directors were obtained when there were ten or fewer, and ten were randomly selected when the number of nonofficer directors exceeded ten. Adequate rosters of officers and directors for 200 corporations were obtained, and from these lists we sampled a total of 2,843 officers and directors, divided as follows: 705 officer-directors, 521 nondirector officers, and 1,617 nonofficer directors. For simplicity, the first two groups are hereafter collectively referred to as officers, while the third group is referred to as directors.

Career information for most officers was compiled from the Dun and Bradstreet directory. Career information on directors and some officers, and data on the involvement of both groups in the governance of outside institutions, were obtained from the 1976-1977 edition of Marquis's *Who's Who in America*. However, only 56% of the individuals in our sample received biographical listings in *Who's Who,* and a separate analysis reveals that the included businesspeople tended to be more "prominent," as indicated by the size of their corporation, the number of corporate boards of directors on which they sat, and membership in major exclusive social clubs. Thus, most of the analysis is of necessity limited to an "up-scale" subset of the full sample. Information on the recent service of the officers and directors on federal government advisory committees was obtained from a complete listing of committee membership for 1976 compiled by a U.S. Senate subcommittee. The roster includes the identities of more than 23,000 individuals who served that year on any of the 1,159 federal advisory committees which, according to the subcommittee's chairperson, "influence the Federal Government in virtually every area of policy making" (U.S. Senate Subcommittee on Reports, Accounting and Management, 1977: iv).

The class segment "location" of the officers and directors is established as follows. For the sectoral division, businessleaders are considered to be a "bankers" if they served as a director or officer of a commercial bank, and they are deemed "industrialists" if they were directors or officers with one of the industrial firms. For the corporate size division, to ensure adequate numbers for reliable analysis and to avoid confounding size with sector, only those in the industrial sector are considered. "Large industrialists" are officers or directors of one of the top sixty industrial firms; "small industrialists" are officers or directors of one of the industrial firms ranked between 451 and 500. The designation of small industrialists is, of course, relative, since such persons are still overseeing firms whose sales ranged between $355 million and $451 million and whose number of employees varied from 1,000⁻ to 26,000. The comparison of large and small industrialists, then, is a conservative one, since the latter category excludes those with very small corporations. Still, the scale of the firms ranked 451 to 500 is less than one-tenth of that of the largest industrials, whose sales ranged from $3.6 billion to $55.0 billion and whose number of employees varied from 7,000 to 797,000.

For the multi-firm division, the businessleaders are divided into four groups according to the number of corporate board of directors they served on, other than the board of the corporation with which they were sampled. The businessleaders are grouped according to whether they hold zero, one, two, or three or more of these "outside directorships." However, to ensure comparability with the other measure of class segments used here, only outside directorships with firms of substantial size are counted. Companies of substantial size are defined as the one thousand largest industrials and the fifty largest companies in each of the six other sectors identified above, as ranked by *Fortune* for 1976.

Our primary measure of outside involvement of the officers and directors is their participation rate in the governance of an outside institution, that is, the percentage of a class segment serving in a governance position. Differential rates will be gauged by calculating a participation rate ratio, which is simply the rate for one segment divided by the rate for another.

Since directors are less intimately tied to the interests of the firm with which they are sampled than are officers, participation rates are initially reported separately for these two groups when comparing the corporate sector and size segments. It should be cautioned that the sectoral placement of both groups is only approximate, inasmuch as many of the businesspeople maintain ties with additional corporations through other linkages, such as kinship and stockholding, that could not be measured here. The bias introduced by the inability to specify these ties is most likely to reduce observed intersegment variation in participation rates. The present analysis, therefore, will tend to yield conservative estimates of class segment differences.

PARTICIPATION IN THE GOVERNMENT

Corporate officers and directors participate in the formulation of government policies and programs in many ways. Among the most important are temporary full-time service as a top government official, direct lobbying of government officials, contributing financially to political candidates and parties, and service on government advisory committees, panels, and boards. Data were only available for three of the several possible modes— service as a federal government official, service on a federal advisory committee, and service on a state or local government advisory body. Service on a federal advisory committee is divided according to whether it occurred prior to 1976 (as recorded in the *Who's Who* biographical listing), or during 1976 (as registered in the U.S. Senate subcommittee compilation).

Table 8.1   Percentage of Corporation Officers and Directors Who Serve on Government Advisory Committees or Who Are Federal Government Administrators, by Outside Directorships, Corporation Size, and Corporation Sector

Officer or Director Location	State or Local Government Advisory Committee	Federal Advisory Committee		Federal Government Admin.	Number of Cases
		Pre-1976	1976		
Outside directorships					
Zero	8.5	8.9	10.2	8.6	(764)
One	11.3	12.9	13.6	11.7	(309)
Two	8.5	14.0	14.8	18.2	(226)
Three or more	18.1	23.8	18.4	17.7	(282)
Ratio:					
three+ %/zero %	2.13	2.67	1.80	2.06	
Industrial corporation size					
Officers	7.6	6.3	3.8	1.3	(79)
Small industrial	5.6	10.2	14.4	4.2	(216)
Ratio:					
large %/small %	0.74	1.62	3.79	3.23	
Directors					
Small industrial	9.9	9.9	4.3	10.6	(141)
Large industrial	12.8	16.6	17.4	19.8	(368)
Ratio:					
large %/small %	1.29	1.68	4.05	1.87	
Corporation sector					
Officers					
Large industrial	5.6	10.2	14.4	4.2	(216)
Commercial bank	11.6	7.1	21.4	8.9	(172)
Ratio:					
bank %/industrial %	2.07	0.70	1.49	2.12	
Directors					
Large industrial	12.8	16.6	17.4	19.8	(368)
Commercial bank	10.9	14.9	14.4	9.9	(202)
Ratio:					
bank %/indus. %	0.85	0.90	0.83	0.50	

Since pre-1976 service precedes the person's current corporate location in a relatively small but unmeasurable number of cases, the distinction between pre-1976 and 1976 service provides a means of screening against the possibility that federal advisory work is the cause, rather than the result of the executive's corporate location.

The participation rates as a function of class segment are displayed in Table 8.1. The percentage of business leaders who are involved in both local and national government advisory service varies, as predicted, by the number of outside directorships. Nine percent of the people with no outside directorships (other than that of their own firm) have been involved as advisers with local and state government agencies; by contrast, 18% of those with three or more outside directorshiops have been involved. The ratio of these partcipation rates is 2.1. Similar patterns are observed for pre-1976 and 1976 federal advisory service, and also for holding a federal administrative post, other than that of a military officer, at some point during the person's career; the participation rate ratios for these three areas are, respectively, 2.7, 1.8, and 2.1.

The participation rates for those associated with the large and small industrial corporations are reported in the second panel of Table 8.1, and, with a single exception, the rates are substantially higher for large industrialists than small industrialists. The ratios for the participation rates range from 1.3 to 4.1 for all comparisons except local and state government advisory service among officers, where the rate inverts to 0.7.

Finally, the corresponding figures for sectoral division are displayed in the third panel of Table 8.1. It is seen that the commercial bank officers are more likely to be involved in three of these areas of governance—local and state advisory service, federal advisory committee service in 1976, and federal government administration (ratios of 2.1, 1.5, and 2.1)—but the predicted pattern does not hold for pre-1976 federal advisory service (ratio of 0.7). Moreover, bank directors are less involved than industrial directors in all four areas of governance (ratios of 0.5 to 0.9).

Consistent with the multi-firm and size hypotheses, then, those with multi-firm connections and those affiliated with large industrial corporations are substantially more likely to participate in the formulation of government policies in various ways than are their respective counterparts. The evidence for the sectoral hypothesis, however, is far more ambiguous. Though bank officers are more frequently involved than large industrial officers in two types of governance, contrary to expectations these patterns are reversed for two other types of governance, and industrial directors are consistently more often involved than are bank directors in all areas.

PARTICIPATION IN BUSINESS POLICY ASSOCIATIONS

Business policy associations play an important role in formulating the concerns and interests of member corporations and in promoting policies that protect these interests, through such activities as "public education" campaigns and efforts to pressure elected and appointed government officials. Business policy associations also provide a means for exercising internal control within the business community by defining and enforcing acceptable forms of business conduct. One commentator on contemporary business practices, for instance, observes that, in response to growing business and public clamor for "rules to . . . discipline management behavior better," the major business policy associations have been conducting discussions "across firm and industry lines" about "general improvements which should be made to codes of conduct" (Dill, 1978: 24; also see Eakins, 1966; Domhoff, 1975; Shoup, 1975; Bonacich and Domhoff, 1977). Thus, differential sectoral participation rates in these associations have implications for the types of internal and external policies they are likely to adopt.

Business policy associations can be divided among three general categories. *National* business policy associations draw their membership from a broad range of business firms located throughout the country and are oriented toward the general interests of business. *Special* business policy associations also have national memberships, but their rosters are typically limited to a single industry, such as oil or steel, and their primary orientation is toward the more parochial concerns of the particular sector. *Regional* business policy associations draw on local executives from a broad range of firms, and their chief concern is development of the regional economy. Drawing on a range of analytic and business sources (especially Bonacich and Domhoff, 1977), we identified ten national associations: American Bankers Association, the Business Council, Business Roundtable, Committee for Economic Development, Conference Board, Council on Foreign Relations, the Foreign Policy Association, National Alliance of Businessmen, the National Association of Manufacturers, and U.S. Chamber of Commerce. The special business associations number in the thousands, and include such organizations as the American Iron and Steel Institute, Biscuit and Cracker Manufacturers Association, and the U.S. Savings and Loan League. Included among the regional associations are such organizations as the Mayor of Chicago's Committee for Economic and Cultural Development, and the Northeast Minnesota Development Association.

Since the more general interests of capital are the chief concern of the national business political associations, it is anticipated that multi-firm businessleaders, large industrialists, and bankers will be more often involved than their corresponding counterparts. Similar, though less pronounced, differences are expected for participation in regional associations, since general business interests, albeit regional in scope, are at stake. By contrast, special associations are not primarily oriented toward overarching business concerns, and little differential involvement is anticipated. Drawing on *Who's Who* information, the corporate officers and directors' participation in the three types of business association is displayed in Table 8.2.

Table 8.2   Percentage of Corporation Officers and
Directors Who Are Members of at Least One National,
Special, and Regional Business Policy Association by
Outside Directorships, Corporation Size, and
Corporation Sector

| Officer or Director | Business Policy Association | | | Number of |
Position	National	Regional	Special	Cases
Outside directorships				
Zero	17.7	6.4	49.7	(764)
One	27.2	12.0	54.0	(309)
Two	34.7	8.1	48.3	(226)
Three or more	39.0	14.9	48.2	(282)
Ratio: three + %/zero %	2.20	2.83	0.97	
Industrial corporation size				
Officers				
Small industrial	8.9	6.3	48.1	(79)
Large industrial	23.6	5.6	55.6	(216)
Ratio: large %/small %	2.65	0.89	1.16	
Director				
Small industrial	11.3	7.1	40.4	(141)
Large industrial	37.2	9.5	47.0	(368)
Ratio: large %/small %	3.29	1.34	1.16	
Corporation sector				
Officers				
Large industrial	23.6	5.6	55.6	(216)
Commercial bank	23.2	16.1	53.6	(172)
Ratio: bank %/industrial %	0.98	2.88	0.96	
Directors				
Large industrial	37.2	9.5	47.0	(368)
Commercial bank	31.7	13.4	52.5	(202)
Ratio: bank %/industrial %	0.85	1.41	1.12	

As expected, multi-firm business elites are far more likely to be active in at least one national association (39% are involved); the participation rate ratio is 2.2. Industrial firm size also predicts participation rates, as anticipated: the large industrial rate is 2.7 times the small industrial rate for officers, and 3.3 times the rate for directors. However, contrary to the sectoral model expectation, commercial bankers are no more likely to be active in a national association than are large industrialists; the participation rates for officers and directors are 1.0 and 0.9.

The regional associations evidence a more mixed pattern of membership. Both multi-firm directors and bank officers are substantially more likely to participate than their counterparts (participation rate ratios of 2.3 and 2.9). However, there is little difference observed for industrial directors (the large firm/small firm rate ratio is 1.3), and for industrial officers the ratio is less than unity (0.9).

None of the three lines of class differentiation is observed to affect rates of participation in the special associations. Nearly half of the corporate officers and directors, regardless of location, are active in at least one special association; no participation rate ratio exceeds 1.2.

Thus, consistent with the multi-firm model, multiple directors overparticipate, compared with single directors, in both national and regional associations. However, seemingly inconsistent patterns are evident for the other two dimensions. Industrial size differentiates participation in the national, but not regional, associations. And, conversely, sector differentiates participation in the regional, but not national, associations. A possible interpretation of these patterns derives from the fact that commercial banks are limited, by law, to regional operations, and, thus, they have an especially strong stake in local economic growth and stability. This may account for the overparticipation of bankers, compared with large industrialists, in regional associations. Similarly, most large industrialists are oriented toward both national and regional concerns, while smaller industrials are likely to be largely local in operation and thus lack the impetus to help formulate national economic policies. This could help explain why size affects involvement in the national, but not regional, associations. Finally, it can be argued that all businessleaders, regardless of location, have a vital stake in the immediate prosperity of their own firm(s), and this would help explain the unvarying rates of involvement in the special business associations.

PARTICIPATION IN CULTURAL ORGANIZATIONS

The creation and perpetuation of dominant ideas, knowledge, and ideologies are of concern to most businesses, and the active involvement of business executives in the governance of organizations responsible for the production and reproduction of culture would not be surprising. But it is also anticipated that the rate of involvement will depend on the location of the business person in the social organization of the capitalist class. Specifically, multi-firm directors, large industrialists, and bankers are expected to be overrepresented in the governing bodies of several types of cultural institutions: art organizations, including museums and performing arts companies; research and scientific institutes and centers, such as the Brookings Institution; and colleges and universities. The latter are further subdivided into a set of elite universities oriented toward the education of those with business elite origins and destinations, and all other higher education institutions. Greater differentiation of involvement in the former than the latter is anticipated, for the educational activities of the most elite universities are prone to receive greatest business vigilance. The elite universities consist of forty institutions that have most often been attended by corporate directors and officers in the present study (this list, available upon request, was partly based on previous studies of elite education by Pierson, 1969, and Useem and Miller, 1975).

The percentages of the corporate officers and directors involved in the governance of these cultural organizations are shown in Table 8.3. While

Table 8.3   Percentage of Corporation Officers and Directors Who Serve on the Governing Boards of Three Types of Cultural Organizations, by Outside Directorships, Corporation Size and Corporation Sector

Officer or Director Position	Cultural Organization				
	Arts Organization	Research Organization	Elite University	Nonelite College or University	Number of Cases
Outside directorships					
Zero	14.9	10.7	6.4	17.8	(764)
One	21.7	14.9	13.6	31.7	(309)
Two	20.3	19.9	22.5	27.1	(226)
Three or more	34.0	29.4	23.8	30.1	(282)
Ratio: three + %/zero %	2.28	2.74	3.72	1.69	
Industrial corporation size					
Officers					
Small industrial	8.9	6.3	2.5	15.2	(79)
Large industrial	12.5	10.2	7.9	20.4	(216)
Ratio: large %/small%	1.40	1.62	3.16	1.34	
Directors					
Small industrial	20.6	12.1	5.7	28.0	(141)
Large industrial	25.0	24.2	20.1	29.1	(368)
Ratio: large %/small %	1.21	2.00	3.53	1.04	
Corporation sector					
Officers					
Large industrial	12.5	10.2	7.9	20.4	(216)
Commercial bank	17.0	12.5	11.6	19.6	(172)
Ratio: bank %/industrial %	1.36	1.23	1.47	0.96	
Directors					
Large industrial	25.0	24.2	20.1	28.0	(268)
Commercial bank	22.3	20.8	17.8	24.8	(202)
Ratio: bank %/industrial %	0.89	0.86	0.89	0.89	

15% of those with no outside directorships serve on the governing board of an art organization, 34% of those with three or more directorships serve. A participation rate ratio of 2.3 for art organizations is paralleled by a ratio of 2.7 for research organizations and 3.7 for elite universities. For nonelite colleges and universities, however, the ratio is far more modest, standing at only 1.7.

Similar differentials are apparent when large and small industrialists are compared. With the exception of nonelite school trusteeships, the rate ratios range from 1.4 to 3.2 for officers, and from 1.2 to 3.5 for directors. Again, the strongest difference is evident in the area of elite university governance, but the expected patterns are observed for art and research organizations as well.

The corporate sector data are far more ambiguous. While bank officers are moderately more likely to be involved in the governance of cultural institutions than are large industrialists (the rate ratios range from 1.0 to 1.5), the rate ratios for the comparison of bank and industrial directors are the reverse of those expected (the ratios all stand at 0.9).

Thus, in this area of participation, the dimensions of multi-firm connections and corporation size are strong predictors of involvement in the governance of outside institutions, while corporation sector is a weak predictor. It is also evident that participation rates are far more strongly differentiated for the elite universities than for other colleges and universities. Though the patterns are less sharp than in the case of elite universities, arts and research organizations are also especially likely to place large industrialists and multi-firm leaders on their governing boards.

INDEPENDENT EFFECTS OF OUTSIDE DIRECTORSHIPS AND CORPORATE SIZE

The three dimensions of class differentiation are themselves related, and it is possible that the observed effect on participation of one dimension may be largely due to its association with another dimension. The average number of outside directorships for small industrial officers is 0.16, for instance, while the average for large industrial officers is 0.43; and bank officers maintain 0.79 outside directorships on average, still more than observed for large industrial officers.

To determine the independent effects of the several dimensions, the corporate sector axis is dropped from further consideration. This dimension did not consistently predict participation rates, and its deletion at this point considerably simplifies the ensuing discussion. Moreover, since the corporate size participation rate ratios were approximately the same for both officers and directors, the officers and directors are combined to ensure adequate numbers for reliable analysis. The need for reliable numbers in the subcategories also led to the dichotomization of the multi-firm variable; businessleaders are divided into those with one or no outside directorships and those with two or more such ties. Even with these steps, too few small-firm executives with multi-firm outside directorships were available, and this category is dropped from the analysis.

We will consider only those areas where the participation rate ratios for both the multi-firm and corporate size comparisons exceeded 1.5 (implying that those with four or more outside directorships were at least 50% more likely to participate than those with no directorships, and that large industrialists were also at least 50% more likely to be engaged than small industrialists). Six areas of governance met this criterion: federal advisory committee membership prior to 1976 and during 1976, federal government employment, national business policy associations, research organizations, and elite universities.

The participation rate ratios are displayed in Table 8.4. The ratio for large industrialists compared to small industrialists ranges from 1.7 to 4.0 when all industrialists are included, but the ratio is reduced somewhat to a range of 1.3 to 3.3 when the number of outside directorships is controlled (by comparing only industrialists with multiple outside directorships). Similarly, the ratio for those with several outside directorships to those with none or one ranges from 1.7 to 3.4 when all industrialists are included, but the ratio is reduced, with one exception, to a range of 1.6 to 2.8 when industrial size is controlled (by comparing only large industrialists). Thus, while controlling for one dimension does reduce the effect of the other dimension, the reductions are seen to be modest in magnitude. All of the controlled values are at least three-quarters of the value of the uncontrolled ratios. And, the controlled participation rate ratios are larger than 1.5 in all cases except one. It is apparent, then, that although the axes of corporate size and multi-firm directorships are related, each of these factors still independently structures the likelihood of participation in a range of governance. A fraction of the uncontrolled predictive power of each axis is a product of the joint impact of the two together, but most of the predictive power of the multi-firm and corporate size dimensions can be attributed to the independent impact of each.

These two dimensions together are, consequently, especially powerful determinants of who participates in the governance of a variety of institu-

Table 8.4 Participation Ratios for Industrial Officers and Directors, Controlling for Industrial Size and Number of Outside Directorships

Officer or Director Location	Federal Government Service		Policy Administration	National Business Research Association	Cultural Organizations		Number of Cases
	Pre-1976 Advisory Committee	1976 Advisory Committee			Elite Organization	Elite University	
Large industrialists/small industrialists							
All industrialists	1.66	3.95	1.95	3.33	1.89	3.22	(586/220)
Those with zero or one outside directorship	1.27	3.27	1.67	3.19	1.62	2.82	(365/181)
Two + outside directorships/zero or one direc.							
All industrialists	1.71	1.73	1.91	1.96	2.00	3.42	(546/260)
Large industrialists	1.74	1.55	1.77	1.66	1.88	2.77	(365/221)

tions. In the case of the national business policy associations, for example, 11% of the small industrialists with no or one outside directorship were active in at least one of the ten associations; 35% of the large industrialists with no or one outside directorship were so involved; and 58% of the large industrialists with two or more outside directorships participated in the affairs of at least one of these associations. The parallel figures for service on the governing board of an elite university were, respectively, 4, 9, and 26%.

THE ROLE OF NATIONAL BUSINESS POLICY ASSOCIATIONS

While it is evident that two dimensions of businessleaders' locations in the corporate structure independently predict their propensity to become involved in the governance of other institutions, the specific features of these dimensions favoring the recruitment of some business elites over others remain unspecified. Among the most important of these features, in all likelihood, are the executives' public visibility, their personal and corporate resources, their reputation for promoting a general business viewpoint rather than the interests of their own firms, and their network of personal and corporate ties both within the business elite and with members of nonbusiness institutions. Evidence is not available on most of these factors, but a reasonable indicator of possession of at least several factors is their involvement in one or more of the national business policy associations.

Participation in the affairs of a national association is likely to mean that the businessperson is sensitized to the general business concerns of the constituent members, and that he or she is part of a transcorporate national network of acquaintanceship. At the same time, association membership enhances visibility and improves contacts with elites in nonbusiness organizations. Involvement in the affairs of a business association also provides other businessleaders with an opportunity to evaluate a person's capacity to promote the general interests of the association's members. When members of the business elite are asked to recommend people for advisory and governing board positions, a consensus is more likely to develop around a proven business activist than around businessleaders whose reliability is unknown.

We have already seen that business executives associated with large industrials and those with multiple outside directorships are considerably more likely to be involved in national business policy associations than are their counterparts, and this would suggest that, indeed, these associations are serving as "screening" devices for the recruitment of businessleaders into positions of outside governance. Moreover, if this thesis is correct, it is also expected that, among those business elites with a similar location in the capitalist class, those who are active in a national business policy association are also more likely to be involved in the governance of other institutions.

To examine this hypothesis, we compared the participation rate of those involved in at least one national business policy association with the rate of those who are entirely uninvolved. This is done for all industrialists together, and then the comparison is repeated for subsets of industrialists for whom corporate size and number of outside directorships are held constant. The participation rate ratios are reported in the upper panel of Table 8.5

The participation rate ratios for all industrialists in pre-1976 and 1976 federal advisory service, federal administration, and governance of research and cultural organizations range from 1.5 to 2.8. That is, industrialists who are active in at least one national business policy association are at least 50% more likely than those with no such association membership to be involved in these five areas of oversight activity. Furthermore, these ratios generally remain substantial even when corporate size and number of outside directorships are controlled. The overall ratio for pre-1976 federal advisory committee membership is 1.7, for instance, while the ratio for large industrialists with zero or one outside directorships is 1.7, and for large industrialists with two or more outside directorships the ratio is 1.3. Similarly, the three analogous participation rates for elite university governance are 2.5, 1.8, and 2.0. The sole exception in the predicted pattern appears in the case of federal administrative appointment, where one of the controlled ratios drops to 0.7. Overall, however, the participation rate ratios conform to the expected pattern, implying that the national business policy associations are playing a major role in channeling members of the business elite into outside governance.

It is evident that involvement in the national business policy associations has an impact on participation that is partly independent of the corporate size and multiple-firm dimensions. Taken together, then, these three factors jointly result in a high degree of differentiation of the businessleaders' propensity to participate in outside governance, as shown on the bottom panel of Table. 8.5. In the case of service on a federal government advisory committee in 1976, for example, only 4% of the small industrialists with few outside directorships and no business association membership so served; among large industrialists with few outside directorships and no business associations memberhips, the rate is 12%; among large industrialists with many outside directorships but no business association memberships, the

Table 8.5 Participation Rate Ratios and Rates for Industrial Officers and Directors, Controlling for Industrial Size, Number of Outside Directorships, and Membership in National Business Policy Associations

Officer or Director Location	Federal Government Service			Cultural Organizations		Number of Cases
	Pre-1976 Advisory Committee	1976 Advisory Committee	Administration	Research Organization	Elite University	
Participation rate ratios: members of one+ national business associatoin/members of no national business association						
All industrialists	1.65	2.07	1.54	2.82	2.50	(211/595)
Large industrialists with one- outside directorship	1.67	1.53	0.72	2.66	1.79	(94/271)
Large industrialists with two+ outside directorships	1.29	1.75	2.28	2.64	2.00	(94/127)
Participation rates						
Small industrialists, one- outside directorship, no national business association	8.5	4.2	7.3	8.5	3.6	(165)
Large industrialists, one- outside directorships, no national business association	9.6	11.8	11.8	10.0	7.7	(271)
Large industrialists, two+ outside directorships no national business association	17.3	15.7	12.6	15.7	18.1	(127)
Large industrialists, two+ outside directorships, one+ national business association	22.3	27.7	28.7	41.5	36.2	(94)

rate is 16%; and among large industrialists with many outside directorships and membership in at least one business association, the rate is 28%. Similarly, for service as a trustee of an elite university, the parallel figures are, respectively, 4, 8, 18, and 36%.

It is also notable that the largest gap in the participation rates of these four groups lies between the latter two—between large industrialists with many outside directorships but no business association activity and a stratum which is otherwise identical except that its members are involved in a business policy association. This further underscores the significance of the national associations' role as a screening mechanism for the selection of businesspeople to represent business to outside institutions. Business elites, otherwise similar in location in the social organization of the capitalist class, are sharply distinguished in their propensity to serve in governance positions according to their involvement in the national business policy associations.

CONCLUSION

Previous inquiry indicated that the differences in secondary economic interests between large and small businessleaders, and between multi-firm and single-firm executives, are sufficiently salient in the United States to have generated distinct class segments. And, consistent with several hypotheses based on this previous research, the present inquiry has confirmed that two lines of economic differentiation have generated corresponding lines of political differentiation as well. Compared with small industrialists, large industrialists are significantly more likely to assist government agencies, oversee a range of cultural organizations, and join major national business policy associations. Compared with single-firm businesspeople, multi-firm directors are also more likely to be involved in each of these areas. In some cases the participation rates of the class segments are observed to vary by factors of two, three, or even more.

While themselves interrelated, the two economic axes are also found to independently structure who represents business to nonbusiness organizations. Further, the national business policy associations appear, according to the data available, to occupy a strategic position in determining who among the large industrialists and multi-firm directors ultimately acquire the relatively few positions available in outside governance. However, business policy association membership, as measured here, is probably only a proxy for more complex processes occurring within and around the activities of these associations, and more refined measures of these factors should further enhance our ability to predict which businessleaders are selected to serve.

Although previous inquiry also pointed to the existence of a cleavage between industrialists and financiers, the present findings suggest that, if the economic cleavage is present, it does not give rise to a corresponding political cleavage. Or, alternatively, it may be that the industrial-financial economic cleavage itself is far less pronounced than the other two axes, and, consequently, it has relatively little impact on any area of corporate or individual behavior, including political participation. It is possible, as Zeitlin (1974: 1111-1112) has suggested, that "the social and economic interweaving of once opposed financial and industrial interests" has so muted this cleavage that it is now of faint salience compared to the corporate size and multiple connections axes.

The present study also provides further evidence that the business elite should not be seen as a unitary, large homogeneous group. The executives who serve as representatives to nonbusiness institutions are not drawn at random or on an arbitrary basis, as might have been expected were the business elite largely undifferentiated. Rather, business emissaries sharply overrepresent two class segments. The voice of business in government circles, cultural organizations, and business policy groups, then, is not a simple aggregate mixture of the many separate voices of the entire business elite. The voice is an unequally weighted mixture, with the expressed needs of two class segments receiving more frequent articulation than the needs of other segments.

Whether large industrialists and multi-firm directors do, in fact, bring a distinct set of commitments and viewpoints to the policy deliberations of the nonbusiness organizations is an open empirical question. There is, however, already ample evidence to substantiate the general principle that businesspeople's values do vary in predictable ways according to their location in the social organization of the capitalist class (e.g., Christ, 1970; Seider, 1974; Russett and Hanson, 1975). If the conclusions of these studies can be generalized, they would suggest that the sectoral interests of large corporations and the general class interests of capital, as carried by the multi-firm leaders, are more prominently expressed than are the interests of other segments or of individual firms. Even if so expressed, it also remains an open question whether the two overrepresented class segments are able to actually impose their views upon the outside institutions in whose governance they directly participate. Scattered evidence suggests that they can significantly influence institutional policies under certain, specifiable circumstances (e.g., Wilensky and Lebeaux, 1958; Useem, 1978b), but direct verification of the impact of the business elite in these specific areas of outside governance is still needed. Until such evidence becomes available, for the moment it is reasonable to assume tentatively that government agencies, cultural organizations, and business policy associations are indeed tending to adopt policies that are at least somewhat more favorable to the interests of the large industrialists and multi-firm directors than to the interests of other segments of capital.

REFERENCES

BALTZELL, E.D. (1964) The Protestant Establishment: Aristocracy and Caste in America. New York: Random House.

BARAN, P. and P. SWEEZY (1966) Monopoly Capital: An Essay on the American Economic and Social Order. New York: Monthly Review Press.

BONACICH, P. and G.W. DOMHOFF (1977) "Overlapping memberships among clubs and policy groups of the American ruling class: a methodological and empirical contribution to the class-hegemony paradigm of the power structure." Presented at the annual meeting of the American Sociological Association, Chicago, September 1978.

CHRIST, T. (1970) "A thematic analysis of the American business creed." Social Forces 49: 239-245.

DILL, W.R. [ed.] (1978) Running the American Corporation. Englewood Cliffs, NJ: Prentice-Hall.

DiMAGGIO, P. and M. USEEM (1978) "Cultural property and public policy: emerging tensions in government support for the arts." Social Research 45: 356-389.

DOMHOFF, G.W. (1975) "Social clubs, policy-planning groups, and corporations: a network study of ruling-class cohesiveness." Insurgent Sociologist 5: 173-84.

——— (1970) The Higher Circles: The Governing Class in America. New York: Random House.

DYE, T.R. and J.W. PICKERING (1974) "Governmental and corporate elites: convergence and differentiation." Journal of Politics 36: 900-925.

EAKINS, D.W. (1966) "The development of corporate liberal policy research in the United States, 1885-1965." Ph.D. dissertation, University of Wisconsin.

FITCH, R. and M. OPPENHEIMER (1970) "Who rules the corporation? part 3." Socialist Revolution 1 (November-December): 33-94.

Fortune Magazine (1978) The Fortune Double 500 Directory. New York: Fortune Magazine.

FREITAG, P.J. (1975) "The cabinet and big business: a study of interlocks." Social Problems 23: 137-52.

GALBRAITH, J.K. (1967) The New Industrial State. Boston: Houghton-Mifflin.

HAMILTON, R.F. (1972) Class and Politics in the United States. New York: John Wiley.

HARTNETT, R.T. (1969) College and University Trustees: Their Backgrounds, Roles and Educational Attitudes. Princeton, NJ: Princeton Univ. Press.

KOENIG, T., R. GOGEL, and J. SONQUIST (1976) "Corporate interlocking directorates as a social network." Unpublished.

KOLKO, G. (1969) The Roots of American Foreign Policy. Boston: Beacon Press.

KOTZ, D..M. (1978) Bank Control of Large Corporations in the United States. Berkeley: Univ. of California Press.

LANDAU, D. (1977) "Trustees: the capital connection." Health/PAC Bulletin 74 (February): 1-23.

MARIOLIS, P. (1975) "Interlocking directorates and control of corporations: the theory of bank control." Social Science Quarterly 56: 425-39.

MARRIS, R. (1964) The Economic Theory of "Managerial" Capitalism. London: Macmillan.

MILLER, S.M. (1975) "Notes on neo-capitalism." Theory and Society 2: 1-35.

MILLS, C.W. (1956) The Power Elite. New York: Oxford Univ. Press.

MONSEN, R.J. and M.W. CANNON (1965) The Makers of Public Policy: American Power Groups and Their Ideologies. New York McGraw-Hill.

O'CONNOR, J. (1973) The Fiscal Crisis of the State. New York: St. Martin's.

PERRUCCI, R. and M. PILISUK, (1970) "Leaders and ruling elites: the interorganizational bases of community power." American Sociological Review 35: 1040-1057.

PIERSON, G.W. (1969) The Education of American Leaders: Comparative Contributions of U.S. Colleges and Universities. New York: Praeger.

POULANTZAS, N. (1975) Classes in Contemporary Capitalism. London: New Left Books.

RATCLIFF, R.E. (1979) "Banks and the command of capital flows: an analysis of capitalist class structure and mortgage disinvestment in a metropolitan area." In Maurice Zeitlin (ed.) Classes Conflict and the State. Cambridge, MA: Winthrop.

RATCLIFF, R.E., M.E. GALLAGHER, and K.S. RATCLIFF (1979) "The civic involvement of bankers: an analysis of the influence of economic power and social prominence in the command of civic policy positions." Social Problems 26: 298-313.

ROSEN, S. [ed.] (1973) Testing the Theory of the Military-Industrial Complex. Lexington, MA: D.C. Heath.

RUSSETT, B.M. and E.C. HANSON (1975) Interest and Ideology: The Foreign Policy Beliefs of American Businessmen. San Francisco: W.H. Freeman.

SALE, K. (1975) Power Shift: The Rise of the Southern Rim and Its Challenges to the Eastern Establishment. New York: Random House.

SEIDER, J.S. (1974) "American big business ideology: a content analysis of executive speeches." American Sociological Review 39: 802-815.

SHOUP, L.H. (1975) "Shaping the postwar world: the Council on Foreign Relations and United States war aims during World War Two." Insurgent Sociologist 5 (Spring): 9-51.

SILVERMAN, B. and M. YANOWITCH [eds.] (1974) The Worker in "Post-Industrial" Capitalism. New York. Macmillan.

U.S. Congress, House Committee on Banking and Currency, Subcommittee on Domestic Finance (1968) Commercial Banks and Their Trust Activities. Washington, DC: U.S. Government Printing Office.

U.S. Senate Committee on Governmental Affairs, Subcommittee on Reports, Accounting and Management (1977) Federal Advisory Committees. Washington, DC: U.S. Government Printing Office.

USEEM, M. (1978a) "The inner group of the American capitalist class." Social Problems 25: 225-240.

——— (1978b) "The inner group and business influence on American colleges and universities." Presented at the Conference on Power Structure in American Education, San Francisco, November.

——— and MILLER, S.M. (1975) "Privilege and domination: the role of the upper class in American higher education." Social Science Information 14: 115-145.

WEINSTEIN, J. (1968) The Corporate Ideal in the Liberal State, 1900-1918. Boston: Beacon Press.

WILENSKY, H.L. and C.N. LEBEAUX (1958) Industrial Society and Social Welfare. New York: Free Press.

ZEITLIN, M. (1974) "Corporate ownership and control: the large corporation and the capitalist class." American Journal of Sociology 79: 1073-1119.

————— W.L. NEUMAN, and R.E. RATCLIFF (1976) "Class segments: agrarian property and political leadership in the capitalist class of Chile." American Sociological Review 41: 1006-1029.

ZEITLIN, M., R.E. RATCLIFF, and L.A. EWEN (1974) "The 'inner group': interlocking directorates and the internal differentiation of the capitalist class of Chile." Presented at the annual meeting of the American Sociological Association, Montreal, August.

9

THE CORPORATE COMMUNITY AND GOVERNMENT: DO THEY INTERLOCK?

Harold Salzman and G. William Domhoff

INTRODUCTION

Beginning with the work of C. Wright Mills (1956), a considerable amount of empirical evidence has been developed by power structure researchers on the large numbers of corporate leaders who go into major positions in nonprofit organizations and the federal government (e.g., Domhoff, 1967, 1970; Freitag, 1975; Mintz, 1975). However, there persists a tendency among many social scientists to minimize the degree of this interchange, and to ignore or explain away what is reported in systematic studies. The degree of interchange between corporations and government is especially sensitive to these problems.

Involvement of former corporate executives in government is sometimes explained away by claiming that a high degree of interchange only occurred during the Eisenhower Administration (e.g., Parsons, 1957). More recently it has been claimed that this interchange is higher during Republican administrations and is declining (Birnbaum, 1978: 110). In the case of sociologist Arnold Rose (1967: 122-123), the claim that the Eisenhower Administration was unique is buttressed by the uncritical acceptance of a superficial

AUTHORS' NOTE: We wish to thank Barbara Wright and the Computer Center staff at the University of California, Santa Cruz, for their invaluable help with parts of the data analysis.

and inaccurate study of the Kennedy Administration by economist Seymour Harris (1962: 25), a study that was redone by Domhoff (1970: 345-346) with very different results. Even the best and most systematic of traditional studies, which showed that the Kennedy and Johnson Administrations were more "big business" than that of Eisenhower, underestimates the degree of corporate involvement in government because of an inadequate definition of the corporate community, a definition that did not include corporate lawyers or trade association executives (Stanley et al., 1967: 37-38).

Those Marxist theorists who emphasize that the government or "state" is of necessity somewhat "autonomous" from the capitalist class also must ignore or explain away the degree of corporate involvement in the government. For example, French Marxist Nicos Poulantzas (1969: 73) argues that "it can be said that the capitalist State best serves the interests of the capital class only when the members of this class do not participate directly in the State apparatus, that is to say when the ruling class is not the politically governing class." However, he does not discuss how his theory would explain the success of the American government despite the presence of a great many members of the ruling class in high positions. Similarly, sociologist Fred L. Block (1977: 10) can write about a "division of labor" between capitalists and "those who manage the state apparatus" without discussing how separate these "managers of the state apparatus" really are. When he does approach the question (1977: 13), he explains the facts away by suggesting that such people become "atypical of their class, since they are forced to look at the world from the perspective of state managers."

Thomas R. Dye, judged by his colleagues to be among the three or four most influential political scientists of the early 1970s (Roettger, 1978), is the most recent and prominent member of the academic community to minimize the exchange of personnel between corporations and government. In a pair of articles and a book *(Who's Running America?)* on elites in American society, Dye and his former students have presented systematic evidence for the year 1970 that is said to show there is little connection among corporate, civic sector, and governmental elites (Dye et al., 1973; Dye and Pickering, 1974; Dye, 1976). (Dye uses the term "public interest" sector for the organizations he includes in this category, but we will use "civic sector" because "public interest" is now used to denote environmental and consumer protection groups organized by citizen activists.)

The most succinct summary of Dye's general claims on the contribution of the corporate community to the other sectors appears in one of the articles and the book (Dye and Pickering, 1974: 913; Dye, 1976: 160):

The corporate sector supplied only 37 percent of the top elites in the public interest sector and only 16.6 percent of governmental elites. Top leaders in government are recruited primarily from the legal profession (56.1 percent); some have based their careers in government itself (16.7 percent) and education (10.6 percent). This finding is important. Government, law, and education apparently provide independent channels of recruitment to high public office. We have already seen that governmental authority is not interlocked with corporate authority in terms of "horizontal" positional overlap. Now we see that high position in the corporate world is *not* [Dye's italics[a prerequisite to high public office, not much "vertical" overlap exists between the corporate and governmental sectors.

Dye qualifies these conclusions somewhat in the text of his book by emphasizing that many of the lawyers and civic association officials who serve in government have close links to and common interests with the corporate elite. He also shows that cabinet-level appointees tend to come from the corporate world, which is the level studied by earlier researchers (e.g., Domhoff, 1967; Mintz, 1975). However, even though Dye's book shows a considerable awareness of the great influence of the corporate elite in American society, his empirical findings sometimes seem to support more sanguine conclusions. Thus, there remains the possibility that other researchers will utilize only his empirical statements and statistics, and in particular those concerning the low levels of interchange between corporations and government, for these statements reinforce the dominant prejudices within the social science community. (For a cross-national comparison which unfortunately used the summary statements on government personnel in just this way to say that C. Wright Mills was "somewhat hasty" in his conclusions, see Birnbaum, 1978: 110.) We therefore will take advantage of Dye's unique data base—the largest and most extensive of its kind to date—as a starting point for a general reconsideration of these questions. We will try to show how more appropriate methodological and theoretical approaches support the conclusion that there is a considerable interchange between the corporate community and both the nonprofit civic center and the federal government. We are grateful to Dye for his willingness to share this data base, making it possible for us to add to it and present a different analysis of these linkages.

DYE'S OVERALL STUDY

Although the most important conclusions of Dye's study concern the relationship between big business and the federal government, the overall study concerned the degree of "interlocking" among major institutional sectors in the United States. Central to the analysis are the following issues (Dye et al., 1973: 10):

> Is there a convergence of power at the "top" of the institutional structure in America, with a single group of individuals, recruited primarily from industry and finance, who occupy top positions in cultural affairs, and the military? Or are there separate institutions, with elites in each sector of society having little or no overlap in authority and many separate channels of recruitment?

To answer these questions, Dye undertook an empirical analysis "to measure the concentration of authority in top institutional positions; to examine the extent of interlocking and specialization among institutional elites; and to describe the pattern of recruitment to top institutional positions" (Dye et al., 1973: 9). Three major sectors of institutional power—corporate, civic, and governmental—were defined in order to determine the extent of interlocking among "those individuals in the United States who occupy formal positions of authority in those insitutions which control over half the nation's resources" (Dye et al., 1973: 10).

The corporate sector used in the research consisted of those corporations in industry, finance, insurance, and transportation-utilities which control approximately one-half of the nation's corporate assets in each field. Dye thus used the 3,572 presidential and directorship positions in these 201 giant corporations as his sample of institutional leaders in the corporate sector. The civic sector consisted of prestigious private universities, major philanthropic foundations, large New York City law firms, and recognized national policy and cultural organizations (Dye et al., 1973: 11). In these four general areas, the positions at the top chosen were: (1) the presidents and trustees of the 12 colleges and universities which possess one-half of all private endowments in higher education; (2) the 12 largest of the 6,803 foundations which gave $10,000 or more in yearly grants; (3) senior partners in the 20 largest New York City law firms; and (4) the governing bodies of six policy organizations such as the Committee for Economic Development and the Council on Foreign Relations, and seven civic groups such as the Metropolitan Opera Guild and the Museum of Modern Art. (For his book, Dye added directors of the major mass media and several Washington law firms to his public interest sector, but these positions were not in the original data base and therefore are not used in his empirical analyses and summary statements in Chapter 6.) All told, the 1,345 positions in these 57 universities, foundations, law firms, and policy and civic organizations contributed the leadership sample in the civic sector.

The governmental elite was defined as "those individuals who occupy formal positions of authority in major civilian and military bureaucracies of the national government" (Dye and Pickering, 1974: 902). These positions of authority were president and vice-president; secretaries, under secretaries, and assistant secretaries of all cabinet-level departments; White House presidential advisors and ambassadors-at-large; congressional committee chairmen and ranking minority committee members in the House and Senate; House and Senate major and minor party leaders and whip; Supreme Court Justices; governors of the Federal Reserve System; the Council of Economic Advisors; and the military bureaucracy. This governmental elite consisted of 286 positions. Fifty-nine of the individuals in these positions were part of the military bureaucracy; 32 were top-ranking career officers in the Army (18), the Air Force (13), the Navy (9), and the Marines (2). The other 27 positions were held by civilians who served as secretaries, under secretaries, and assistant secretaries of the Departments of Army, Navy, and Air Force.

Taken together, the corporate, public interest, and governmental sectors provide a data base with 5,203 formal positions of authority. These formal positions were held by 4,000 different individuals, several hundred of whom held three or more positions. Dye made three different analyses of these data that are relevant to our concerns in this chapter. First, he determined the number of positions in a sector which were concurrently interlocked with other positions in that sector, meaning that two or more positions were being held at the same time by one individual. Second, he calculated the number of positions in each sector that were concurrently interlocked with positions in other sectors. The concurrent interlocking used in these two analyses was termed "horizontal" interlocking. Dye's third analysis focused on the previous positions held by his positional elites. This sequential interlocking or career pattern was termed "vertical" interlocking.

The major conclusion of his first two analyses was that a majority of positions are "specialized" in that they are neither concurrently interlocked with other positions in their own sector nor with positions in other sectors. Dye recognizes that "specialists" may be something of a misnomer, however. He points out that many of the individuals in these specialized positions may hold positions in other large corporations and important nonprofit organizations, as indeed they do by all accounts, including that of Dye (1976: 130):

> Many of these "specialists" held other corporate directorships, governmental posts, or civic, cultural, or university positions, but not top positions as we have defined them. We will observe later than even our "specialists" fill a wide variety of lesser positions (directorships in corporations below the top

hundred; positions on governmental boards and commissions; trusteeships of less well known colleges and foundations; and directorships of less influential civic and cultural organizations) in addition to their top positions.

Although this qualification of the basic generalization is an important one that brings Dye's findings closer to those other other power structure researchers, the emphasis on relative specialization nonetheless remains, and in particular specialization within a specific sector, whether it be corporate, civic, or governmental. Not surprising to us was the fact that there was virtually no concurrent or horizontal interlocking between corporate and governmental positions, for it would be a minor scandal if corporation presidents and directors were to continue to hold their jobs while serving in full-time government posts. In that sense, this finding is a nonfinding.

For Dye's third analysis the question was: "How many positions of authority in all types of institutions have top leaders *ever held* [Dye's italics] in their lifetime?" (Dye and Pickering, 1974: 910). In addition to gathering information on the number of previous positions, Dye categorized individuals in terms of their "principal lifetime occupational activity." His determination of vertical interlocks among sectors "depended largely on an individual's own designation of principal occupation" in *Who's Who in America 1970-1971* (Dye et al., 1973: 26). In all, 2,026 of the 4,000 individuals in the sample were listed in that volume.

This third analysis showed that many of these positional elites had held numerous major positions over their careers. However, as already noted, the categorization in terms of principal occupational activity suggested there was little contribution by the corporate sector to the civic sector (37%) or the federal government (16.6%).

Our reconsideration of the claims in Dye's work will begin with an analysis of the horizontal interlocking in and between the corporate and civic sectors. Such a reconsideration will show why other researchers have found the organizations and institutions in his two sectors to be so interwoven as to form the basis for a power elite in America. We will then turn to the question of vertical interlocking between the corporate community and the federal government.

INTERLOCKING IN THE CORPORATE AND CIVIC SECTORS

In reviewing Dye's work, we were struck by the unusual method of calculating the degree of horizontal interlocking. It is this unorthodox method which accounts for most of his differences with the findings of earlier studies. Unlike previous researchers, who have measured interlocking by the degree to which *institutions* are interlocked by common directors, he measured the degree to which *positions* were held by individuals who occupy at least one other position in the sample. For example, there were 3,572 positions in the corporate sample, and 1,570 of these positions were filled by a person holding another position in the sample. Thus, 43.8% (1,570/3,572) of the corporate positions are said to be horizontally interlocked, and 56.2% (2,000/3,572) are termed "specialized."

The traditional focus on institutional interlocks, we believe, is more in keeping with the theoretical emphasis which social scientists put on the nature of organizations and their relationships with their "environment" of surrounding institutions. The sociological functions of interlocks are those of establishing channels for information-sharing, coordination, and development of shared outlooks. It is not necessary for most positions to be interlocked to a high degree for these functions to be carried out, especially when it is understood that the directing bodies of most organizations in the corporate and public interest sectors consist of fifteen to thirty people. Indeed, a high degree of positional interlocks among the very largest organizations would mean that several hundred individuals would have to direct a great many of these organizations, leaving them little time for involvement in the many other important corporations and organizations in which they are involved already. Positional interlocking among only the very largest organizations would mean there would be very little possibility of information-sharing and coordination throughout the entire structure of the corporate community and its affiliated organizations.

The contrast in the conclusions led to by the two different methods of calculating interlocks can be seen by again considering the interlocks of those in the corporate sector. By Dye's positional method of calculation, "Approximately 44 percent of all top corporate positions were interlocked with other top positions, most of which were in the corporate sphere" (Dye and Pickering, 1974: 907). From an institutional perspective, however, we found that these 1,570 interlocked positions provide 190 of the 201 corporations in the sample with at least one interlock to one other corporation. Even more impressively, these 1,570 positional interlocks link 164 of his corporations with at least *five* other of the 201 corporations. It is findings such as these which led sociologists John Sonquist and Thomas Koenig (1975: 204), in their study of corporate cliques based on interlocks among large corporations for 1969-1970, to say that the level of connectedness among the 797 corporations was so high that the data would "show up as one big clique" if they defined a link between corporations as one or more overlapping board members. Even when they defined a link between two corporations as two or more common directors, they found "a tightly connected central core of 401 corporations" and 32 clusters or cliques within that central core (Sonquist and Koenig, 1975: 204-205). Similar conclusions on the tightly knit nature of the larger corporate community in the United States have been reached in studies by Dooley (1969), Bearden et al. (1975), Mariolis (1975), Bunting (1976b), and Allen (1978), and historical studies indicate that these relationships have existed throughout the twentieth century (Bunting and Barbour, 1971; Bunting, 1976a; Mizruchi and Bunting, 1979).

The differences in methods and conclusions can also be seen when we turn to what Dye defined as the civic sector. By his method, a mere 474 of 1,345 civic positions (35.2%) were horizontally interlocked with other institutional positions in his sample. Of these 474 interlocked positions, only 54.8% were with corporate positions. Viewed from the more relevant institutional perspective, however, the results are quite impressive. Our reanalysis shows that 150 of the 201 corporations (75%) have at least one interlock with one or more institutions in the civic sector, and many are linked with several civic organizations.

We also analyzed these institutional linkages from the point of view of the civic organizations. That is, we determined how many of the civic organizations have interlocks with these 150 corporations. The results support the finding of interwoven networks among corporations, foundations, universities, policy groups, and law firms that has been reported in other studies (e.g., Domhoff, 1967, 1970, 1974; Hartnett, 1969; DiMaggio and Useem, 1978; Useem et al., 1976). All of the 12 universities have at least one trustee who is a corporate director from one of these 150 corporations, as do all 13 policy and cultural organizations. Ten of the twelve foundations have interlocks with at least one corporation, and twelve of the twenty New York City law firms have at least one senior partner who sits on a board of directors in the sample. Moreover, 57% of the organizations in the civic sector have interlocks with four or more corporations.

The extensive connections of corporations to corporate law firms deserves further consideration, for these organizations are usually considered to be a part of the corporate community by those who have studied them (e.g., Klaw, 1958; Smigel, 1964; Goulden, 1972; Hoffman, 1973; Green, 1975). Happily for us, the first large and systematic study of directorship and financial interlocks between corporations and law firms was carried out for the years 1970 and 1971 (Hudson, 1972). It used the reports corporations must file with the Securities and Exchange Commission if they paid legal fees to a law firm which had a partner on the corporation's board. In general, the study revealed that in 1971 the 1,919 corporations with law partners on their boards paid $157.5 million in legal fees to the law firms from which these partner-directors came. However, William J. Hudson, Jr., the former stock analyst who hired five research assistants to help him search through fifty-five large file cases at the Securities and Exchange Commission, emphasizes that his findings on legal fees "represent only the tip of the iceberg" *(Business Week, 1972: 23)*. This is because they include only those fees corporations pay to law firms which have a partner on the board of directors. His findings on interlocks, on the other hand, represent the greatest proportion of this aspect of corporation-law firm interactions. The fact that only 1,182 law firms were involved with the 1,919 companies suggests the multiple directorships held by many major law firms. Indeed, 18 of the 20 law firms in Dye's sample had two or more such interlocks, and several had 10 or more. The findings concerning the distribution of 155 corporate interlocks among these 20 firms for 1970 are presented in Table 9.1. Also shown in Table 9.1 are the number of interlocked firms which appear on the Fortune list of 797 top-ranked corporations in all major sectors of the economy.

To show the way in which the policy organizations in Dye's civic sector unite organizations from both the corporate and civic sectors, two organizations were singled out for further study. These policy groups are the Council on Foreign Relations and the Committee for Economic Development, whose importance in policy formation has been suggested by a number of studies (e.g., Schriftgiesser, 1960, 1967; Eakins, 1966, 1969; Domhoff, 1970, 1979; Shoup and Minter, 1977; Dye, 1976). For this analysis we included all members of these two groups who were already in the Dye sample, for these organizations are forums where policy can be discussed in a variety of settings by members, and not just by the leadership of the organization.

Consistent with earlier studies, 64% of the 201 corporations in the Dye sample have at least one director who is a member of the 1400-member Council on Foreign Relations. More specifically, 125 corporations have 293 positional interlocks with the Council. Twenty-three of the largest banks and corporations have four or more directors who are members of the Council. The Council's connections to organizations in the civic sector are also extensive. All twelve universities have at least one trustee who is a member, as do six of the twelve foundations. All seven cultural institutions include one or more Council members on their boards, as do five of the other six policy groups. The details of these overlaps are shown in Table. 9.2.

The Committee for Economic Development, which draws over 90% of its members from large corporations, has concurrent interlocks with the

Table 9.1   Interlocks between Corporations and Law
Firms

Law Firm	Total Corporate Directorships	Fortune Corporate Directorships
(1) Simpson, Thacher & Bartlett	20	6
(2) Sullivan & Cromwell	17	12
(3) Shearman & Sterling	14	7
(4) White & Case	13	5
(5) Willkie, Farr & Gallagher	11	1
(6) Davis, Polk & Wardwell	10	5
(7) Mudge, Rose, Guthrie & Alexander	10	2
(8) Royall, Koegal & Wells	9	1
(9) Cahill, Gordon & Reindel	8	5
(10) Milbank, Tweed, Hadley & McCloy	8	4
(11) Cravath, Swaine & Moore	7	6
(12) Kelley, Drye & Warren	6	3
(13) Breed, Abbott & Morgan	5	4
(14) Cadwalader, Wickersham & Taft	5	3
(15) Chadbourne, Parke, Whiteside & Wolff	4	2
(16) Lord, Day & Lord	2	1
(17) Cleary, Gottleib, Steen & Hamilton	2	1
(18) Winthrop, Stimson, Putnam & Roberts	2	1
(19) Donovan, Leisure, Newton & Irving	1	0
(20) Dewey, Ballatine, Bushby, Palmer & Wood	1	0
Total	155	69

boards of ten of the twelve universities, five of the seven cultural organizations, four of the other five policy groups, and four of the twelve foundations. We believe these interlocks provide an impressive communication and persuasion network into the civic sector for a two hundred-member businesspeople's organization. As expected, the Committee also has interlocks with a great many of the top corporations—twenty-eight of the largest fifty banks, eleven of the largest eighteen insurance companies, eleven of the thirty-three largest transports and utilities, and fifty-one of the top one hundred industrials. A breakdown of the results for Committee interlocks with civic organizations is presented in Table 9.3.

Although our findings on the degree of interlocking between the corporate and public interest sectors disagree with those of Dye, our conclusions do not differ from the generalizations he makes in his book. This is because he too thinks in terms of how institutions, not positions, are interlocked when he develops his overall picture of the two sectors:

> The same individuals who occupy top posts in the leading corporate, governmental, and mass media institutions are frequently the same individuals who direct the leading foundations, civic associations, and cultural organizations. In the next few pages, we shall see many of their names again, when we

Table 9.2   Council on Foreign Relations Members on
Civic Sector Boards

Foundations		Cultural Organizations	
Rockefeller	11	Metropolitan Museum	14
Carnegie	9	Museum of Modern Art	13
Sloan	5	American Red Cross	10
Ford	4	John F. Kennedy Center	6
Hartford	2	Metropolitan Opera Guild	4
Mellon	1	Smithsonian Institution	3
		National Gallery of Art	1
		Universities	
Princeton	12	John Hopkins	7
Harvard	11	Stanford	6
Yale	11	Dartmouth	4
Columbia	9	Pennsylvania	4
Chicago	7	Cornell	4
MIT	7	Northwestern	1

Other Policy Groups	
Committee for Economic Development	29
American Assembly	11
The Brookings Institution	7
Conference Board	3

examine the trustees of the nation's leading universities. The purpose of "nam-
ing names," even when they become repetitive, is to suggest frequent interlocking of top elites in different institutional sectors. [Dye, 1976: 116].

Thus, the major conclusion we would draw from our institutional reanalysis of concurrent or horizontal interlocking is that the corporate and civic
sectors as defined by Dye are integrated to such a great extent that they are in
fact one large "private sector," with the major corporations, foundations, and
policy groups at the center. We would argue further that this corporate-based
network of foundations and policy organizations is the core of a power elite
in the United States, a power elite that Domhoff (1970: 106) roots in the
upper class by defining it as "active, working members of the upper class

Table 9.3   Committee for Economic Development
Members on Other Civic Sector Boards

Foundations		Cultural Organizations	
Sloan	3	Museum of Modern Art	2
Ford	2	Metropolitan Museum	1
Rockefeller	2	National Gallery of Art	1
Hartford	2	American Red Cross	1
		Smithsonian Institution	1
		Universities	
Chicago	5	Yale	2
MIT	5	Princeton	2
Northwestern	4	Stanford	1
Dartmouth	3	Cornell	1
Harvard	2	Pennsylvania	1

Other Policy Groups	
Council on Foreign Relations	29
Conference Board	6
The Brookings Institution	5
American Assembly	3

and high-level employees in institutions controlled by members of the upper class." (For evidence that the power elite has its base in the upper class, see Domhoff [1967, 1970], Dye [1976: 151-156], and Bonacich and Domhoff [1977].) From a class-based theoretical perspective, it is this power elite that should be the relevant starting point in assessing the flow of personnel from the corporate community to the federal government. However, for this chapter we will define the "corporate community" only in terms of *Fortune*-listed corporations and large corporate law firms.

We now turn to Dye's conclusions on the vertical interlocks between corporations and government, which emphasize the relative independence of the federal bureaucracy. We will look closely at all the corporate connections of executive department appointees for 1970 and only secondarily supplement our findings in terms of their involvement in the larger power elite network.

THE CORPORATE COMMUNITY AND GOVERNMENT OFFICIALS

Dye found that only 16.6% of his government sample had their principal occupational activity with major corporations before their appointment to government, and that only 25% had held any top position in a large corporation (Dye, 1976; 135, 160). As noted, there is the possibility that his conclusions on the minimal connections between the corporate elite and government will be seen as differing from those of Mills (1956) and other power researchers. In actuality, the differences are not as great as they first appear. It will be the purpose of this section to explain the differences, and to show that the connections between the corporate community and the executive departments are greater than Dye concluded.

The first reason for the differences is that Dye used a larger and more diverse sample of government officials. His study included congressional leaders, career military officers, Supreme Court Justices, White House advisers, the Council of Economic Advisors, and the Governors of the Federal Reserve System, whereas earlier studies usually focused on the major departments of the executive branch. Since no studies claim that any of these other parts of government except the Federal Reserve System are horizontally or vertically interlocked to any significant degree with the largest corporations of the business world, they can be treated briefly here.

There is general agreement that congressional leaders come more often from smaller businesses and smaller corporate law firms, with roots in the politician's home state or district. It is also clear that the top military officers entered the military academies and worked their way up the military hierarchy. Studies of the Supreme Court show that the justices are lawyers, albeit sometimes corporate lawyers. Similarly, members of the three-person Council of Economic Advisors are usually professional economists, although it can be added that they often have advisory connections to major policy groups such as the Committee for Economic Development and The Brookings Institution. As for White House advisers, they are a mixed group that ranges from political operatives to academic experts to very important corporate executives.

The case of the seven-member Board of Governors of the Federal Reserve System is slightly more complicated, for it is only one part of a larger system which includes twelve district boards and thirty-seven regional boards that have very important roles within the overall system. This system had not been studied positionally in detail until 1976, when a congressional committee (U.S. House, 1976) showed the overwhelming representation of major bankers and other corporate executives on the district and regional boards. It is employees and former employees of these district and regional boards, along with academic economists and career Treasury Department employees, who ususally sit on the Board of Governors.

However, the different samples do not explain all the discrepancies, for Dye still found very few connections between top corporate leadership and the appointed officials of the executive branch. It is to this problem that we will devote the remainder of this section. Two factors explain these different findings. First, some of the differences are due to the fact that Dye's study makes it necessary for top corporate leaders to accept *secondary* government positions. Let us introduce this point with a look at four of the top nine appointees to the Treasury Department:

Name	Most Recent Corporate Position
David M. Kennedy Secretary of Treasury	Chairman, Continental Illinois Bank
Charls E. Walker Under Secretary	Executive Vice President, American Bankers Association
Paul A. Volcker Under Secretary (Monetary Affairs)	Vice President, Director of Planning, Chase Manhattan Bank
John R. Petty Assistant Secretary (International Affairs)	Vice President, Chase Manhattan Bank

Reading through these four positions holders and their major occupations previous to government appointment, it is clear that they come from the corporate community. However, by Dye's criteria, only the bank chairman who became a secretary is a member of the corporate elite. The secondary corporate officials who took secondary government positions are lost from view. This finding for the Treasury Department holds for other departments as well. The Under Secretary of Defense, David Packard, sat on several corporate boards and qualifies for Dye's list. However, the Assistant Secretary of Defense for Manpower and Resources, Roger T. Kelly, who came to this post from a vice presidency at Caterpillar Tractor, does not qualify. Secretary of Labor George P. Shultz, dean of the business school at the University of Chicago and a director of several major corporations, is counted as a link between the corporate community and government, but his Assistant Secretary for Policy Development and Research, Jerome M. Rosow, an Exxon executive from 1955-1966, and a manager of employee relations for its European subsidiary, ESSO Europe, for the three years immediately before his appointment, does not count.

It is our contention, then, that Dye's analysis overlooks an important distinction between different levels of positional power across sectors. Interorganizational personnel flow, we would argue, occurs on corresponding levels of power from one organization to another. Secondary positions in government are filled from secondary positions in the corporate community. The president of Ford Motors, by this reasoning, is no more likely to accept a post as Assistant Secretary of Treasury than he is to accept the position of vice-president at Chrysler Motors. Indeed, the president of Ford Motors is not likely to accept the position of Secretary of Treasury if he or she sees it as a step down in power. This seemingly hypothetical example may have occurred in 1960, according to journalist David Halberstam (1972: 223), when Ford Motors president Robert McNamara refused to head Treasury:

> He was called to Washington and met Kennedy, who immediately liked him and offered him either Treasury or Defense. The Treasury job had little attraction; he asked one member of the Kennedy team what the Secretary of Treasury does, and was told he sets the interest rates. "Hell, I do more at Ford about setting the interests than the Secretary of Treasury," he answered.

Shortly thereafter, McNamara was appointed Secretary of Defense.

The second reason Dye's findings seem at odds with those of other studies is that he has treated the legal profession, which contributed 56.1% of the government leaders in his sample, as a category separate from business leaders. However, as we have argued and demonstrated in the previous section with the work of other analysts, there is one kind of lawyer who must be considered part of the corporate community, and that is the corporate lawyer. The failure to take this fact seriously is one of the major reasons why studies of governmental appointees by traditional scholars (e.g., Stanley et al., 1967; Prewitt and McAllister, 1976) are not of great use to power structure researchers. Once again, Dye (1976: 99) gives every indication that he agrees with our general conclusion about corporate lawyers when he writes that "The great law firms are, of course, 'the spokesmen for big business'," but this understanding is not reflected in his categories or quantitative analyses.

The role of the corporate lawyer in government can be seen by turning to two more of the top nine positions at the Treasury:

Name	Most Recent Corporate Position
Eugene Rossides Assistant Secretary (Enforcement & Operations)	Partner, Royall, Koegal & Wells,

Edwin S. Cohen   Counsel, former partner, Barrett,
Assistant Secretary   Knapp, Smith & Schapiro
(Tax Policy)

Royall, Koegal & Wells, the firm in which Rossides was a member and/or partner 1954-1956 and 1961-1969, is one of the twenty New York City law firms on Dye's list; it had nine corporate interlocks in 1970. Barrett, Knapp, Smith & Schapiro, where Cohen was a partner from 1949 to 1965 after thirteen years at the more prestigious Sullivan & Cromwell firm on Dye's list, is a smaller New York corporate law firm with one corporate interlock.

In our view, then, five of the top nine positions at Treasury were held by members of the corporate community. These five positions were vertically interlocked with major corporate organizations—Continental Illinois Bank, Chase Manhattan Bank (2), Royall, Koegal & Wells, and the American Bankers Association. A sixth was connected with a smaller corporate law firm. (The final three positions at Treasury were held by two career government employees and an economics professor.)

This consideration of the involvement of the corporate community in the Treasury Department through second-level executives and top corporate lawyers as well as through top corporate officials prepares the ground for our more general study. In order to determine the involvement of the corporate community in the executive branch of the federal government in a systematic way, we studied the occupational careers of one hundred twenty-one secretaries, under secretaries, and assistant secretaries for 1970 from twelve cabinet-level departments and the departments of Army, Navy, and Air Force. All of these departments are included in the Dye study. Using a variety of sources, including the *Biographical Directories Master Index, Martindale-Hubbell Law Directory,* and *The New York Times Index,* we were able to find the necessary biographical information on all but one of these people. Unlike Dye, who determined occupational classification partly by the person's self-designation at the beginning of his or her biography in *Who's Who in America 1970-1971,* we placed a person in one of our several categories, to be described in a moment, on the basis of his or her predominant occupational involvement prior to the beginning of the Nixon Administration in 1969. In most cases such a determination was relatively unambiguous. However, there are a few cases that could be considered ambiguous. Three of those cases will be discussed after we have presented our general results in order to demonstrate the complexities of categorical judgments.

Several of the categories used in this study derived from our interest in whether or not the person had been involved with the major institutions of the business sector prior to government service. These "big business" or "corporate community" categories are as follows: chairperson or president of a corporation listed as among the largest in its field for 1970 (*Fortune*, 1970: 216-218); director or partner in one of the forty largest investment banking firms for the years 1960-1969 (Hillstrom and King, 1970: 28); partner in a large corporate law firm (the definition of this category will be explained in the next paragraph); executive of a corporate trade association; and second-level executive with a *Fortune*-listed corporation or one of the top forty investment banking firms. In addition to the "big business" categories, we also had a "small business" cluster made up of small business executives, partners in small corporate law firms, and partners from the accounting firms which audit the books of large and small corporations.

The above categories are unambiguous except for those containing the corporate lawyers. Although it is clear that some lawyers and law firms specialize in work for corporations, criteria are needed to identify which these are, for they are small in number as a percentage of all lawyers in the United States. For our purposes the two best criteria, due to the availability of public data, are (1) listing as a corporate law firm in the *Martindale-Hubbell Law Directory* or (2) having a partner on a corporate board in *Inside Counsel, Outside Director,* the compilation based on Securities and Exchange Commission records that was discussed in the previous section of this chapter. We divided corporate law firms into large and small in the following way: A large corporate law firm is one that has one or more clients listed in the 1970 *Fortune* rankings of the largest companies in various sectors of the economy, or, if it does not reveal its clients (as many large firms do not), has twenty-five or more partners in the firm (Carlin, 1963). A small corporate law firm is a firm which identifies itself as a corporate firm but has no *Fortune*-listed clients and less than twenty-five partners.

Our remaining categories derived from a careful reading of the career information on each government appointee: The most important are:

> *Career government employee.* This category includes people who spent a majority of their occupational careers in government positions at any level of government, including military personnel and high school teachers. However, most people in this category had worked as civilians at the state or national level.
>
> *University or college administrator.* In terms of our data, this category includes deans of specific schools within universities and presidents or chancellors of colleges and universities.
>
> *Professor or researcher.* This category includes people with specialized academic training who work for colleges, universities, or nonprofit research

organizations as teachers and researchers. Some people in this category had worked for both universities and research organizations, a not unusual pattern for highly specialized academicians.

Politician. A politician was defined as an elected official who had spent the majority of his or her occupational career in elected offices.

The remaining categories are self-explanatory and contained very few people—noncorporate lawyer, farmer, trade union official, and civil rights leader.

Utilizing these categories, we found that 35% of appointees to the fifteen departments under scrutiny came from large organizations of the corporate community. Nine of the appointees were top executives of corporations or investment banking firms, twenty-one were secondary executives at large corporations or subsidiaries of large corporations, nine were members of large corporate law firms, and three were trade association executives. Another twenty-four of the people in our sample were small-business executives, partners of small corporate law firms, or partners in major accounting firms, bringing the contribution of the business community as a whole to 55% of the appointees.

Career government employees accounted for thirty-three positions in the study. There were eight professors and researchers, five college administrators, two noncorporate lawyers, and two politicians. There was one journalist, one labor union official, one farmer-turned-state agricultural commissioner, and one civil rights leader.

These findings suggest the extensive involvement of the corporate community in the executive branch of the federal government in 1970. However, the general findings of this analysis tell only part of the story, for there was considerable variation in occupational background depending on the level of the appointment. The major executives of large corporations tended to cluster at the level of secretary and under secretary. Three of the four exceptions were assistant secretaries in the most prestigious department, the Department of State. Partners from large corporate law firms were found at all levels of appointment due to the fact that two such men were assistants in the Department of Justice, but partners from small corporate firms were found mostly at the assistant secretary level. Most of the other noncareer appointees tended to cluster in the assistant secretary categories, although there were two politicians, Melvin Laird at Defense and John Chafee at Navy, who headed their departments.

These findings on the predominance of major business executives in top executive department positions for 1970 are not atypical. Freitag (1975) and Mintz (1975) report similar findings for 1897-1972. Stanley et al. (1967:

33-37), although their data are not presented systematically in terms of size of business when it comes to cabinet ranking, seem to suggest the same pattern for 1933-1965. Thus, the Nixon Administration is not especially "big business," any more than was the Eisenhower Administration.

One of our most striking findings concerned career employees, the appointees who could provide evidence for the claim that the federal bureaucracy is an independent channel of recruitment to top government positions. Only one of these people, Secretary of the Air Force Robert Seamans, headed a department. Three were under secretaries, and the remaining twenty-nine were assistant secretaries. (A summary of the findings for occupational backgrounds and level of appointment can be found in Table 9.4.)

Moreover, the career employees at the assistant secretary level, with the exception of the foreign service officers at the State Department, tended to have the most perfunctory positions in their departments. Eleven of the twenty-one career government employees not in the State Department were assistant secretaries for administration, accounting (comptroller), or public relations. The most typical of these appointments was as Assistant Secretary for Administration, a position that had been designated since 1950 as one to be filled from the ranks of career employees if possible (Heclo, 1977:

Table 9.4   Occupational Backgrounds of Appointees by Government Position

	Secretary	Under Secretary	Assistant Secretary	Total
Top corporate executive	3	2	4	9
Secondary corporate executive	0	4	17	21
Large corporate law partner	3	3	3	9
Trade association executive	0	2	1	3
Total "corporate community"				42
Small business executive	3	2	8	13
Small corporate law partner	1	1	7	9
Accounting firm partner	0	0	2	2
Total "small business"				24
Career government employee	1	3	29	33
College administrator	2	0	3	5
Professor-researcher	0	0	8	8
Politician	2	0	0	2
Labor official	0	0	1	1
Farmer	0	1	0	1
Other lawyer	0	0	2	2
Journalist	0	0	1	1
Civil rights leader	0	0	1	1
Total	15	18	87	120

76-78). However, even this toehold for civil servants began to be undermined under Kennedy and Johnson, and was all but abolished by Nixon in his second term. As Heclo (1977: 78) reports:

> The new-style "political" appointees [to this position] generally came from the private sector and possessed technocratic skills but little prior experience in either government or politics. In 1976 almost all the career ASAs [Assistant Secretaries for Administration] had been replaced by men with little or no government experience, and the experiment in top-level administrative continuity was, for all practical purposes, a dead letter.

Thus, one of the few positions at the top that supports the claim of an independent federal bureaucracy (Birnbaum, 1978) was returned to "outsiders" shortly after Dye collected his data.

FOUNDATIONS, POLICY GROUPS, AND GOVERNMENT

Government appointees who were trustees or members of major foundations or policy-discussion groups were found in the higher levels of the departments. University of Nebraska Chancellor Clifford Hardin, a trustee of the Rockefeller Foundation and a director of a major insurance company, was Secretary of Agriculture. Banker David M. Kennedy, a past trustee of both The Brookings Institution and the Committee for Economic Development, was Secretary of Treasury. Industrialist David Packard, a trustee of the Committee for Economic Development from 1963 until his appointment to government, was Under Secretary of Defense. Secretary of Labor George Shultz, already mentioned as the dean of the University of Chicago School of Business and a director of several large corporations, was on the Committee for Economic Development's research advisory board from 1965 to 1968. Rocco Siciliano, a Washington lawyer and president of the Pacific Maritime Association before becoming Under Secretary of Commerce, was a member of CED's Committee for the Improvement of Management in Government. Another business policy group, the National Association of Manufacturers, had two recent directors at the secretarial level. Maurice Stans, an investment banker and corporate director, was Secretary of Commerce, and Winton Blount, a major owner in one of the one hundred largest construction firms, was Postmaster General.

Six of the nine Council on Foreign Relations members in the sample were at the State Department. Under Secretary of State Elliott Richardson, a corporation lawyer and politician who will be discussed further in a moment, headed the list. Two other noncareer appointees to State, Nathaniel Samuels and John Richardson, Jr., both investment bankers with major Wall Street firms, also were Council members, as were three career employees at the assistant secretary level, Samuel DePalma, Joseph Sisco, and Phillip Trezise. Also in government were Council members Stanley Resor, from a large Wall Street law firm, as Secretary of the Army; William Chartner, a vice president at the Wall Street investment firm of Goldman, Sachs, as an Assistant Secretary of Commerce; and John R. Petty, an aforementioned Chase Manhattan Bank executive, as an Assistant Secretary of Treasury.

As noted, there were several ambiguous cases in the sample. These cases are among the most instructive in understanding the complexity of the connections between big business and government. One such ambiguous case was Under Secretary of State Elliott Richardson, whom Dye (1976: 62-64) uses as an example of a person whose career is relatively independent of the corporate community. This is because Richardson had served as a senatorial assistant in 1953-1954, as an Assistant Secretary of Health, Education, and Welfare from 1957-1959, as a U. S. Attorney from 1959 to 1961, and as Lieutenant Governor and Attorney General of Massachusetts from 1964 to 1969. However, in between those governmental involvements Richardson was a member of the most distinguished corporate law firm in Boston, Ropes & Gray, which interlocked with nineteen corporations in 1970. He also had served as a director of a Boston savings bank, New England Trust Company, from 1953 to 1957 (Burch, 1980). Perhaps we are wrong in classifying this scion of what Dye tells us is a millionaire family as a corporate lawyer from a large law firm, but readers can decide from themselves whether or not Dye (1976: 64) is more accurate in saying that Richardson was "not recruited from the corporate or financial world."

Another ambiguous case that we finally classified as a small businessman was Barry J. Shillito, an Assistant Secretary of Defense in 1970. After finishing his Air Force service in 1945, Shillito worked four years as the general manager of a small supply company in Dayton, Ohio, which he left to become chief procurement officer for the Air Force at nearby Wright Patterson Air Force Base. In 1954 he joined Hughes Aircraft, rising to vice-president in 1959, when he became vice-president and then president of Houston Fearless Company in Los Angeles. In 1962, Shillito accepted the presidency of the Logistics Management Institute, a nonprofit organization set up about that time by Secretary of Defense Robert McNamara to bring "the most experienced and creative business management to logistics problems" (*Missiles and Rockets*, 1963: 117). The need for such an institute was considered crucial because about 70% of the Defense Department's program is concerned with supply inventory, procurement of new equipment, and other logistical matters. The board of the Institute at the time included retired executives from Sears, Roebuck, National Cash Register, and General Electric, as well as military officers and business school professors. Shillito headed Logistics Management Institute from 1962 until he was appointed to the Department of Navy in 1968 and the Department of Defense in 1969. Is Barry J. Shillito a career government employee or a defense company executive?

Another somewhat ambiguous case that we classified as a small business executive was Spencer Schedler, an Assistant Secretary of the Air Force. Born in 1933, Schedler worked as a petroleum engineer and executive for Humble Oil, Houston Oil Field Materials, and Sinclair Oil from 1958 until he served as an assistant director of the budget in New York City from 1965 to 1967. He then returned to private industry for two years before his federal appointment.

WHERE ARE THEY NOW?

The relationship between the corporate community and government can be examined from another angle by studying the subsequent careers of the one hundred twenty appointees on whom we found preappointment occupational information. Because nine years had passed when we did our study of these 1970 appointees, it was possible to determine "where they are now" in terms of subsequent occupational careers. Did the businesspeople and corporate lawyers in this sample return to their previous occupations? Did people not previously involved in major businesses or corporate law firms take jobs with such firms after government service, thereby providing the corporate community with another channel of communication and persuasion to government officials?

In general, a great majority of the eighty-seven noncareer appointees returned to the occupations they had left to join government, and a small majority of the career employees stayed in government. Among the minority who pursued new occupations, there was a strong movement into the corporate community. Thus, the corporate community not only regained most of the members who had gone to government, but was infused with new members who had gained what is thought to be valuable government experience. The specific findings for the various occupational categories, including career government employees, will be found in the following paragraphs.

Twenty-two of the thirty executives from large corporations returned to the corporate community. Four turned sixty-five or died shortly after government service. Four remained in government service for most of the 1970s. Of the twenty-two who returned to business, twelve returned to their old companies, ten joined new corporations. The three trade association executives in the sample also returned to the corporate community; two became executives of major corporations and one opened his own lobbying firm for corporations. The picture for the nine corporate lawyers from large firms was much more mixed. Three went back to their old firms, one joined a new firm, three accepted further executive appointments, one became a judge, and one (John Mitchell) went to jail for his part in Watergate. Overall, however, most of the forty-two appointees from what we have defined as the corporate community remained closely affiliated with that community.

Fourteen of the fifteen small businesspeople and accountants in the sample returned to private life. Two moved up to executive positions in major corporations, one moved into partnership in a major law firm, and one became president of a major trade association. (Two of the four who moved "up," Barry Shillito and Spencer Schedler, were among the ambiguous cases discussed earlier. Shillito became a vice-president at Teledyne, Inc., a *Fortune*-listed firm; Schedler became a general manager and vice-president at Continental Can, another *Fortune*-listed firm.) The remaining ten small business executives returned to the predominantly family firms from which they came, sometimes adding one or two directorships they had not had before government. Four of the nine small corporate lawyers moved into large corporations or law firms after their government service. Two of those four joined large Washington law firms, one as a partner, one as a consultant, and two became vice-presidents, for Peabody Coal and Weyerhaeuser Timber. Two of the nine small corporate lawyers became federal judges, and the remaining three returned to small corporate law firms.

Seventeen of the thirty-three career employees in our sample either stayed in government or retired, but seven of the remaining sixteen moved into the corporate world in a variety of executive positions. For example, a foreign service officer became an ITT executive in 1973, and an Assistant Secretary of Interior went to work for Atlantic Richfield in the same year, first as the director of a development project, then as its Washington representative. Other corporations hiring career employees into executive positions were General Electric, Pan American, Xerox, and Signal Corporation. By way of contrast, one former career employee went to work for the AFL-CIO, representing government employees in disputes with agency and department leaders. Other positions taken by one or two career employees were university administrator, trade association executive, and consultant at a major policy-formulation organization.

The trend into the corporate community was even stronger for the former college administrators and politicians in the sample. Three of the four college administrators who survived beyond their years in government became executives of major corporations. Clifford Hardin left his post as Secretary of Agriculture to become vice-chairman of the board of Ralston Purina; George Shultz became a senior vice-president at Bechtel Engineering (one of the largest construction firms in the world); and Curtis Tarr became a vice-president at Deere & Co. The fourth former college administrator became a consultant to government agencies, and the fifth died shortly after leaving government. Both politicians in the sample became part of the corporate community. Melvin Laird, appointed Secretary of Defense after many years in Congress, left the Nixon Administration in 1974 to become a senior consultant at *Readers Digest* and a director of seven corporations over the next few years. John Chafee, a former governor of Rhode Island who was appointed Secretary of the Navy, returned to private life in 1973 as a corporate director and a partner in a major corporate law firm. (Chafee went back into politics as Senator from Rhode Island in 1977, but retained his directorships with two medium-sized Rhode Island companies.)

People in the remaining categories—professor-researcher, noncorporate lawyer, farmer, labor official, journalist, and civil rights leader—returned to private work closely related to their previous occupations. Only one of the fourteen, a former professor, stayed in government for any length of time, and only one, a noncorporate lawyer, joined a major organization in the corporate community.

We believe this post-1970 study provides further impressive evidence for the close relationship between the corporate community and the federal government. Not only does the corporate community contribute a great many executives and partners to government who then return to big business or corporate law, but many career employees, politicians, college administrators, small business executives, and small corporate lawyers become part of the corporate community when they leave government. The fact that so many of these corporate-connected people move in and out of government in a relatively short time span suggests that it is possible to talk about interlocks between corporations and government at some level nearly akin to the "concurrent" or institutional level. The continuous circulation of corporate officials into and out of government, which has been documented in more general terms in other studies (Stanley et al., 1967; Heclo, 1977), means that the major corporations constantly are "interlocked," through different persons, with the federal government.

However, we believe that what we would term the revolving interlocks between corporations and government make possible a different relationship between the corporate community and government than is possible with the concurrent interlocks within the corporate community. While concurrent interlocking establishes channels for immediate information-sharing and coordination, revolving interlocks with government would seem to provide a certain degree of "temporary autonomy" from the concerns of specific firms or business sectors, thus enabling appointees to become "atypical of their class" (Block, 1977: 13) and to act on behalf of the more general interests of the corporate community. We stress "temporary autonomy" because we infer from our post-1970 findings that most appointees remain oriented toward a return to or entry into the corporate community, and therefore do not have the time or the inclination to become fully independent of corporate concerns and develop a perspective that incorporates the interests of other sectors of society.

Those who have been called "structural Marxists" assert that the general interests of a ruling class and its power elite may be best served when its members do not occupy formal positions of governmental authority (e.g., Poulantzas, 1969; Offe, 1974; Block, 1977). This is because they believe members of the ruling class usually cannot transcend their short-run interests and narrow, profit-oriented consciousness. However, as we suggest here, it may be that a species of sequential interlocking we call revolving interlocking gives members of the corporate community enough freedom to fulfill the larger role that is required of them when they are in government. In this respect, the "relative autonomy" of the state in America may be attained through the "temporary autonomy" of its corporate appointees.

CONCLUSION

We have done this analysis to show that there is in fact a great deal more interchange of personnel between the corporate community and government than has been claimed by Mills's critics (e.g., Parsons, 1957; Rose, 1967; Birnbaum, 1978), or has been found in the methodically inadequate studies by Stanley et al. (1967), Dye (1976), and Prewitt and McAllister (1976), none of which has an adequate conception of big business and all of which exclude corporate lawyers from the corporate community.

Whether the symbiotic relationship we describe is either necessary for or useful to the corporate community, it does exist in the United States, and it would seem to be a worthwhile endeavor for structural Marxists and others to explain why it does exist in future comparative studies. We believe that the degree of involvement in government by members of the corporate community should be seen as a dependent variable which may vary from epoch to epoch and society to society in relationship to a variety of possible factors, including the history of a society, the intensity of the class struggle within the society, the degree of cohesion within the ruling class, and the place of a nation within the world system of capitalist countries.

For now, we are content to have shown that all major investigations by power structure researchers from Mills (1956) to Freitag (1975) and Mintz (1975) to this present study are in agreement on the interchange of personnel between the corporate community and the executive branch of the federal government. This clears the way for what should be the future tasks of such research, explaining why this interchange occurs and determining in more detail the effects it may have on how the United States is governed.

REFERENCES

ALLEN, M. (1978) "Economic interest groups and the corporate elite." Social Science Quarterly 58, 4: 597-615.

BEARDEN, J., W. ATWOOD, P. FREITAG, C. HENDRICKS, B. MINTZ, and M. SCHWARTZ (1975) "The nature and extent of bank centrality in corporate networks." Presented at the meeting of the American Sociological Association, San Francisco, August.

BIRNBAUM, P. (1978) "Institutionalization of power and the integration of ruling elites: a comparative perspective." European Journal of Political Research 6: 105-115.

BLOCK, F. (1977) "The ruling class does not rule: notes on the Marxist theory of the state." Socialist Revolution 7, 3: 6-28.

BONACICH, P. and G.W. DOMHOFF (1977) "Overlapping memberships among clubs and policy groups of the American ruling class." Presented at the meeting of the American Sociological Association, Chicago, September.

BUNTING, D. (1976a) "Corporate interlocking, Part I—the money trust." Directors and Boards 1, 1:6-15.

——————— (1976b) "Corporate interlocking, Part II-the modern money trust." Directors and Board 1, 2: 27-37.

BUNTING, D. and J. BARBOUR (1971) "Interlocking directorates in large American corporations, 1896-1964." Business History Review 45: 317-355.

BURCH, P. (1980) Elites in American History: The New Deal to the Carter Administration. New York: Holmes & Meier.

Business Week (1972) "The high cost of corporate law." July 22: 23.

CARLIN, J. (1963) Lawyers on Their Own. New Brunswick, NJ: Rutgers Univ. Press.

DI MAGGIO, P. and M. USEEM (1978) "Cultural property and public policy." Social Research 45: 356-389.

DOMHOFF, G.W. (1979) The Powers That Be. New York: Random House.

——————— (1974) The Bohemian Grove and Other Retreats. New York: Harper & Row.

_____ (1970) The Higher Circles. New York: Random House.

_____ (1967) Who rules America? Englewood Cliffs, NJ: Prentice-Hall.

DOOLEY, P. (1969) "The interlocking directorate." American Economic Review 59: 314-323.

DYE, T. (1976) Who's Running America? Englewood Cliffs, NJ: Prentice-Hall.

DYE, T., E. DECLERQ and J. PICKERING (1973) "Concentration, specialization, and interlocking among institutional elites." Social Science Quarterly 54: 8-28.

DYE, T. and J. PICKERING (1974) "Governmental and corporate elites: convergence and specialization." Journal of Politics 36: 900-925.

EAKINS, D. (1969) "Business planners and America's postwar expansion," in D. Horowitz (ed.) Corporations and the Cold War. New York: Monthly Review Press.

_____ (1966) "The development of corporate liberal policy research in the United States, 1885-1965." Unpublished Ph.D. dissertation, University of Wisconsin.

Fortune (1970) "Alphabetical index of [top] corporations." May: 216-218.

FREITAG, P. (1975) "The cabinet and big business: a study of interlocks." Social Problems 23: 137-152.

GOULDEN, J. (1972) The Super Lawyers. New York: Weybright & Talley.

GREEN, N. (1975) The Other Government: The Unseen Power of Washington Lawyers. New York: Grossman.

HALBERSTAM, D. (1972) The Best and the Brightest. New York: Random House.

HARRIS, S. (1962) Economics of the Political Parties.New York: Macmillan.

HARTNETT, R. (1969) College and University Trustees. Princeton, NJ: Educational Testing Service.

HELCO, H. (1977) A government of Strangers. Washington, DC: Brookings Institution.

HILLSTROM, R. and R. KING (1970) A Decade of Corporate and International Finance, 1960-1969. New York: Investment Dealers' Digest.

HOFFMAN, P. (1973) Lions in the Street. New York: Saturday Review Press.

HUDSON, W. (1972) Inside Counsel, Outside Director. New York: New York Law Journal Press.

KLAW, S. (1958) "The Wall Street lawyers." Fortune (February): 107-120.

MARIOLIS, P. (1975) "Interlocking directorates and control of corporations: the theory of bank control." Social Science Quarterly 56: 425-439.

MILLS, C.W (1956) The Power Elite. New York: Oxford Univ. Press.

MINTZ, B. (1975) "The president's cabinet, 1897-1972: a contribution to the power structure debate." Insurgent Sociologist 5, 3: 131-148.

Missiles and Rockets (1963) "LMI has growing effect on planning." March 25: 117.

MIZRUCHI, M. and D. BUNTING (1979) "The structure of the American corporate network: 1904-1919." Presented at the meeting of the American Sociological Association, Boston, August.

OFFE, C. (1974) "Structural problems of the capitalist state," in K. von Beyme (ed.) German Political Studies. Beverly Hills: Sage Publications.

PARSONS, T. (1957) "The distribution of power in American society." World Politics (October). Reprinted in G.W. Domhoff and H. Ballard (eds.) C. Wright Mills and The Power Elite. Boston: Beacon Press, 1968.

POULANTZAS, N. (1969) "Problems of the capitalist state." New Left Review 58: 67-78.

PREWITT, K. and W. McALLISTER (1976) "Changes in the American executive elite—1930-1970," in H. Eulau and M. Chaudnowski (eds.) Elite Recruitment in Democratic Politics. New York: Halstead Press.

ROETTGER, W. (1978) "Strata and stability: reputations of American political scientist." PS 11: 6-12.

ROSE, A. (1967) The Power Structure. New York: Oxford Univ. Press.

SCHRIFTGIESSER, K. (1967) Business and Public Policy. Englewood Cliffs, NJ: Prentice-Hall.

————— (1960) Business Comes of Age. New York: Harper & Row.

SHOUP, L. and W. MINTER (1977) Imperial Brain Trust. New York: Monthly Review Press.

SMIGEL, E. (1964) The Wall Street lawyer. New York: Free Press.

SONQUIST, J. and T. KOENIG (1975) "Interlocking directorates in the top U.S. Corporations: a graph theory approach." Insurgent Sociologist 5, 3: 196-229.

STANLEY, D., D. MANN, and J. DOIG (1967) Men Who Govern. Washington: Brookings Institute.

U.S. Congress, House (1976) Federal Reserve Directors: A Study of Corporate and Banking Influence. Washington, U.S. Government Printing Office.

USEEM, M., J. HOOPS, and T. MOORE (1976) "Class and corporate relations with the private college system." Insurgent Sociologist 4, 4: 27-35.

10

ORGANIZATIONAL ANALYSIS AND POWER STRUCTURE RESEARCH

Nancy DiTomaso

The major contribution of power structure research over the last two decades has involved a demystification of the notion of social structure by identifying the familial, recreational, educational, business and political connections of the wealthiest people in the United States. People have been put back into the roles that sociologists are wont to discuss at length. This focusing on the everyday institutional contexts which bind particular strata of people together is fundamentally sociological.

But power structure research still presents significant shortcomings, insofar as it has tended to ignore the contributions of sociological work on organizations, which would help to specify several dimensions of the questions raised by power structure research. While these researchers have sought to identify the dominant traits of an upper class (and in some cases of a ruling class), and more specifically its disproportionate membership in various types of organizations, they have not attempted to establish the significance or the relevance of these organizations and of their interrelations to the domination of the society. Nor have they aimed at showing the role played in this regard by specific positions or committees within those organizations as well as outside of them.

To be sure, an historical analysis of power structure literature makes it easy to understand why researchers have sought to identify interactions among upper-class members before specifying the structural characteristics and the meaning of the positions they hold. Yet, it has become necessary to link this type of research to the organizational literature for two reasons. On the one hand, to establish that a large number of people are connected in various ways and through various organizations is to raise the question of what difference it makes. On the other hand, the "segregation" of power structure and of organizational researchers is sufficiently artificial both from a scientific and a political viewpoint to make it necessary to elaborate further the meaning and functioning of positional power.

Thus, the purpose of this chapter is to highlight some of the insights which could be drawn from organizational theory and research to enlighten the questions which power structure researchers are facing at the present time. The chapter does not constitute an exhaustive, nor a noncontroversial review of organizational sociology. By extrapolating from major articles and presenting my own understanding—and critique—of organizational sociology, I aim to show the contributions of this type of sociological work to power structure research.

Despite the continuing interest of many sociologists in studies of the "power structure," research of this type has been widely attacked among political sociologists in the last few years. From the early work by Mills (1956) and the responses by Rose (1967) and others, to the current work by Domhoff (1967, 1970) and the critiques by Esping-Andersen et al. (1976), power structure research has raised as many questions as it has answered regarding domination within society. These questions come out of the criticisms that have been leveled against power structure research from both the right and the left.

All studies of domination force one to answer questions of boundaries, limits, and alternatives. Power structure research, as Domhoff (1976) argues, was originally an attack on the pluralist conception of power in the United States. In that pluralists argued that power was dispersed, the burden of proof for power structure research was to show that power was concentrated and unified. But as all who have studied relations of power understand, these are questions of degree, precisely because power is a relationship and not an attribute per se. Furthermore, each statement regarding the distribution of "power," for example, invokes associated questions regarding the dimensions being used to define it and the meaning and consequences of its distribution.

The questions which I argue are critical for explaining the significance and defending the implications of power structure research are the following:

(1) *What is the meaning of fragmentation and conflict within the dominant class?* This question results from the controversy over the concentration versus the dispersion of power. Insofar as power structure research focuses on the concentration, it must also explain existing evidences of internal fragmentation and conflict within the upper class. In other words, it must explain how unity emerges out of diversity.

(2) *How do a few (fragmented and competitive) people maintain control, coordination, and loyalty from the many?* This question is related to the first in that once one draws boundaries around something called the "upper class," then one must also explain the relationship between those who are defined as part of it and those who are not. This question could be rephrased as, "what difference does it make?"

(3) *How can one explain the "successful" opposition at times by subordinate classes to the control of a dominant class?* This question is raised by the relational nature of power. Insofar as power structure research focuses our attention on the "powerful," it also elicits questions about the active versus passive character of those over whom the powerful have power. The successful opposition of subordinates is in a sense the boundary to the power of the upper class.

(4) *How does the control of upper-class members in one organization relate to the control of other organizations and to the rest of society?* This question is raised by the continual criticism that power structure research has insufficiently explained how domination is actually constructed by those in powerful positions, such that their activities have the effects which are claimed by power structure researchers. To answer this question is to explain why one studies power by looking where power structure researchers have been looking.

In short, the conclusions which can be drawn from power structure research remain ambiguous as long as answers to these questions are not offered. My chapter provides some answers by combining power structure research with research on organizations. Thus, the rest of the chapter suggests answers by extrapolating from the sociological literature on organizations.

FRAGMENTATION OF THE UPPER CLASS

Power structure researchers have sought to answer their critics regarding conflict within elite groups by minimizing the fragmentation through their studies of consensus-seeking organizations, such as the Council of Foreign Relations or the Business Council. By uncovering the operation of such groups, power structure researchers have helped us to understand that the "upper class" does not exist automatically, but rather, that it must be created through the active recruitment and socialization of members into it. The perpetuation of domination by the upper class requires its members to be socialized both to the general values of capitalism and to the specific interest of the faction of capital to which they belong. The work of Mills (1956),

Baltzell (1964), Domhoff (1967, 1974), and others on intermarriage, membership in social clubs, recreation resorts, and attendance at the same elite educational institutions, indicates part of the process of socialization of upper class-members into the general values of capitalism. Combined with the work on consensus-seeking groups, such research is directly related to the formation of homogeneity of policy within the upper class.

But there is a more specific aspect to the question of socialization and recruitment. One must also show why it is necessary that administration and management of specific major political and economic organizations are staffed with those people who are related to each other through the common experiences of education, recreation, and intermarriage. Such questions cannot be taken for granted because a number of conceptions of social structure postulate self-perpetuating and internally evolving systems which do not require "leaders" or "managers" to guide their development. Studies of power in organizations help enlighten this issue. First, organizational sociologists are interested in the processes of socialization into the goals and values of particular organizations and the relationship such socialization has to predicting future behaviors (see, for example, Buchanan, 1974; Ondrack, 1975; Shirom, 1976; Feldman, 1976; Steers, 1975; and Graen et al., 1977). Such studies recognize the importance of socialization and training for strengthening the existing distribution of power in an organization and hence for avoiding unexpected changes in the direction of an organization's functioning.

Second, the studies of key positions within organizations have indicated that people whose backgrounds are similar to those who control the organization are chosen for leadership positions. The most important aspect of background in this regard is socioeconomic position (See Pfeffer et al., 1976; Lord, 1977; and Pfeffer, 1977). Especially for those positions where the circumstances under which decisions are to be made cannot be predicted in advance, where evaluation of tasks is ambiguous, and where circumstances are new or rapidly changing, upper-class owners need to rely on internal values of managers rather than on external control of behavior. Socioeconomic background is a means to predict what the internal values of managers will be. Thus, the implication for power structure research is that people with upper-class backgrounds will occupy disporportionately those positions that have a wide latitude in decision-making, especially if the decisions that are made are critical to the survival of the organization and are uncertain, new, or rapidly changing.

Choosing people with similar backgrounds to one's own is a means of building in predictability about the actions those people will take in the future. However, organizational theorists have also long recognized that organizations insure the predictability of behavior within them by structuring the situations in which people perform their tasks so that they do not have to make many decisions. Built-in patterns of response and "standard ways of operating" within organizations are called the "institutionalization" of an organizational structure (Selznick, 1957; Simon, 1961; and Perrow, 1972). That the early structuring of relationships within an organization embody defined relations of power via institutionalization of a tradition regarding how things are done has also been recognized by political scientists in their studies of governmental organizations (see, for example, Rourke, 1969; Seidman, 1976; and Biggart, 1977). Kimberly (1975), for example, found that the values or goals of the organizations he studied varied with the time period in which the organizations were founded. (Also see Stinchcombe, 1965; and Brown and Schneck, 1979.)

If one means to power is to build it into the relationships within organizations from the beginning, then any rearrangement of an organization is also a redistribution of power. Invariably, reorganization leads to conflict among actors (Biggard, 1977). The implication for power structure research is to look for whoever is gaining or losing power when there is a reconstitution of membership within critical organizations or a rearrangement of the manner in which tasks are performed within an organization. If this is correct, then one should also expect to find upper-class involvement in the reorganization of those organizations which begin to effectively represent the interests of subordinate classes. Usually such attempts fall under the rubric of the "professionalization of reform" or the development of "efficient management" (see, for example, DiTomaso, 1977, 1978; Molotch and Lester, 1973).

But, if there are conflicts and fragmentation within organizations, the study of conflicts between organizations is also relevant to the issue of identifying the tensions occurring within the upper class. The power of organizations increases with their ability to control resources (Pfeffer and Salancik, 1978), and conversely, coordination among organizations emerges out of their mutual need for each other's resources (Aiken and Hage, 1968; Franko, 1974; Pfeffer, 1973). Such findings flesh out how either consensus or accommodation is worked out among the conflicting interests of fragments of the dominant class. Indeed, consensus developed within such groups as the Council of Foreign Relations is insufficient and must also be concretely developed in the relationships, for example, among General Motors, Volkswagen, and Toyota. The inter-organizational literature points to attempts by competing organizations to find alternative markets, to interlink themselves with their competitors through boards of directors, the formation of coalitions, cartels, or joint programs. Such work is relevant to power structure research insofar as it shows the significance of interlocking directorates among corporations or of the need for representation in lawmaking bodies or regulatory commissions. Organizations act toward each other to reduce the "turbulence" of their own environments (Terryberry, 1968), to use the terminology from organizational sociology.

THE FEW AND THE MANY

Understanding how the few can dominate the many has been a central question in political sociology, long before power structure research. For example, Engels argued in his response to Dühring:

> The simple fact that the ruled and exploited have been at all times far more numerous than the rulers and exploiters, and that therefore the preponderance of actual force has rested with the former is by itself sufficient to make clear the absurdity of the whole force theory. The problem of explaining relations of mastery and servitude still remains. [Moore, 1957: 39].

Power structure research has tended to answer this question by documenting the interrelationships and the disproportionate participation of upper-class people at top positions within political, social, and economic organizations. Yet, they have not specified the rank ordering of these positions, their determinants, nor their consequences on patterns of domination.

Before addressing these particular questions, however, it is important to note the alternative directions that this issue has taken in various fields, including both politial sociology and complex organizations. The first argues that a few people can dominate a large number of people because the few control the most important positions. The second argues that the structure of the situation itself creates the dynamics of interactions among all of the people within it. In political sociology, and specifically in regard to power structure research, this debate has taken the form of a controversy on the relative merits of "structuralist" or "instrumentalist" explanations of power (see Esping-Andersen et al., 1976; and reply by Domhoff, 1976). Although power structure researchers have assumed that this debate creates a false dichotomy between "people creating structures" and "structures creating people," a similar debate has been waged within organizational theory as well over the relative explanatory power of "leadership" versus the "structure" of the organization.

In organizational theory, traditional management theories of organizations placed most emphasis on the causal effects of different types of leadership (see, for example, Chandler, 1962). In contrast, sociologists have tended to focus on the development of organizational structures, as determined by the conditions of organizational needs and goals, independent of the motivations or personal characteristics of leaders. (See, for example, Hall, 1972; and Haas and Drabek, 1973, for reviews of the development of organizational sociology during the 1960s). Partly in response to the traditional management studies of leadership and psychology, sociological studies of organizations in the 1960s came to be known as "structuralist." Of late, however, organizational sociologists have become disillusioned with the limitations of "structuralist" explanations, while political sociologists have been placing increased emphasis on structural determination. Given that the debate has been more extensive and continual in organizational sociology, it could significantly enlighten the study of power structures, because in organizational sociology the debate has sought to specify the conditions under which differences in people are important and, alternatively, the conditions under which structure constrains the personal motivations, actions, or characteristics of people.

In fact, organizational sociologists are divided over the relative weight to be given to "choice versus constraint" (Aldrich, 1979:137), "structure versus flexibility" (Pfeffer and Salancik, 1978:81), "system versus action" (Crozier, 1979). In my own terminology, this debate is about the tension in organizations between the need for "domination" on the one hand and "flexibility" on the other. Mintzberg (1973), for example, argues that managers simply follow the exigencies of the structure rather than make their own plans and choices, whereas Child (1972) argues that under "strategic" circumstances, the choices of managers are critical to the direction taken by the organization. Pfeffer and Salancik (1978) strongly suggest that managers come to make the choices and have the preferences demanded by the structures they find themselves in.

This debate has contributed to the discussion over which positions within organizations are more important than others. The general consensus among organizational theorists is that those positions which control the allocation of resources (Pfeffer and Salancik, 1978), uncertainty (Crozier, 1964), and those that are linked to the outside ("boundary-spanning roles"; see, for example, Aldrich and Heker, 1977) are both the most powerful and the most important positions within any organization. The implication of this work for power structure research is that one would expect disproportionate membership of the upper class in such positions, because these are the ones that are powerful. For example, one is much more likely to find the board of directors and the executive committee to share upper-class backgrounds than their middle management counterparts. And one is more likely to find people with upper-class backgrounds disproportionately in finance, for example, where resource allocations are decided, than in the production department of a corporation, where the activities are probably more easily standardized. Many examples could be given, but little of the work on power structure research has differentiated positions in this way (for an exception, see Soref, 1976).

If organizational theory suggests which positions are more powerful than others, it also suggests why. Although organizations are created in order to coordinate the actions of a number of people in the performance of predetermined tasks, organizations, nevertheless, have limited domains, both internally and externally. Not only must organizations deal with "men who are not machines," to quote Simon (1961), but they must also deal with continually changing environments. Survival depends on their ability to predict the circumstances under which they must function and to adapt to changes as they occur. Internally, this means that all tasks, no matter how menial, involve to some extent the use of "discretion" on the part of the person doing it (Bendix, 1956).

Although all organizations attempt to elicit the voluntary cooperation of members of the organization at all levels, the use of discretion against the interests of the organization in the case of those positions which have more consequence is far more costly to an organization than in the case of lower-level positions (Bendix, 1956). In lower-level positions, the use of discretion can be limited by placing constraints on the tasks themselves (dividing them into little parts or making them interdependent with the tasks of other people), but at higher positions, in boundary-spanning positions, and in positions of "uncertainty," tasks are more likely to be nonroutine. When the owners of the organization cannot control discretion by surrounding people with constraints, they must predict how they will use discretion by selecting people who have internalized the same goals as they themselves have. It is important to understand in this regard that the flexibility of some positions must be maintained in organizations. One could, in fact, redefine the concept of "key positions" as those positions in which the use of discretion is authorized and encouraged. (See Ouchi and Dowling, 1974; Ouchi and MacGuire, 1975; and Ouchi, 1977 for discussions of two types of control within organizations.)

Last, organizational theory specifies the means by which those in "key" positions successfully dominate others within organizations. The early management theory by Barnard (1958) argued that organizations are cooperative systems in which the "contributions" of subordinates are gained by the organization's management offering "inducements" in exchange. Alternatively, of course, inducements could be withdrawn or withheld, and would then lead to the withdrawal of the contributions by subordinates. This view of an organization, of course, assumes mutually beneficial exchange.

Although the mainstream organizational literature still tends to rely on this view, other research suggests additional means by which managements gain control and cooperation of subordinates, and this has important implications for power structure research. Thus, Bendix (1956) argued that the dominant class developed "ideologies of management" which tied workers to their own organizations, while allowing managers to join in collective action to pursue their interests. Bendix's work on the United States, for example, stresses the adaptation of management ideologies, as needed, to the resistance of workers to the authority of the factory. Braverman (1974) focuses on the same kinds of issues, but he places more stress on the use of Tayloristic management practices which separate the planning of work tasks from the doing of them and constrains the behavior of subordinates by limiting their knowledge of the work process.

There has been extensive research on the question of organizational control (see, for example, Etzioni, 1961), and especially on the determinants of "effective" supervision and "span of control" (see, for example, Blau and Schoenherr, 1971). Some recent research is of particular interest for understanding the differences between management and operational personnel in organizations. Ouchi and MacGuire (1975) found that the type of control differs for those positions at the top and those at the bottom of organizations. In those positions where the tasks are well defined and the process of performance of those tasks is well known (i.e., predominantly lower-level positions), control is maintained by supervising the behavior of employees. In contrast, in those positions where the tasks are not well defined and where the process of their performance is not well understood (i.e., predominantly the same positions which were earlier identified as "powerful"), control is maintained by monitoring output, but not by direct supervision. That is, only the results count for key positions, but both the means and the ends are examined for lower-level personnel. Taking this work together indicates that those in key positions within an organization maintain their domination by rewards and punishments, supervision, and by the division of labor and the organization of work, such that resistance or the use of "unauthorized" discretion is minimized. The important implication for power structure research is that it helps explain both how a small number of people can dominate a large number of people and contributes to specifying where and how this is done.

RESISTANCE TO DOMINATION

By focusing on the identification of members of the upper class, power structure research may tend to give the impression that subordinate classes are themselves not actively involved in resistance. This, of course, was the central theme of the article by Dreier (1975), who advocated more attention to class struggle in studies of the power structure. Although this was perhaps not intended, power structure research has been more focused on the formation of consensus and coordination of behavior than on the rearguard actions that the upper class adopts as a result of the resistance and opposition of subordinate classes.

In contrast, the problems raised by the resistance of subordinates to the powerful have always been central to organizational theory, because the primary problem of "management" is to gain cooperation and prevent opposition. Beginning with Taylor's early work on the "irrationality" of lower-level personnel (1911) to the studies in sociology in the 1950s on the way in which the "informal culture" within organizations influenced employee behavior (see, for example, Gouldner, 1954), the need for supervision and control has been a key concern or organizational theorists.

Indeed, the "unpredictability" of the behavior of subordinates has induced a number of studies on the active means of dealing with resistance, opposition, misunderstanding, "goldbricking," and lack of motivation in organizations (see, for example, Mechanic, 1962; French and Raven, 1968; Warren, 1968; and Julian, 1966). The implications for power structure research are several. The inclusion of this work would not only round out the picture by showing the extent to which members of the upper class have to actively confront the resistance of subordinates, but it would also broaden the scope of power structure research by focusing attention on other kinds of organizations, like management training schools, special seminars by private consultants, etc.

DOMINATION AMONG ORGANIZATIONS

Although power structure researchers have made extensive studies of the disproportionate membership of upper-class people in various "key" organizations, there has been little if any discussion of how some organizations control others. In contrast, organizational theorists have examined at length the relations among organizations and have examined the bases of power among them (see, for example, Aiken and Hage, 1968; Aldrich, 1971;

Aldrich and Pfeffer, 1976; Benson, 1975; Evan, 1966; Levine and White, 1961; Litwak and Hylton, 1962; Marrett, 1971). In addition to the research on the conditions under which some organizations try to or are forced to cooperate with others, the study of interorganizational relations also includes how particular organizations are either affected by or manage to shape their own environments. The principles of interorganizational relations could be adapted to understanding the differences among organizations and the linkages between those which gain the primary attention and participation of the upper class and those which do not. How, for example, do the policy preferences of major corporations get negotiated concretely with local governments? Or, how do universities work out their research agendas to fit the needs of nearby corporations? These questions and others could be analyzed in terms of interorganizational relations, in combination with the identification of the family or social ties among participants.

Also important to power structure research is the work of those organizational sociologists who have tried to specify the relationship between organizations and societal development (see, for example, Touraine, 1971, 1976; Karpik, 1972; Crozier, 1979). This work specifically traces the role played by organizations in the relations of power within society and vice versa. For example, Touraine (1971) analyzed the relationship of the "firm" to national planning. Such work could be used in power structure research to elaborate the dissemination of policies formulated by upper-class organizations in both the "public" and the "private" spheres.

CONCLUSION

I have tried to argue in this chapter that answers to questions which are currently of issue for power structure research could be found in part in the sociological literature on organizations. Precisely because organizational sociology is mostly concerned with specifying the conditions under which some behaviors are more important than others, some people are more important than others, and some positions are more important than others, as well as the interrelations among them, it could enlighten our understanding of the implications of the work on power structures which has already been completed, and it could possibly point to new directions for future research.

If research were pursued along these lines, it could help avoid the difficult questions of how many people need to be from upper-class backgrounds to call it a "power structure" and how it is that the interests of the dominant class are maintained even when managers do not have upper-class backgrounds. It also points to specific research questions regarding which positions are most important and powerful and under what circumstances members of the upper class are either substituted for or replaced by nonupperclass members. Further, such research points to the active means by which upper-class members attempt to engender control, in contrast to some current assumptions which imply the inevitablity of such processes. In other words, the exercise, and not only the attribution of power, belongs in power structure research. In this regard, to call power structure researchers "instrumentalists" is a misnomer, because the instrument of power—organizations—is what has been missing from such research.

REFERENCES

AIKEN, M. and J. HAGE (1968) "Organizational interdependence and intraoranizational structure." American Sociologist Review 33 (December) 912-930.

ALDRICH, H. (1979) Organizations and Environments. Englewood Cliffs, NJ: Prentice-Hall.

——— (1971) "Organizational boundaries and interorganizational conflict." Human Relations 24 (August) 279-287.

——— and J. PFEFFER (1976) "Environments of organizations" pp. 79-105 in A. Inkeles (ed.) Annual Review of Sociology, Vol 2. Palo Alto, CA: Annual Review.

BALTZELL, E.D. (1964) The Protestant Establishment. New York: Vintage.

BARNARD, C.I. (1958) Functions of the Executive. Cambridge, MA: Harvard Univ. Press.

BENDIX, R. (1956) Work and Authority in Industry. New York: John Wiley.

BENSON, J.K. (1975) "The interorganizational network as a political economy." Administrative Science Quarterly 22 (March) 1-121.

BIGGART, N.W. (1977) "The creative-destructive process of organizational change: the case of the Post Office." Administrative Science Quarterly 22 (September) 410-426.

BLAU, P.M. and R.A. SCHOENHERR (1971) The Structure of Organizations. New York: Basic Books.

BRAVERMAN, H. (1974) Labor and Monopoly Capital. New York: Monthly Review Press.

BROWN, J.L. and R. SCHNECK (1979) "A structural comparison between Canadian and American industrial organizations." Administrative Science Quarterly 24 (March) 24-47.

BUCHANAN, B., II (1974) "Building organizational commitment: The socialization of managers in work organizations." Administrative Science Quarterly 19 (December) 533-546.

CHANDLER, A. (1962) "Organization structure, environment, and performance—the role of strategic choice." Sociology 6 (January) 1-22.

CROZIER, M. (1979) L'acteur et le systeme. Paris: Seuil.

——— (1964) The Bureaucratic Phenomenon. Chicago: Univ. of Chicago Press.

——— (1977) "The Department of Labor: class politics and public Bureaucracy." Ph.D. dissertation, University of Wisconsin, Madison.

DITOMASO, N. (1978) "The experience of the means of administration: class struggle over the U.S. Department of Labor." Kapitalistate 7: 81-106.

DOMHOFF, G. W. (1979) The Powers That Be. New York: Random House.

——— (1976) "I am not an instrumentalist." Kapitalistate 4-5: 221-224.

———— (1974) The Bohemian Grove and Other Retreats. New York: Harper & Row.

———— (1970) The Higher Circles. New York: Random House.

———— (1967) Who Rules America? Englewood Cliffs, NJ: Prentice-Hall.

DREIER, P. (1975) "Power structures and power struggles." Insurgent Sociologist 5 (Spring) 233-244.

ESPING-ANDERSEN, G. et al. (1976) "Modes of class struggle and the capitalist state." Kapitalistate 4-5: 186-220.

ETZIONI, A. (1961) A Comparative Analysis of Complex Organizations. New York: Free Press.

EVAN, W. (1966) "The organization-set: toward a theory of interorganizational relations," in Approaches to Organizational Design, James Thompson (ed.) Pittsburgh: Univ. of Pittsburgh Press.

FELDMAN, D.C. (1976) "A contingency theory of socialization." Adminsitrative Science Quarterly 21 (September) 433-452.

FRANKO, L.G. (1974) "The move toward multidivisional structure in European organizations." Administrative Science Quarterly 19 (December) 493-506.

FRENCH, J.R.P. and B. RAVEN (1968) "The bases of social power," pp. 259-269 in D. Cartwright and A. Zander (eds.) Group Dynamics. New York: Harper & Row.

GOULDNER, A. (1954) Patterns of Industrial Bureaucracy. New York: Free Press.

GRAEN, G. et al. (1977) "Effects of linking-pin quality on the quality of working life of lower participants." Administrative Science Quarterly 22 (September) 491-504.

HAAS, J. E. and T. E. DRABEK (1973) Complex Organizations. New York: Macmillan.

HALL, R.H. (1972) Organizations, Strucutre and Process. Englewood Cliffs, NJ: Prentice-Hall.

JULIAN, J. (1966) "Compliance patterns and communication blocks in complex organizations." American Sociological Review 31 (June) 382-389.

KARPIK, L. (1972) "Le capitalisme technologique." Sociologie du Travail 13 (January-March) 2-34.

KIMBERLY, J.R. (1975) "Environmental constraints and organizational structure." Administrative Science Quarterly 20 (March) 1-9.

LEVINE, S. and P.E. WHITE (1961) "Exchange as a conceptual framework for the study of interorganizational relationships." Administrative Science Quarterly 5 (March) 583-610.

LITWAK, E. and L. HYLTON (1962) "Interorganizational analysis: a hypothesis on coordination." Administrative Science Quarterly 6 (March) 395-420.

LORD, R.G. (1977) "Functional leadership behavior: measurement and relation to social power and leadership perceptions." Administrative Science Quarterly 22 (March): 114-133.

MARRETT, C. (19710 "On the specification of interorganizational dimensions." Sociology and Social Research 56 (October) 83-99.

MECHANIC, D. (1962) "Sources of power of lower participants in complex organizations." Administrative Science Quarterly 7 (December) 349-364.

MILLS, C.W. (1956) The Power Elite. New York: Oxford Univ. Press.

MINTZBERG, H. (1973) The Nature of Managerial Work. New York: Harper & Row.

MOLOTCH, H. and M. LESTER (1973) "Accidents, scandals, and routines." Insurgent Sociologist (Summer).

MOORE, S. (1957) The Critique of Capitalist Democracy. Boston: Beacon Press.

ONDRACK, D.A. (1975) "Socialization in professional school: a comparative study." Administrative Science Quarterly 20 (March) 97-103.

OUCHI, W.G. (1977) "The relationship between organizational structure and organizational control." Administrative Science Quarterly 22 (March) 95-113.

————— and J.B. DOWLING (1974) "Defining the span of control." Administrative Science Quarterly 19 (September) 357-365.

OUCHI, W.G. and M.A. MacGUIRE (1975) "Organizational control: two functions." Administrative Science Quarterly 20 (December) 559-569.

PERROW, C. (1972) Complex Organizations: A Critical Essay. Glenview, IL: Scott, Foresman.

PFEFFER, J. (1977) "Toward an examination of stratification in organizations." Administrative Science Quarterly 22 (December) 553-567.

————— (1973) "Size, composition, and function of hospital boards of directors: a study of organization-environment linkage." Administrative Science Quarterly 18 (September) 349-364.

————— and G.R. SALANCIK (1978) The External Control of Organizations: A Resource Dependence Perspective. New York: Harper & Row.

————— and H. LEBLEBICI (1976) "The effect of uncertainty on the use of social influence in organizational decision making." Administrative Science Quarterly 21 (June) 227-245.

ROSE, A. (1967) The Power Structure. London: Oxford Univ. Press.

ROURKE, F.E. (1969) Bureaucracy, Politics, and Public Policy. Boston: Little, Brown.

SEIDMAN, H. (1976) Politics, Position, and Power. New York: Oxford Univ. Press.

SELZNICK, P. (1957) Leadership in Administration. Evanston, IL: Row, Peterson.

SHIROM, A. (1976) "On some correlates of combat performance." Administrative Science Quarterly 21 (September) 419-432.

SIMON, H.A. (1961) Administrative Behavior. New York: Macmillan.

SOREF, M. (1976) "Social class and division of labor within the corporate elite: a note on class, interlocking, and executive committee membership of directors of U.S. industrial firms." Sociological Quarterly 17: 360-368.

STEERS, R.M. (1975) "Problems in the measurement of organizational effectivenss." Administrative Science Quarterly 20 (December) 546-558.

STINCHCOMBE, A.L. (1965) "Social structure and organizations," in J.G. March (ed.) Handbook of Organizations. Chicago: Rand McNally.

TAYLOR, F. (1911) Principles of Scientific Management. New York.

TERRYBERRY, S. (1968) "The evolution of organizational environments." Administrative Science Quarterly 12 (March) 590-613.

TOURAINE, A. (1976) The Self-Production of Society. Chicago: Univ. of Chicago Press.

————— (1971) Post-Industrial Society. New York: Random House.

WARREN, D.I. (1968) "Power, visibility, and conformity in formal organizations." American Sociologial Review 22 (December) 951-970.

WEICK, K. (1969) The Social Psychology of Organizing. Reading, MA: Addison-Wesley.

ABOUT THE AUTHORS

IRVINE ALPERT completed his undergraduate work in sociology at the University of California, Santa Cruz, in 1978 and is doing graduate work in city and regional planning at the University of California, Berkeley.

NANCY DiTOMASO received her degree in sociology from the University of Wisconsin and teaches sociology at Northwestern University.

G. WILLIAM DOMHOFF received his degree in psychology from the University of Miami and teaches psychology and sociology at the University of California, Santa Cruz.

MARVIN G. DUNN received his degree in sociology from the University of Oregon and teaches sociology at Lewis and Clark College.

ERIC LICHTEN is completing his dissertation in sociology at the Graduate School and University Center, City University of New York, and is currently teaching political sociology at the College of Old Westbury of the State University of New York.

ANN MARKUSEN received her degree in economics from Michigan State University and teaches planning and economics in the Department of City and Regional Planning at the University of California, Berkeley.

SUSAN A. OSTRANDER received her degree in sociology from Case Western Reserve University and teaches sociology at Wake Forest University.

RICHARD E. RATCLIFF received his degree in sociology from the University of Wisconsin and teaches sociology at Washington University.

HAROLD SALZMAN completed his undergraduate work in psychology and economics at the University of California, Santa Cruz, in 1977 and is doing graduate work in sociology at Brandeis University.

MICHAEL USEEM received his degree in sociology from Harvard University and teaches sociology at Boston University.

J. ALLEN WHITT received his degree in sociology from the University of California, Santa Barbara, and teaches sociology at Brown University.

RICHARD L. ZWEIGENHAFT received his degree in psychology at the University of California, Santa Cruz, and teaches psychology at Guilford College.